"*Art and Social Interaction* is an extraordinary example of student learning and community engagement in the major domestic issues of our time, including crime; mental illness; child, spousal and substance abuse; frail elderly concerns, and poverty."

Dr Robert A. Scott, *President Emeritus, Adelphi University*

"Dr Peck's book on the healing of disenfranchised and marginalized populations via shared expressive art activities with college students is a breath of fresh air. An artist and an educational icon, she leads the next generation of students to appreciate the value and imperative nature of this endeavour."

Kathleen Monahan, *DSW, LCSW, LMFT, Associate Professor, School of Social Welfare, Stony Brook University*

"What makes Peck's book different is the authenticity of her broad experience, and its relevance to professors, students and institutional administrators. The kind of work encouraged and fostered here draws on an altruism that is fading. This work facilitates social change and builds sorely needed connection between institutions and communities."

Andy Teirstein, *PhD, Arts Professor at NYU Tisch School of the Arts*

"*Art and Social Interaction* is truly a book for this moment, when those with educational privilege are called to use their skills to advance social justice. Professor Peck demonstrates the way visual art levels the playing field and facilitates critical insight into identity and society. *Art and Social Interaction* is a must read for university administrators and faculty as we work to educate the next generation of compassionate and skilled leaders."

Francine Sherman, *Clinical Professor Emerita, Boston College Law School; President of I Am Why, Iamwhy.org*

I0894594

Art and Social Interaction

This second edition expands upon a program that teaches expressive visual arts activities to college students to share with individuals in jails, nursing homes, psychiatric facilities, domestic abuse shelters and youth care centers.

Creating expressive art through interaction with those affected, students gain an intimate awareness of crime; mental illness; substance, child, domestic abuse; and aging—critical issues of our time. Specially designed projects in drawing, painting, collage, sculpture and crafts are supplemented with student reflections on how the experience influenced their lives and future careers plus institutional evaluation on the effectiveness of the program on their clientele.

Delivering everything needed to set up the course in any liberal arts college, the book covers planning, execution, projected outcomes and evaluation, offering students an education relevant to their lives and careers while giving institutions a dynamically effective program of self-enhancement through the arts.

Color versions of many projects can be viewed online at www.routledge.com/9781032972008.

Judith Peck is a sculptor with work in 80 public and private collections including the Yale Gallery of Art and the Ghetto Fighters Museum in Israel. Peck holds a doctoral degree from New York University and two master's degrees from Teachers College, Columbia University.

Art and Social Interaction

How College Students Spark Creativity, Purpose and Joy in Institutional Settings

Second Edition

Judith Peck

Routledge
Taylor & Francis Group
NEW YORK AND LONDON

Designed cover image: Student Cindy Klein with participant

Second edition published 2026
by Routledge
605 Third Avenue, New York, NY 10158

and by Routledge
4 Park Square, Milton Park, Abingdon, Oxon, OX14 4RN

Routledge is an imprint of the Taylor & Francis Group, an informa business

First edition published by Routledge 2022

Library of Congress Cataloging-in-Publication Data
Names: Peck, Judith author
Title: Art and social interaction : how college students spark creativity, purpose, and joy in institutional settings / Judith Peck.
Description: Second edition. | New York, NY : Routledge, 2026. | Includes bibliographical references and index.
Identifiers: LCCN 2025009935 (print) | LCCN 2025009936 (ebook) | ISBN 9781032971995 hardback | ISBN 9781032972008 paperback | ISBN 9781003592693 ebook
Subjects: LCSH: Social work with criminals—Study and teaching | Psychiatric social work—Study and teaching | Social work with older people—Study and teaching | Internship programs
Classification: LCC HV7428 .P43 2026 (print) | LCC HV7428 (ebook) | DDC 365/.66—dc23/eng/20250811
LC record available at https://lccn.loc.gov/2025009935
LC ebook record available at https://lccn.loc.gov/2025009936

ISBN: 978-1-032-97199-5 (hbk)
ISBN: 978-1-032-97200-8 (pbk)
ISBN: 978-1-003-59269-3 (ebk)

DOI: 10.4324/9781003592693

Typeset in Palatino, Futura and Rockwell
by Apex CoVantage, LLC

Access the Support Material at www.routledge.com/9781032972008

This book is dedicated to Ramapo College of New Jersey, the newest State college in New Jersey, whose fresh ideas of intercultural, experiential and interdisciplinary education welcomed a program like Art and Social Interaction and helped it flourish.

Contents

Foreword

Robert A. Scott, PhD

President Emeritus and Professor Emeritus, Adelphi University

Art and Social Interaction by Judith Peck, EdD

Hands-on learning through internships have been shown to be life-changing experiences for students. Internships in human service institutions such as jails, nursing homes and psychiatric facilities, as designed and described by Professor Emerita Judith Peck of Ramapo College of New Jersey, enrich the experiences of undergraduate college students no matter their major course of study.

Internships require planning, lead to discovery, promote the application of learning, and interns benefit from reflection on what they have experienced and learned. Professor Peck shows that internships in human service settings are especially rich in helping students discover new knowledge and understanding and in providing opportunities to reflect on the human condition and societal ideals.

The value of the internship is further enhanced when it involves creative visual arts. This is especially true if the art included is more than the process of art creation or the product of artistic effort, but when art is employed as a vehicle for engagement with others who live in different and often difficult circumstances.

The college experience is intended to give students the confidence to take initiative, solve problems, formulate ideas and develop the skills of language, learning and leadership. The goals of the liberal arts and general education are to emphasize reasoning in different modes, clear and graceful expression in written and oral communications, organizational ability, tolerance and flexibility, and creativity. Such an education cannot be gained in the classroom alone or by solitary immersion in a book. It requires active participation and learning in groups. Internships provide this benefit.

Art and Social Interaction is an exemplar of this form of student learning and community engagement. The program, now nearly 50 years in operation, has given students an opportunity to meet, speak to and make art side by side with people central to the major domestic issues of our time: crime; mental illness; child, spousal and substance abuse; frail elderly concerns, and poverty. At a time in their lives when students are most open to learning, they are introduced to an intimate form of caring. Many choose careers in the helping professions, but almost all gain a new awareness of life beyond the mainstream and a pride in their adventure and accomplishments. Realizing the courage to set oneself in unfamiliar, slightly scary places to help others is inspiring.

The activities covered are designed to stimulate memory, acknowledge experience and achievement, and improve self-esteem. Accessible projects in drawing, painting, collage, sculpture and crafts are described with explanation of their purpose and process of creation, all accompanied by fetching illustrations.

Art and Social Interaction serves as an excellent manual to assist faculty in adopting this approach to internships in their own manner and adapting it for their own teaching objectives. This new edition of the book contains seven new chapters, including one with inspiring excerpts from students affirming the life experiences gained; a second from representatives of the diverse institutions served affirming the need for the program for their constituents. Other chapters relate to careers in art therapy and social work; the correlation of brain function with making art and viewing it; and the effect of music education in prisons. The unique success of the program in jail environments is given its own chapter as is a sampling of participant artwork. Welcome to a marvelous, innovative program for student learning and community service.

Robert A. Scott, PhD.

Robert A. Scott, PhD. President *Emeritus* and University Professor *Emeritus*, Adelphi University; President *Emeritus* and Professor *Emeritus*, Ramapo College of New Jersey; Author, *How University Boards Work*, Johns Hopkins University Press, 2018; and Co-Author, with Drew Bogner, PhD, *Letters to Students: What it Means to be a College Graduate*, Rowman & Littlefield, 2024

A Personal Perspective

There is a sensation, an undercurrent of empathy and emotion, that strikes a student in the middle of an art workshop, that she is doing something *wonderful*. A feeling that she has helped someone in a way both she and they have never experienced. She stands amazed to be no longer afraid. The people seated at her table and walking about are folks she's come to know—heard their stories, grown familiar with their odd behaviors. She has begun to understand them in the context of their surroundings. And become newly aware of herself within her own home and family.

I know this by reading the students' logs, written after each session conducted with their team at the site they have chosen. But also from my own encounters with the populations we serve. Each time I leave a site after my twice-a-semester observation of my students at work there—limited because my presence alters the dynamics of the interactions—I feel that sense of wonderful. To me it is clear that freedom is at the core of this sensation. The freedom inherent in creative art which soars through the rooms in opposition to the confinement that suffuses the air. The first impression and a lasting one for anyone entering a jail or prison is the clang of the doors opening then clanging shut just as startlingly behind you. Entrance and exit are restricted similarly in the psychiatric hospital wards, though with silent digital technology.

The eccentricities within the individual institutions are evident on first approach, walking along the halls and feeling the wary stares. Dismissive among incarcerated men gathered sometimes in mass sleeping quarters like a gym or standing behind a screen of bars, though not the same entering with the undergrads at which time we are whistled and *whoo-hood* a sizzling, albeit scary welcome. In the psychiatric facility we are stared at—if patients are diverted at all from the ubiquitous TV. Eyes are empty of connection or the opposite when we are physically approached and often touched, believing we can rectify some deeply lodged injustice. Then ten weeks later as students and participants chat and laugh together at the final session, which is a mini party with certificates presented to those completing the series, a sense of pride hovers in the air. It settles among participants in the form of a slight rekindling of self-worth. Among students, the pride takes many forms: new-found courage, competence, the surprise of having touched someone else's life, But more than anything, what lasts is a sense of humility. To have been given the privilege to see behind the doors of lives, so in many ways ill-fated, but lovely in their special ways. And that, I share.

Judith Peck

Other Books by Judith Peck

Leap to the Sun: Learning through Dynamic Play
Sculpture as Experience: Working with Clay, Wire, Wax, Plaster and Found Objects
Sculpture as Experience 2nd Expanded Edition
Smart Starts in the Arts: Fostering Intelligence, Creativity and Serenity in the Early Years
Art Activities for Mind and Imagination
Artistic Crafts: Inventive Creations from Cast-offs
Seeing in the Dark: Arielle's Story, novel
Naked Under the Lights, novel
Runaway Piggy Bank, children's picture book
The Bright Blue Button and the Button-Hole, children's picture book
Dynamic Play and Creative Movement: Powering Body and Brain
Art and Social Interaction 1st edition

Introduction

Art activities have garnered acceptance as a helpful intervention in facilities which care for the elderly, the mentally ill and underserved youth. Although not as commonly employed with individuals incarcerated for criminal offences or drug abuse, creative arts have proven of value in the goal of reintegrating these men and women into society as productive individuals.

What is missing to make art activities more universally accepted is a venturesome attitude among site administrators welcoming it into their understandably restricted environments. Then if welcomed, to have in hand the how-to material to deliver a program to meet their institution's specific needs. The material provided in this text is fashioned to meet that need: how to start, maintain and succeed in producing a creative arts program in a facility not in the least geared for it.

Because funding to bring trained art teachers and materials into a facility is often the first hurdle, the concept of combining college coursework with student community service is a viable avenue to embrace. The marriage has the advantage of being of unique benefit to both students and community. The university is fulfilling its educational mandate by providing relevant academic learning and an opening to career opportunities while well prepared faculty and students serve sites that will benefit.

The coordinate need is to give interested faculty in visual art or social work the methodology to create a course that combines creative art and social interaction within a fieldwork framework. This text provides that avenue and does so in the following ways:

Program Concepts and Components

- Provides college students the opportunity to advance their undergraduate academic coursework with hands-on experience to enhance their knowledge of diverse people in often closed-off communities with whom they would never otherwise come in contact.
- Provides colleges an opportunity to attract community institutions which can be effective in stimulating students' future study and career opportunities.
- Provides human services staff with the information they need to institute a creative arts program in their facilities.

DOI: 10.4324/9781003592693-1

- Provides participants exposure to a magic mix of creative expression and social interaction with trained college students whose attendant study is dedicated to their well-being.

Few programs exist that have the potential to be so mutually beneficial for all involved: college purpose, student learning, institutional support and participant welfare. It is the author's hope that the book at hand will facilitate this lively exchange.

Part One

Art and Social Interaction

Concept and Design

Figure 1.0 Psychologist Sam Menahan, student Judy Ferber and therapist Barbara Stein draw with oil pastels, West Bergen Mental Health Center, Ridgewood, NJ

DOI: 10.4324/9781003592693-2

Chapter 1

Background and Overview

There is only one subject-matter for education and that is Life in all its manifestations.
Alfred North Whitehead

Concept

Life surely manifested itself in the unfamiliar situations that students discovered inside the institutions they ventured into with their pencils, paints and brushes; their expressive ideas but limited experience of people beyond their safe suburban coterie of family, friends and peers. The diversity of institutions served and spectrum of people with whom the students worked side by side are fully described in these pages. That the education that did manifest itself was mutual during the weeks of the program's progression in each site is paramount.

Art and Social Interaction—originating as "Art on the Outside"—was, by information known, the only undergraduate project of its kind nationwide to train *undergraduate* students from diverse areas of the college in artistic media to serve and thereby come to understand people in non-mainstream settings. Students accomplished this service by presenting a series of art workshops with an emphasis on evocative participation within an informal atmosphere of social interaction.

The objectives of the program at its start and still ongoing are these:

- To generate productive creative activity among individuals who for complex reasons are confined or may live in the community but are out of the mainstream; to do this with a view toward improving self-esteem and confidence in personal expression.
- To provide students with an educational experience not available in purely theoretical academic study; an opportunity to have personal contact with individuals they might otherwise never meet and become aware of the distinctive problems of these individuals.

DOI: 10.4324/9781003592693-3

Beginning in 1973, the program then received funding for three years, 1975, 1976 and 1977 from the New Jersey Department of Higher Education under Title I. Continuing in operation to the present as a college fieldwork course, the objectives, approach, projects, conduct and evaluation through the years have been crystallized and standardized.

There was a need to create a type of manual when the course as a program became relied upon as an institutional service and attractive as an interdisciplinary course offering. Administrators of participating institutions requested that it continue each semester and a waiting list began forming for others who wanted to initiate it. Nevertheless, departmental needs did not permit expansion within the college, and due to the complexities of delivering "free" visual arts expression in rigid institutional environments, there existed no safe and efficient method to reproduce it elsewhere. This text is therefore intended to serve as a guide for replicating the program's concept, structure and methods for service in other worthy places and, in addition, to expand the how-to's of art and social interaction to internships in the social work arena where admirable service fieldwork is already in place.

Distinguishing Characteristics of the Program

The groups addressed in the art and social interaction program are:

Jail inmates (Prison inmates could be, but it was not logistically expedient)
Individuals in drug rehabilitation centers
Nursing home residents and elderly in adult day-care centers
Hospitalized and outpatient psychiatric patients
Hospitalized veterans
Abused and emotionally disturbed youth residing in child-care facilities
Children and adults living in shelters for domestic violence
Youth of the low-income housing projects
The physically and intellectually challenged

The unifying objective for these very different participants is to stimulate personally productive activity that may help to improve self-image and confidence, promote positive social behavior and enrich life in situations of confinement, emotional isolation, physical difficulty or neurological deficiencies.

The pilot program revealed a history of problem-solving to reach its objectives. Difficulties arose out of the understandably closed-door atmosphere of places which confine (to hold or to help) the law-breakers, the mentally ill and the physically and sexually abused. Regrettably, even the aged, the infirm, the physically or intellectually challenged and the poor have sometimes in our society been added to the rosters of "peripheral" people.

Addressing these problems through art generated a surround of vibrant color and texture as memory and personal experience was expressed and shared. The freedom inherent in art activity contrasted with the restraints of the institution, while friendly social interaction triggered the formation of unexpected and often unlikely kinships. On a philosophical level, the brightly engaged college students coming in contact with the dark despair of institutional life showed the stark polarities that the human spirit can contain. Not infrequently, this feeling stayed with students inspiring careers in the helping professions. In the meantime, they learned and began to care about society's timeless issues: crime, old age, mental illness, child abuse, drug abuse, poverty, physical disability and the American institutions that try but do not always succeed in helping.

Book learning and events in the news surely address these issues but not with the integrated emotional and cognitive experience that comes from some direct involvement with the community and the opportunity to know people not as classified groups but as individuals with personal concerns. As students contemplate the breadth and depth of these concerns and their ultimate effects on society, they not only learn but begin to perceive their own lives in a wider context.

Equally compelling are the benefits to the community that students and other volunteer presenters are able to offer. Institutions and agencies are often understaffed and underfunded and thus the services offered to constituents may be less than optimal. The art activities and responsive interrelationships that develop through the program support institutional objectives.

The combined freedom and control in artistic expression may be a new experience for participants. So too may be the opportunity to be received as they are; presenters are not concerned with judgments others make who have an investment in their performance, such as courts, family members, custodians and attendants. Creating side by side, presenters are in a position to view the participants as individuals, folks like themselves with surprises appearing on paper that go well beyond classifications.

Terms

The book utilizes the following terms for the sake of simplicity. Those presenting the art and social interaction workshops—whether college students enrolled in a course, college interns, volunteers serving independently or designated activities personnel—will be termed *presenters*. Those receiving the workshops, for want of a universally appropriate term for the broad constituency served, will be termed *participants*. The institutional and agency facilities hosting the program will be termed *sites*. The art and social interaction series will be termed the *program*.

Presenters of the Program

The book is intended to serve all of the diverse groups listed above, but the content can be adapted to start an art program in a single facility such as a nursing home. Similarly, it can become an adjunct to programs already in place such as in music, drama, dance and creative writing. Interrelating the arts in institutional settings, as in mainstream education, supports the program's objectives.

Content included in the book

- The overall objectives and special approach of the program to be used by any group of presenters, namely college students, or community volunteers, or activities staff within the institution.
- Methods for organizing, preparing for and presenting the program in a spectrum of institutions and agencies.
- Designs for evaluating accomplishments and needs.
- Procedures for structuring the program specifically as a college course offering and securing support for it both internally and within the community.

The program as described is prepared for these broad areas of users:

- Social work and visual arts faculty,
- College administrators,
- Faculty advisors in psychology, American studies, disability studies, education, law and society, gerontology,
- Social workers and mental health counselors,
- Activities personnel working in the institutions,
- Students enrolled in the program as a course,
- Students and their faculty advisors looking for internship opportunities,
- Agency personnel bringing college students or community volunteers into their facilities whom they will supervise.

Presenters in all instances should value artistic expression although they need not have studied art. They should have a willingness to provide to others the motivation to engage in creative means of personal expression.

The Program for Use by College Faculty and Students

Increasingly, demands are made on higher education to provide learning opportunities that can relate liberal arts to vital contemporary issues. Increasingly, too, the college is expected to be a source of cultural stimulation to the community. For both of these reasons, the concept of a credit-bearing course that offers *instruction to the community while receiving instruction from the community* is a viable one for colleges located in an area where appropriate human service facilities exist.

Although there are many graduate college courses and several undergraduate courses that study the use of artistic activity as a vehicle for social growth, and there are fieldwork courses that serve some of the populations addressed in this text, such courses are geared toward students with a particular interest in the field of art therapy or psychology. The course described in these pages is geared toward students from virtually any department of the university, designed as a liberal arts opportunity.

Many undergraduate students have not yet decided about their precise field of study and in some cases even their major. They are often pressed, however, to think about job opportunities and a potential career. The art and social interaction program while interfacing with a significant number of academic courses (see Insert 7.1 "Academic Courses Relevant to the Art and Interaction Program") exposes students to a wealth of potential career opportunities, and not infrequently, jobs as well.

The program can be adapted for both undergrad and graduate students as an independent fieldwork course or internship, work/study or independent study project. The diverse ethnicity and age range of today's student body forms a good constituency to attend to the varied groups of people the program serves.

The complete methodology for establishing the program as a college course is offered in subsequent chapters.

The Program for Use by Activities Staff

Staff personnel may have direct responsibility for group activities and use the book to enrich their offerings. Or to train other staff who have a specific interest in the arts. Or to supervise students, professionals or outside volunteers coming into the institution either individually or under group sponsorship.

The Program for Use by Volunteers and Professionals

Volunteers and even professional teachers coming into an institution for the first time are generally unfamiliar with the special needs and requirements of institutional life. Making applicable sections of the text available to presenters who are bringing creative programs in from the outside can save time for staff supervising such programs and help to avoid unpleasant and perhaps dangerous situations.

Participants in the Program

Appropriate settings for the art and social interaction program include:

Nursing homes
Adult day-care centers
Senior citizen clubs
Psychiatric hospitals
Outpatient mental health clinics
Veterans' hospitals
Urban housing projects
Youth care facilities—pre-school through adolescent
Residences for abused children
Centers for individuals with physical and intellectual disabilities
Correctional facilities for adults
Correctional facilities for youth
Shelters from domestic abuse

Group Structure

Because the program functions most effectively in an atmosphere of informal socialization, a *group* of presenters is preferable to a single individual. Consisting of two to five people, this should function as nearly as possible as a group, not a leader working with assistants. Group interaction via the art activities is the modality of the workshops, not an instructor/student or leader/follower format, and comfortable coordination among presenters can do much to set a positive tone. Participants observe such interactions keenly. The participants meet as a group as well, all taking part in the workshops together.

Safety and Precautions

Having a successful outcome for each session requires taking precautions and observing them continually. In the situations of confinement (and often isolation) described, problems will occur and should be apprehended quickly so that the achievements of the session are not undermined. Regular staff working in these institutions are aware of hazards that may never occur to an outsider coming to the facility for brief periods of time. The program can only exist if it adheres to its purpose, which is to enhance and certainly not impede the institution's mission. That rather obvious statement may become lost in the enthusiasm of presenters as the program gets underway; the art activities can sharply contrast with the dour quality of custodial care sometimes seen in long-term institutional settings. Nevertheless, for the welfare of everyone and indeed for the program to be allowed to continue at all, it is essential that participants understand the factors pertaining to safety. If the guidance at times appears over-protective, it is to indicate areas worth treating with extra care.

That said, the imaginative "go for it" energy that presenters bring to the sessions will be in their own individual style. As long as institutional needs and precautions are observed, those qualities will form the style of the program. Adaptation and innovation are intrinsic to the program and in the end will determine its distinctive "personality."

Figure 1.1 Students Rick Larken, Denise Colette and Barbara Van Driel enter jail with supplies

Figure 1.2 Student paints with child in a Paterson housing project

Figure 1.3 The author draws along with female detainees in the female wing of the jail

Chapter 2

The Magic Mix
Art and Social Interaction

The workshop sessions have a dual thrust of artistic activity and social interaction. Both occur together in the successful program to form a *free atmosphere within a controlled structure*. This format creates an effective means for participants to join with others in personally productive ways.

The Limitations of Product-oriented Art Programs

Readers who are activities personnel may already be including art activities in their recreational programs. This is creditable but unfortunately, much of this activity is product-oriented, involving little or no creative process. The "arts and crafts" of non-creative activities is purposeful in that a sense of productivity is afforded to overcome listless behavior, but activities of much deeper and lasting personal value can be explored within a similar timeframe, place and materials requisition. Busy work fills the hands but may leave the mind and heart unfulfilled. Equally important, the precious time of the individual whose hands are so occupied is not used as well as it might be.

Creating art involves accepting one's personal vision and making a journey through memory, imagination and experience to transform an idea via art materials into an image. This understandably is an unchartered journey and somewhat feared. Activities personnel working with adults may resist offering expressive creative projects for two reasons: insecure about their own artistic abilities and aware that their clients tend to relate art activity to childish play. Responses to the latter attitude is addressed under the heading "Barriers in Instituting the Workshop Series." As for the former, the processes for engaging in the projects are designed specifically to counter hesitancy to begin. When activities staff experience the spontaneity of approach connected with most projects, they should feel more confident to introduce them.

Engaging in expressive art activity may take some doing in the chronic wards of the psychiatric hospital where individuals may be heavily medicated and lethargic. In these situations, more verbal interaction is usually needed to stimulate folks to engage in the project.

DOI: 10.4324/9781003592693-4

After laying out supplies, presenters should then start on their own creative piece, as this may start things off.

In the different situations that presenters encounter, the goal may have to alter a bit and the process changed to adapt, but the creative opportunity should be used, however minimally. Try to provide a meaningful event within the limitations imposed. If you succeed in getting participants and staff to discard the notion of "talent" and instead think about honest personal expression, you've made a good start.

Evocative Artistic Activity

> *Art is a human activity, consisting in this, that one man consciously, by means of certain external signs, hands on to others feelings he has lived through, and that other people are infected by these feelings, and also experience them.*
>
> Leo Tolstoy

Through the artistic processes described in this text, personal experiences such as the joys and the loss of freedom; illness; tragedy; and other such difficult, lived-through events can be expressed and communicated. When imagery about these thoughts and feelings is shared, others deepen and further their understanding. Evoking experiences through art can also organize and focus them. The inmate productions described in Insert 2.1 illustrate both concepts.

Communication in art is nonverbal and as such may be particularly valuable for individuals for whom verbal communication is difficult or severely limited. Artistic activity supports communication—the personal expression of one's inner and outer worlds—and integrates emotional, intellectual and cultural growth.

Imagination, Curiosity and Intelligence

A growing body of research supports the value of artistic engagement in everyday life. We now know after decades of scientific understanding of the brain, that there is a biological reason behind this engagement. We can speculate about what is going on in this scenario of a college student sitting with an inmate or frail elderly adult or other individual in difficult circumstances as they engage in expressive art together. A small sampling of commentary on this is offered here, much more in Chapter 24 titled *The Brain and Art in Collaboration*, detailing neurological connections relating the brain to creativity and art.

Insert 2.1 Descriptions of Two Inmate Productions

Inmate Drawing and Poem "A Child Is"

The drawing of a child wearing sleepwear is in the center of the paper. A cell door, open and waiting, is drawn. Inside the cell the artist has written the words, "Confusion, pressures, jail, insanity, crime, drugs, alcohol, death, robbery, rape and murder." Along with this there are representations of barbiturates, reefers, a revolver, packets of heroin, a cooker and syringe. To the left of the child in the same drawing is the artist's poem.

A child is tender when it's born,
Not knowing its heart will soon be torn.
A child is tender when it's born,
Not knowing the world or its evil scorn . . .
A child is tender when it's born,
To raise a family or be a pimp of whores.
A child is tender when it's born,
To be a renegade or kind and warm.
A child is tender when it's born,
To be a writer of words or a singer of songs.
A child is tender when it's born,
Not knowing it's here and will soon be gone! We've got to save the children!

Juan, Essex County Jail, 1979, recorded by Rick Larkin, student

Inmate Painting, "A Coke Trip"

A female jail inmate, who had never painted before even as a child, was given the theme, "Where do you want to be in ten years." She selected acrylic paints and produced an explosive pattern which emanated from the center of the page outward. She said it was "a coke trip." She was both startled and excited by the visual feelings she had produced. The students, at the same time, had a vivid visual experience of her "trip."

Most of us are familiar with some level of creativity and the analogy to art making and the brain to cooking could begin here. To make an appealing dish, we begin with the ingredients. How lucky if these can already be found in our fridge and cabinets. Lucky we are for nature already did all that shopping and storing, preparing our brains at the start for use and as kids we used every bit of it: curiosity, imagination, fantasy, searching out and bringing in what we see—and don't see but invent to satisfy the delights of our play, and with it of course our learning. These intelligence-building ingredients have been spread out on the counter since we were babies for our minds to spoon out and stir up. When we knowingly use the brain's food and condiments we feel self-assured and terrific, creating something new and wholly our own, even admired by others who share our delight in having produced such a dish.

Sadly, through the years the use of that playful creativity and its components of curiosity and imagination fall by the way as verbal intelligence is established and skill at reading and communicating through proper language dominates the school years. But educational theorists have seen other kinds of intelligence emerge, often resistant to the formal tests of achievement that accompany those skills. Temple Grandin, in her book *Visual Thinking*, argues that visual thinking, rather than through language alone, is another way that the brain processes information. You might be able to tell if you are a visual thinker if you are musical, good at art, or good at putting mechanical things together, or use a combination of verbal and visual thinking to navigate the world. She discusses Michaelangelo as an extreme example of a visual thinker. His spatial skills show in the extraordinary details in the monumental David and the frescoes on the Sistine Chapel. Geniuses like Leonardo are extreme examples of visual-spatial thinkers producing monumental original thought (Grandin, 2022, 173).

Guy Claxton who writes on body brain connectivity in his latest book, *Intelligence in the Flesh*, claims imagination as an area of higher mental process in which body and mind link up for learning. "Using our imagination to solve problems, fantasize possible futures, rehearse presentations or see other people's points of view is clearly a valuable and highly intelligent asset." It is possible to see specific parts of the brain engage when imagination is in play in thinking. Rhythmic or repetitive movement often accompanies the burgeoning of ideas, such as when in the shower or on a walk or driving to work. "There seems to be something about repetitive activity that puts the brain into a state conducive to creative thinking." (Claxton, 2015, 163).

Your Brain on Art by Susan Magsamen and Ivy Ross includes a plethora of studies on the correlation of the brain with artistic enterprise. How one's sense of well-being is tied to using the brain's resources of curiosity, play, laughter and how its urge for newness and change enhance brain plasticity, all elements embodied in art.

Bessel Van der Kolk in his classic text on healing, *The Body Keeps the Score*, writes that imagination is critical to the quality of our lives:

> Our imagination enables us to leave our routine everyday existence by fantasizing about travel, food, sex, falling in love, or having the last word – the things that make life interesting . . . It fires our creativity, relieves our boredom, alleviates our pain, enhances our pleasure, and enriches our most intimate relationships . . . Without imagination there is no hope, no chance to envision a better future, no place to go, no goal to reach.
>
> (Van der Kolk, 2014, 17)

When participants in Art and Social Interaction who in the dull routine of simple survival have long forgotten the inventiveness of imagination and are suddenly given permission to sink into it with an encouraging companion sitting alongside doing the same, something new and lively occurs. A sense of play emerges, and as inventive images appear on paper the memory of someone who used to be pretty good at all that emerges, and the self who belongs to that someone feels a sweet sense of satisfaction.

Art Therapy

The use of art for diagnosis and treatment of mental health issues is now highly regarded, and there is ample literature on advances made in that field over decades of work by scholars and practitioners (Naumberg, Kramer, Uhlman, Rubin, McNiff, Malchiodi, Moon, Levick, Wadson and many others). The approach and projects in this text, however, although designed to be used in institutions and agencies and in a broad sense are therapeutic, do not represent clinical art therapy. Extensive training is required of art therapists, both in art and in clinical psychology, training which this text does not provide. Presenters are therefore cautioned against trying to care for emotional problems using the material in this text. Because individuals using the book may develop an interest in the field of art therapy, information about that field is provided in Chapter 22 and in the Appendices and Annotated Bibliography.

Projects of the Text

The projects included are those offering the most creative potential. It is likely that presenters will embellish these with new ideas, using them as springboards for ideas inspired by the personalities and experiences of the group. The projects, as in all other components of the text, should be viewed as flexible instructions which can adjust to a wide range of temporal and eclectic human factors.

The art activities to be used in the presentations include projects in:

Drawing and design
Collage
Painting
Sculpture
Fabric pictures
Jewelry-making
Puppet-making

Presenters must explore the art projects in advance to become familiar with the processes and materials. Students will be afforded class time for this. All of the projects described in this text will not be used for reasons of insufficient time or space or feasibility. Of the ones explored, student teams will decide each week upon a project they decide most suitable for their specific site.

The method of presenting the projects is a "join-in" approach. That is, materials are distributed and the project is initially explained by a presenter. Then both presenters and participants become involved in creating their own work side by side with others, sharing ideas, comments and materials. Sometimes, though still side by side, they will work in silence.

Figure 2.1 Student Cindy Klein and an inmate from the county jail painting together

Social Interaction

We are social creatures. We need other people, though we often fail to acknowledge it, not willing to make the effort to socialize, feeling inadequate in one way or another, or preferring the surety and familiarity of our own company. One is indeed fortunate to be able to enjoy one's own company, but being open to the company of others invites insights into those other lives, and through that, discoveries into our own. Lives starkly different from our own have even more to share. Chermayeff, S. (1973, 9) wrote:

> There are no mixing places in our culture. The designing of the environmental process must include the making of mixing places—public places where young and old, middle aged and adolescent, will find themselves as a matter of daily necessity . . . Indeed, it particularly behooves us to become sensitive to the needs and aspirations of those we don't know, because they may very well become the catalysts we need in order to transform ourselves.

The social interaction in the art sessions is often an unfamiliar one, occurring between individuals who would likely never have met outside the art session. Happily, the climate created by sharing an art activity is conducive to informal conversation. When individuals work side by side, conversation might begin with the project at hand—"the tree you drew reminds me of one in my yard long ago"—and go on to personal concerns—"I hated to leave that house, that town." Such *easy* communication may be a new experience for some who customarily find social intercourse trying. Not being able to communicate socially tends to compound already prevalent notions of poor self-image and feelings of inadequacy. Therefore, modest success in this endeavor with someone who appears genuinely to care may have an effect, at least temporarily, on self-esteem.

The social interaction that takes place during the art workshops between presenters and participants may also be noticeable among participants who do not normally relate to one another outside of the sessions. If that happens, some improvement in social skills may develop, for with a reduced fear of bad consequences, efforts toward other social interactions may follow. An effort may be made toward personal attractiveness, which may generate an increase in social contacts, each encounter promoting positive feelings of self-worth.

Figure 2.2 Student Jody Dramen in the Ridgewood Nursing Home, NJ, shows an elderly woman examples of a project they will be making together

Figure 2.3 Students showing children how to paint with watercolors in a Paterson New Jersey housing project

References

Chermayeff, S. "The Shape of Humanism." In G. Battcock, ed. *New Ideas in Art Education: A Critical Anthology*. New York: E. P. Dutton, 1973, p 9.

Claxton, G. *Intelligence in the Flesh*. New Haven and London: Yale University Press, 2015.

Grandin, T. *Visual Thinking*. New York: Riverhead Books, 2022.

Magsamen, S. and Ross, I. *Your Brain on Art*. New York: Random House, 2023.

Van der Kolk, Bessel, M.D. *The Body Keeps the Score*. New York: Viking, 2014.

Chapter 3

The Program as a Learning Experience for Presenters

Cultural Significance

For presenters from the college or community, the informality of the sessions offers a way to interact with people in our society who would not normally be available to them. It is regrettable but true that most of us rarely leave mainstream society in our spectrum of activities, and our knowledge of non-mainstream institutions and their populations is second-hand, derived from terrifying or titillating stories in books, film, TV and news media. Moreover, we tend to choose our friends from our own economic, intellectual and ethnic backgrounds and thus voluntarily close off access to groups unrelated to ourselves.

Certain populations are segregated for protective needs such as prison inmates, psychiatric patients and children suffering from abuse removed from dangerous homes. But other estrangements exist for more obscure reasons reflected in cultural attitudes: the frail elderly, those with disabilities in a society emphasizing youth and physical vigor, the poor where buying power is advertised to reflect belonging and often central to occupying a place in the mainstream.

Yet individuals in these groups constitute the human element at the root of most of the major social problems of our time: crime, mental health, ageing, disability, domestic violence, child welfare and poverty. Understanding these populations, not as classified groups but as individuals with specific problems, may place the overall domestic issues of our day in clearer focus and stimulate interest in related social or psychological concerns. Most immediately, personal contact by means of shared creative activity and private conversation offers a perspective not to be found in other sources.

Personal Significance

In addition to learning about others, presenters perceive their personal lives in a wider social context. Their problems concerning family relationships, friends, jobs, money and other matters are viewed in a less isolated way. The wider viewpoint may result in a more positive outlook toward their own situation and achievements.

DOI: 10.4324/9781003592693-5

Figure 3.1 Student drawing with an inmate at a county jail

Staff, students and volunteers who are attracted to this type of program tend to be men and women who are concerned with helping people; open to learning more about the social and psychological conditions of people with whom they are unfamiliar; and more inclined toward becoming personally involved in social problems (this observation is based on information supplied by students in the pilot program.)

Helping others in the course of the program results in an individual feeling satisfied that they are functioning well. The presenter might see this by a participant's restored feeling of independence in making choices in materials and subject matter. But helping is a two-way street; building trust and empathy of the others' situation is needed for the relationship to succeed. On both sides, mutual liking, respect and acceptance support helping relationships that foster growth and development.

The growth that ensues to presenters through this direct engagement is helpful in another way. Each contact can help in an examination of oneself and one's future: aging and feelings of alienation and loss; crime and the consequences of breaking the law; poverty and being deprived of home and mobility; child abuse and feelings of neglect or rejection; mental illness and the inability to cope. All could be perceived as happening to oneself in extreme circumstances; all are extensions of self. What if?

Informational Significance

Subject matter that will enhance the education of presenters and at the same time help the program run more smoothly are given in Insert 3.1 Suggested Site Information to Provide

Presenters, a list of topics that institutional representatives might discuss. Several of these points are aimed at fitting the program to constituents' needs, but others are clearly aimed at making presenters more knowledgeable about the institution, its problems and its place in the framework of society. Such information can alleviate understandable fears that presenters might have in entering a jail, a state mental hospital or a nursing home for the first time. Sensations involving sight, smell and sound cannot be adequately prepared for as these are intimate and personal and of the moment. But other preparations of an intellectual or academic nature can help to fit impressions into a composite picture of a place, its people, its problems and some solutions.

Questions will surely be raised by presenters about the personal life and predicaments of the participants. While specific information on client charts will usually not be divulged, some background information might be given to presenters about the place and the people they will be servicing. Information that does not violate the code of ethics of the institution should be forthcoming throughout the program series.

Presenters coming into the institution from the outside may not find it easy to obtain responsible information. Some staff will be too busy, others will seem not to care about providing it, merely appreciating the time off while their charges are occupied. Nevertheless,

Insert 3.1 Suggested Site Information to Provide Presenters

- The rules and objectives of the institution. Regardless of the length or extent of one's role as a presenter, not knowing the rules of the institution can be physically or emotionally harmful to oneself and to others. Moreover, one may work at cross-purposes and confuse rather than enrich the participants.
- The history of the institution with respect to changes in present versus past functioning. What part do changing social values play? Newly discovered medications? National, state and local economic priorities? Laws pertaining to equal access and opportunity for the disabled?
- An overview of the kinds and amounts of care and services.
- Operational aspects of the institution: what is the cost per day to maintain an inmate, a patient, a resident? Where do funds come from? What kind of staff does the institution attract? What special problems are connected with security, food and shelter, staff training and consistency?
- The long- and short-term goals of the institution. What does it hope to accomplish?
- Admission to the institution. How are the courts involved? What part does family play? How are the schools brought into the picture?
- What is the rate of recidivism in jails; special youth facilities; mental health clinics and hospitals? What are some causal factors resulting in recidivism?
- How are case histories prepared and used in the institution? How are they shared? How is privacy protected?
- What is being done through social programs and government action to prevent, deter or deal with institutional problems?

for the benefit of all concerned, presenters should urge that some information be provided. A professional or administrative representative is more suited to provide this than line staff whose knowledge may be confined to more limited aspects of their work.

Good information can improve the quality of the sessions, for when presenters are aware of such participant tendencies as testing, manipulation for rewards and conning, they may be able to handle themselves and the group more diplomatically. Moreover, they will have the opportunity to hear the institutional side of the story: the hard facts about why people are confined and what the institution is prepared to do and not do for them. Later, in the informality of the art workshops, they will hear the participants' side of that story. From this perspective, presenters are likely to get a more complete picture of the institution and the potential of their own role.

The Use of Media

Films, DVDs and video tapes provide a method of covering direct or tangentially related subject matter in an expedient manner. Brief but focused documentaries on child abuse, street crime, prison programs, the use of art in therapy and any number of other relevant topics can directly enrich the presenter's knowledge of the institution and its special problems. A 17-minute film and video tape of the pilot program, called "Art on the Outside" is also available: Appendix 2.B, along with a 9-minute You Tube version https://www.youtube.com/watch?v=zdjPyMonTd0. The information offered may stimulate further readings and research, all of which will add to the quality of the workshops and to the educational enrichment of presenters. See the Annotated Bibliography for additional resources.

Part Two

Participating Groups

An Overview

Figure 2.0 Student Carol Stein paints her picture with watercolors next to a little girl painting her own picture in an urban day-care housing project

DOI: 10.4324/9781003592693-6

Chapter 4

Group and Site Distinguishing Characteristics

Presenters in the college course will ideally be working with two groups throughout the semester in two different sites. But if the course credit allocation or other factors do not allow for this time they will work with one group in a facility for the ten-week period. Clearly, institutional or agency populations will have different problems and needs. The sections below contain brief overall descriptions of specific groups, their special needs and ways that presenters might assist those needs. This will give the undecided reader a perception of what type of population might best be suited to his or her temperament or interests.

The Frail Elderly and the Intellectually and Physically Disabled

He who is of a calm and happy nature will hardly feel the pressure of age, but to him who is of opposite disposition, youth and age are equally a burden.

Dialogues of Plato

That may be so but despite good humor the frail elderly suffer, alienated from the personal world of which they may once have been the center and enduring repeated loss of persons and of powers. Presenters should try to respond to the needs of the frail elderly with genuine caring and acceptance, trying to get to *know* them—their family, careers and life experiences—as opposed to being solicitous and tolerant. The elderly have had too many years of human relationships not to recognize the difference.

The future is not as compelling as the past in the nursing home and in the hospitalized veteran's center. Therefore, new challenges, per se, are not needed; moreover, there is no need to discover new ways of failing. In exploring the past, however, with its rich resources of experience and memory, there is the promise of a compelling present. Therefore, ways to summon the past creatively should be found. Use the content of the art projects to build in this direction.

DOI: 10.4324/9781003592693-7

Understanding Physical Disabilities

The overt consideration in working with the frail elderly and the disabled are their individual physical limitations. Such difficulties may include partial or complete blindness; deafness; missing or inadequate use of arms and legs; trembling; lack of muscular strength and mobility of the hands due to arthritis; memory loss due to dementia or Alzheimer's disease; emotional disturbances; and neurological impairments due to strokes. Some handicaps necessitate advance preparation by presenters to minimize manual requirements during the session. Simple tasks such as cutting and connecting can be taxing and even painful to the aged and disabled and may defeat the aims of the projects before they are able to get underway.

With respect to physical limitations, presenters must try to understand the implications of weakness in a new way. Physical infirmity and personality weakness are not synonymous. In our society, strength and power have perhaps been stressed to the point that weakness may be equated with failure. The frail elderly are indeed in weakened physical condition, but they have succeeded, not failed, to arrive at that time in the natural order of life in which physical weakness occurs. Feeling empathy with this state of the elderly as opposed to presenting kindly but insipid notions of respect, you might, for example, talk more loudly to be heard but not down to them as though they were small children.

One way of empathizing with the physical and emotional state of the frail elderly and the sense of inadequacy they may feel because of their declining abilities is to try to experience some of the handicaps. Do this by such efforts as wearing someone else's glasses and trying to thread a needle; by wearing ear plugs and trying to hold a conversation; if right-handed, draw or paint with the left hand. Recall the pain of a constant backache, menstrual cramps or toothache while someone else encourages you to paint. Tightening a belt or wearing shoes that are too small are other ways of incurring a state of relentless pain. Another act, more subtle, is to sit in one place and wait for your needs to be met by someone else—the need for a glass of water, a trip to the bathroom, a move to a bed to lie down.

The physical weakness of the frail elderly and the disabilities encountered among these participants and others do require that extra hands and additional help be available for executing various aspects of a project. Therefore, more presenters may be needed in these situations as opposed to other settings. The project may also require extra encouragement be given to overcome possible past feelings of failure, and assurance given that the effort will be worth the results. Individuals should be reminded of their previous successes when they claim as they might that they "can't do it." Pointing to earlier completed projects is useful as participants frequently forget what they have made.

Adapting materials and technique to the particular disabilities of participants is the key. The physically and intellectually disabled demonstrate their capabilities in diverse ways. Their artistic productivity can be surprising and rewarding for presenters, taking little coaxing for them to venture into projects that appeal to them, so familiar are they with overcoming challenge.

Support from other patients is a consistent source of encouragement. Interest in one another's work occurs if presenters succeed in creating a climate of shared experience and enterprise.

Figure 4.1 Student Karen Plant helping a frail elderly woman place fabric on her picture

Figure 4.2 Student Bernadette Mandese chatting with a resident of the Ridgewood Nursing Home, NJ

Choosing to Work with the Frail Elderly or Disabled

Reproduced below are excerpts from students' logs, describing some of their reactions to presenting the program in a nursing home:

> This is a place of extreme contradictions. One is aware of an incredible mixture of pleasure and pain, pathos and joy, reminiscing and forgetfulness. One can leave feeling extremely rewarded or overwhelmingly frustrated, or in possession of both emotions at the same time.
>
> *Marilyn*

> Ronald is an active old man who pinched the bottoms of any young women that he could get near, yet he said that his hands were too weak to do the art projects. Cynthia, a tall athletic student with smiling eyes, told Ronald that if he could pinch, then he could draw and it was time to start. From that day on, he became an active participant in the art program, a firm friend of Cynthia and a non-pincher.
>
> *Elovitz (evaluator)*

> It was tempting just to sit and talk since she really is a lovely person, but I decided our projects would never get done that way.
>
> *Debra*

> The fun we had today . . . the past and the future linked in the present, links in a chain of life. I remember, particularly, getting a lovely notation on a log, then I painted a picture I got lost in and carried my feelings to the nursing home where they helped others, especially a lethargic, hostile Mrs. A. to be free, and my double pleasure that I took home and bestowed on my six year old who transcribed his excitement into a card for a patient, and taking that card back to the patient . . . then I reported it in another log and again got a lovely notation . . . a cycle of good will . . . links in a chain.
>
> *Ellen*

Presenters who elect to work with the frail elderly or the disabled should be warmly compassionate individuals with a positive approach toward the natural order of life's stages. They should be accepting of differences in people and their disparate situations, and while perceiving the need for assistance and encouragement, acknowledge the uniqueness of each individual.

Residents of Correctional Facilities: Jails and Drug Rehabilitation Wards

The jail, as distinguished from a prison, is a short-term holding facility. Inmates, sometimes designated detainees, are awaiting trial or have been tried and are awaiting removal to other facilities. Short sentences can also be served out in the jail. The maximum holding time for any detainee is usually set at one year, but in practice, they are often held longer. Thus, the jail places a wide range of offenders and "presumed innocents until proven guilty" together in a volatile climate of apprehension while enforcing a strictly limited range of movement (see the schedule reproduced in Jail Routine, Insert 4.1). Prisons were not served in the pilot program mainly because of geographic proximity, but there is no reason why they should not be included when feasible.

Insert 4.1 Jail Routine

6:00 AM	Reveille	1:00 PM	Work Programs Begin
6:00 AM	Head Count	3:00 PM	Work Details End
6:30 AM	Breakfast-Optional	3:00 PM	Head Count
8:00 AM	Head Count	4:00 PM	Head Count
8:00 AM	Work Programs Begin	4:45 PM	Supper
11:00 AM	Work Ceases	5:50 PM	Recreation
12:00 Noon	Lunch	11:00 PM	Head Count/Lights Out

Source: Bergen County Jail Annex, Joseph F. Job, Sheriff; undated.

As detainees wait for events to occur which may radically change their lives, a sharp edge of anxiety might hang over every workshop. Presenters will hear talk circulating of trials delayed, cellmates dispatched to Federal prisons to serve long sentences and inmates returning from hearings, parole denied or free at last to leave. Because of this, a sense of anxiety runs through the sessions. That anxiety is an energy. All art requires energy and it is far better used than stored. Bitterness, anger, hate, nostalgia for family, revenge against deceivers: these are some of the emotions entrapped within the confinement of the art workshop space. They are, for the most part, not reflective but striking-out emotions. Challenges are wanted and needed and can be embedded in artistic activities which can utilize it well.

Of course, detainees have individual dispositions and problem situations, bringing more or less emotion to their artwork. As they continue their creative efforts in the workshops, new sensibilities may be discovered that can be used in art and beyond. In any case, creativity and attentive social engagement in this taut and highly controlled environment surely relieve for a time the strain of confinement. Not to be discounted, the act of organizing thoughts and feelings into material form can be rewarding when one's whole life may seem haphazard.

Notes About Art Workshops in the Drug Rehabilitation Units

Detainees in jail drug rehabilitation units (DRUs), encouragingly, are being provided services toward re-entry to the community. They may live in a less restricted environment within the jail or other facility, such that an art program (depending on the forward thinking of the local Sheriff or director) is, if not encouraged, at least allowed. It is understood that in every jail, security is the main concern and letting the outside in, by its nature, causes extra concerns and more work. Detainees understand that incarceration in a drug rehab unit is a positive alternative to serving time in the main facility; they know that participation in the rehabilitative schedule is required. This both eases and complicates the art workshop presentations. A usual situation is that the workshops at first may seem childish—after all, they only drew and painted as children—or it may appear they only enjoy the proximity of attractive co-eds (which it does to jail officers). But in surprisingly short order the art, together with a bit of self-discovery attending the activities, makes its magical way into the sessions and the workshops are looked forward to.

The women in the DRU section of the facility are open to the art workshops from the start. Because the sessions are often held in the same room as living quarters, the sessions feel to presenters easy and comfortable. Moreover, the women are fewer in number than the males, have less activities scheduled and are closer knit to one another, therefore more open to sharing the art-making activities. Often, the women have children at home for whom they want to send finished pieces.

In all situations, after the first session in both male and female jail facilities, during which presenters are understandably nervous, the weekly art workshops tend to feel like folks getting together to share a productive adventure.

Attitudes and Values

Presenters inject attitudes of achievement into the jail environment through discussions about their own interests and activities: their school and work; their doubts and aspirations. These are natural topics of discussion, just as descriptions of jail life and inmates' interests are natural in the exchange of conversation. It is not impossible that a new set of attitudes and values might originate because of that association. And with that, inmates may feel the presenters' lives, though different from their own, are not so unobtainable for themselves. That it might be an inverse exchange and the presenters receive the deviant values of the prisoners is not likely since among other things, the situation of incarceration is an undesirable one.

It is argued—and guards often do—that socializing for a criminal is merely a "point-scoring tactic," a manipulative means to build himself up before peers and outsiders. Nevertheless, even by following that tactic—ingratiating himself with presenters for his own gain—he is involving himself in a potentially more positive sphere of influence.

Many factors must be present to change a lifestyle and the odds for such change are not good. The economic, social and moral forces preventing an individual from breaking away from reinforced, self-destructive behaviors can be deeply entrenched. However, the goal of the presenters is not to *change people* but rather, by their presence and the creative atmosphere they bring, to *change an environment*, so that one may reach into it and possibly change oneself.

Choosing to Work with Incarcerated Men and Women

Presenters are a little frightened to go into a jail environment which is natural and understandable; however, following the rules of the facility and the safety messages of the art and social interaction program, they are in no danger. The rules for the program are to protect both the presenter and the program. Unless they are followed, there will be no program. A rule applicable in all sites is to provide first names only. No information about address is to be given. If asked, the simple response "It's a rule of the program" will suffice. Individuals at all sites are used to rules and will normally not jeopardize their situation or the program by pressing the issue, particularly so in detention facilities. Another rule is that any acts inconsistent with the program's intent, such as the passing of affectionate notes, sexual innuendo or inappropriate remarks of other nature should be promptly reported to the liaison or officer in charge.

Presenters may build sympathetic ties with detainees, seeing them solely in their safely confined situations and conversing with them in a relaxed social manner. This kind of interaction is the tenor of the program. It can, however, be misunderstood in the friendly exchanges while backgrounds of both parties are put on back burners. Presenters can get an incomplete persona of the participants they talk to. Thus, it is not unwise for presenters to be made aware at some point—preferably, well into the series—of the actual offenses detainees are charged with. Due to privacy regulations, this information may not be transferrable, but presenters would do well to take it upon themselves to read about crime and punishment beyond class requirements.

Reproduced below are excerpts from student logs which might give the reader notions about presenting the program in a jail. Chapter 21, The Jail Experience, includes additional student reflections on their experiences.

> I was very nervous the first time I went in and at the end I was so comfortable. It was like going to see a group of friends, just to get together, to rap, to do art . . . I have learned so much in the past several months. We had nothing to fear when we first came and they had nothing to fear from us. But now, we both know that.
>
> *Allison*

> Sally put on the TV and watched a wedding on a soap. She was crying. Later, she told me that she was leaving Monday and that she was thinking about what she would cook for her first meal home. We chatted about cooking and various recipes.
>
> *Marilyn*

Tonight, Alice told me she was in for a Federal offense—smuggling cocaine from Colombia—and was sentenced to eight years but eligible for parole in 32 months. Her husband was in a jail in New York. Tonight, she had a collection of beautiful and fun-filled photographs of her husband and herself on a cruise, taken three days before they were arrested. They sure didn't look like the typical criminals. They also had an adorable little daughter.

Denise

On the way out, the Undersheriff told us why some of the inmates were there. The woman on my right had murdered her boyfriend; the young girl who sat opposite me was a drug addict and a pusher; the sweet sixteen-year old to my left had coaxed a six-year old into the car during a recent kidnapping in Long Island. In a way, I am glad I was told why these people were under arrest because based on my observations, I would have insisted that they were all in jail by some trivial mistake.

Elizabeth

Hasaad was sitting by himself. I introduced myself to him and we began talking. He had a lovely picture with him that was for his daughter . . . that he had done in his cell.

Micheline

The thing that bothered me most was the prisoners' age. It seems unbelievable that a person could be in enough trouble by the time she is sixteen to affect her whole life.

Debra

And yet . . . if I can walk in sad or in a bad mood and walk out smiling, something was given to me by the inmates. We helped each other.

Cindy

Through their artwork, the inmates slowly learned that it is safe to open up, try new things like sketch a self-portrait, express a future goal and seek positive ways of resolving a conflict.

Katherine

Presenters who select the jail site must be responsible, mature and thoughtful about their mode of dress and both their verbal and nonverbal behavior so that they can be trusted by the jail administration to meet the demands imposed by a tight security system. While they should be good listeners—alert, interested and compassionate—they must also have the intelligence to recognize their ignorance by understanding that the subject of crime has many more facets than those with which they are coming in contact in the jail. There are no easy answers, and presenters must seek to temper emotional responses with good judgment and the open-mindedness to seek more knowledge.

Presenters should also be somewhat versatile in their artistic competency. They should feel confident doing the projects in the book and perhaps competent in other arts such as calligraphy, print-making, cartooning, portraiture, sketching or pastel work. Many inmates are anxious to acquire skills in art, either to please themselves or impress others with their capabilities or to produce something to sell. Presenters who can further such efforts add dimension to the program. Unfortunately, security restrictions on supplies impede the extent of projects permitted to be introduced.

Adult Patients of Psychiatric Hospitals and Mental Health Centers

The constituencies of these institutions are as different as are the facilities themselves and are grouped together only for the expediency of space and organization. Acknowledging the distinctive individuality of each participant, three types of facilities are briefly described: the chronic wards of the psychiatric hospital, the acute wards of the hospital and outpatient mental health centers.

The Chronic Wards

Patients residing in the chronic wards of a state psychiatric hospital are usually severely disturbed, many hospitalized for long periods of time. Their verbal responses to art activity and to presenters may vary from silence to a stream of disconnected or incoherent remarks to overt delight. In most cases, whatever the eventual response, many are willing to sit down and try what is offered. This willingness may be due in part to the docility produced by long institutionalization rather than genuine interest. But whatever the source, the result is that art activity and social participation do occur and this is rewarding.

As presenters become involved with specific patients, they may be able to encourage further adventurousness in subject matter and materials. It is advantageous to learn about the background of individual participants: how long ago they entered the institution and for what reason, whether they are visited by anyone and how they tend to behave when not engaged in the session. Building a good relationship with responsible staff helps to procure this information.

Presenters should be aware that their goal in the chronic wards may simply be to make life richer within the institution since after lengthy institutionalization some patients might never be able to function outside that protective environment. Accepting this, you will feel less discouraged about seeing little overt change in patient responsiveness. The simple goal of making life more engaging is a valid one when life in the hospital is the only environment that can be sustained.

The Acute Wards and Out-patient Mental Health Centers

Patients in the acute wards of the psychiatric hospital and out-patients receiving therapy in mental health centers are more open to change, positively and negatively. Presenters should take note of this as the sessions progress. Wide disparities may exist in the competency of these individuals to cope with new people and events but more active participation than in the chronic wards is to be expected. Field supervision must always be accessible to quickly and ably respond to needs. Essential in this regard is an advance orientation to the facility and dialogues after each session to help presenters understand how to make appropriate responses to patient expressions and requests.

Some patients may have prior experience in art media, and the projects selected by presenters should take account of this. A patient might only be interested in particular subject matter, for example, trees or flowers, and practiced at rendering that. Think then of imaginative ways to expand the subject, perhaps combining pictures with a story. Be sensitive, however, to accepting work as is, and moving forward when it seems helpful.

Choosing to Work with Psychiatric Patients

Excerpts from logs written by students who presented the program in the chronic ward of a state psychiatric hospital provide insights into what to expect.

> Then, there was Margaret. I can recall the time she told us that she had seventeen children and they were all twenty feet tall. And she had four cats that were her grandchildren and they used to talk to her about everything . . . she told us that she sang at Carnegie Hall and the Met. But she got fired because the lady song critic told her she sang beautifully but had a terrible voice.
>
> *Diane*

> Harriet told in detail about her mansion in Florida with 99 servants who wore pink and gold waistcoats. She talked about her swimming pools and tennis courts and yachts . . . Harriet had been admitted when she was 22 and has been a resident of Rockland for 39 years.
>
> *Marilyn*

> When patients such as these are disposed around a lounge, watching television, they look like institutionalized mental patients. They may be withdrawn, or hallucinating, or asleep. Most look to be out of contact. I was impressed how the same patients during the art session, although visibly chronic patients, nevertheless approach the norms for acceptable social interaction. Patients, for example, moved about freely and naturally [and] there was a good deal of interaction with students.
>
> *Humphreys—evaluator*

> Rita was against getting her hands dirty, and also it became evident that she was intimidated by the clay. It seemed to her impossible to make anything. Then she

discovered a turtle appearing out of her pulling and patting. She said, "Look, a turtle!" She kept repeating this the whole session.

Sally

When the patients came to the College to see the exhibition of their work, I saw some people looking at them in the cafeteria and I thought, "They're not seeing them like I see them. I see them beyond their differences."

Sally

We have to cut through some of our own barriers and realize that people are people even though they might be behaving in a bizarre way. It is an utterly "other" kind of place and before you know it, you're flowing right with it. Not that you're acting crazy, but you do let up. You can be absolutely free.

Martha

Presenters who choose either a psychiatric hospital or mental health facility should have open-minded and flexible dispositions with a great deal of patience and calm. They should have a desire to be helpful but not a compulsion to effect change. Presenters should be able to work with patients at their own pace, helping them to take only what they can from the artistic and social opportunities of the program. As in the jail sites, special art skills are useful to extend the competency of some individuals to whom mastery and proficiency may be important.

It merits repeating that engaging in art activity for any purpose that involves diagnosis or treatment of a patient's illness is not an objective of the program and should not be contemplated unless the projects are used in conjunction with a supervised art therapy program.

Children with Special Needs Relating to Abuse, Trauma, Poverty and Disabilities

Many factors work toward making the artistic experience effective with youth such as the stimulating nature of the project or its materials; mastery of new skills; the focus on personal subject matter; and the shared "play" with college students. Introducing art activities with youth of the low-income housing projects who have few material possessions, a precarious sense of individuality and limited opportunity for shared creativity with interested adults has a chance to affect self-esteem or at minimum excite a child toward other learning adventures. These same notions apply when working with children who suffer from issues stemming from abuse and neglect.

Creating art productions that derive from a child's unique vision and with his or her own input promotes a sense of individuality. This is, of course, the goal in all of the art sessions,

Figure 4.3 Student Nancy Halloway modeling in clay with children at the day-care center in the urban housing project

to create from experience, memory, feelings and the sights that abound all around. Originality can be challenging under the pervasive influence of commercial media setting a slick picture-perfect standard. Or the distraction from iPhones about what other people are doing and images flooding in from elsewhere.

Children with physical and intellectual disabilities are used to challenge and often approach art with a try-it-out attitude that others could be inspired by. Because they require *being* helped in various ways, the children love opportunities to help others. Therefore, setting up projects to do in partners is a good idea, partnering with other children or adults, possibly each with separate tasks.

Young children may be fascinated by brilliant color and the magic of making colors change, by being allowed the mess of clay and paint, or simply by their power to control events.

Elementary-grade children are generally highly responsive to art activities. Bringing in media they have not previously worked in by exploring some of the projects new to you described in Chapter 15 should prove rewarding on many levels.

Middle-school-age youth feel pride in discovering new skills in drawing, painting, sculpture and jewelry-making and in discovering personal ways of communicating their outer and inner worlds. Certain activities, such as creating puppets and devising a play around the characters, can have social significance beyond the project.

On the other hand, pre-teen and teen-age youth in the housing projects or youth detention centers who have been in trouble with the law do not readily agree to channel energies into artistic activity. It might be said at the outset that conducting the art and social interaction workshops with these youth will not be easy for presenters. Challenging projects of a utilitarian nature, which involve more sophisticated and higher energy processes than those described in this manual, will prove more successful. Projects such as, for example, carving objects in wood and stone or fabricating movable constructions might be received with some enthusiasm. (The author's book, *Sculpture as Experience*, referenced in the Bibliography, describes techniques for 3-D projects. Appropriate projects for teens in a range of 2-D and 3-D projects are described in two other books by the author referenced in the Bibliography: *Art Activities for Mind and Imagination* and *Artistic Crafts*.) Artistic resources to adapt to the goals of the program involving use of technology might be found on various internet sites for this age group. Be sure to create the project yourself and check with a supervisor before presenting.

Attitudes and Values

"Tough" youth often communicate with one another by a body show of strength and language which they use to get what's wanted and defend one's turf. When handing out materials, try to ensure that each child has an adequate amount needed for the project so that sharing and turf problems are minimized.

Crowding, a persistent condition of the housing projects, adds to aggressive and antisocial attitudes. It can be surprising to see this behavior begin as early as the grade school years. It seems like *war* on an everyday basis as children defend their person, territory and goods.

Because hyperactivity or lack of patience and emotional control is evident in some children, it helps if projects are completed in one session to produce a sense of accomplishment. A clear objective of the art sessions is to make children aware of their own capabilities, so take time in advance to select alluring projects with good potential for a successful outcome by each workshop's end. A pattern of accomplishment develops through completing the art projects and the respect from peers, staff and presenters which follows.

Because many of the youth in these disparate facilities are attention-starved, they may develop overtly responsive behavior to presenters—hugging, pulling and tugging. Males may assume aspects of the wanted parent for children in single-parent households. If you are successful, you will likely be regarded as an accepting adult with whom the children feel comfortable. The relationships may then go on further to your becoming a role model, and with that, the idea of going to college just like you is not far behind.

Supervision

Supervision at each session is a necessity in all youth sites. Without this, the testing that children apparently must do to assume mastery over new situations may be relentless and debilitating. Moreover, the absence of agency supervision places presenters in a disciplinary role, which undermines administering the workshops in a friendly and informal manner.

Responsible representatives can supply background information to increase a presenter's understanding and effectiveness: for example, reasons for children's tantrums and hyperactivity, and reasons for certain punitive staff responses that might otherwise appear perplexing.

Unfortunately, the lack of funding provided for youth facilities (as in many other social agencies) results in poorly staffed operations and thus ideal support services may be lacking. Therefore, presenters should be prepared that stamina, patience and quick thinking are among the many needed personal ingredients at these sites.

Choosing to Work with Youth

These excerpts from student logs give the flavor of the program in an urban housing project. Excerpts relating to working with children with special needs were not available but references on this appear at the end of the book citing art therapy resources.

> I had never seen slums like that in my life and it was a completely different experience for me. Once I got in there, I realized that these people are just like us, only not as lucky, that's all . . . They met us at the car every time we pulled in and they would help us carry our supplies in . . . For the first 15 minutes it was complete chaos. You can't get them under control at first because they're so full of energy . . . but by the time we get things set up, they've started to calm down . . . They walk in and out most of the time because it's really hot in the room and it smells and there are rats, supposedly. One of the kids has to run to his own apartment to get Lysol and spray it.
>
> *Lynne*

> The worst part was when a few started fighting. It seemed to spread to each one so that if it wasn't broken up immediately, the whole bunch of them went wild . . . The puppets were a complete success; they enjoyed making them and had even more fun wrecking them. I asked several of them to tell me about their puppets and each one identified it with another child there. Instead of creating a personality for it, they borrowed one from a friend and called it by that name.
>
> *Arlene*

> They had never been exposed to such an abundance of materials before and they took advantage of this chance to take as much as possible. The preschoolers were not as obsessed with the materials as the other children.
>
> *Jennifer*

> He would tell people to shut up and was very nasty to everyone. He had a puppet in each hand and I asked him some questions about them. He said they didn't know

each other. When Sue asked why he didn't introduce them, he replied that they don't want to be friends and that people aren't really your friends.

Linda

Those who decide to work in the youth facilities should first and foremost enjoy being with children. They should be able to tolerate the high energy and noise levels of children and be effective in transferring this energy to the projects. They should be able to accept shifting emotional reactions and respond appropriately; they should feel competent in pursuing the program's goal of self-discovery through creative activity.

Chapter 5

Site Characteristics Relevant to the Program

Institutions vary greatly in the scope and quality of the services they offer to their constituents. Some institutions whose primary purpose is security, as in the jail setting, may elect to provide few if any social services. Others may lack personnel with the farsightedness to extend services beyond those necessary for basic needs. Others who want to provide services might lack the funds to do so, as in the housing projects. (Suggested funding for these and other such programs is described in Chapter 8.) Although the various sites designated for the art and social interaction program have sharply disparate characteristics, some of the needs and objectives with reference to the program are similar and are listed below:

Responsiveness to the Needs of the Participants

Non-judgmental Relationships

Presenters who do their job well will create interpersonal relationships that are non-judgmental, without expectations for future performances and without recriminations about past actions. The burden of judgment, though necessary in courts of law and expected in family settings, schools, workplaces and so on, is not the domain of the art workshops where individuals should be accepted as they are. The release of that burden may allow other resources of the individual to emerge. (Non-judgmental attitudes in the context of the art experience are discussed at length in Chapter 16.) It is expected that participants will take a while—shorter or longer—to accept you in their midst. They may even feel uncomfortable with the peers they live and break bread with, as they might with the staff among them, let alone strangers coming through the doors. But all, individually and collectively, are members of the community, a community which you represent and in most instances which they are expected to re-enter. Your acceptance of them together with the intriguing bounty that you bring can help in this transition.

DOI: 10.4324/9781003592693-8

Responsibility, Order and Control

There is a need in the institutional setting to make and keep order out of possible chaos. And so there are rules that must be abided by. Within that structure people are expected to take control of their lives, to be responsible. Actions of responsibility occur in the making of art: decision-making—choosing colors, sizes and forms; discipline—bringing a piece to completion; concern—for the care of tools and materials.

The process of art-making has unique elements of responsibility in an institutional setting: it places the creator in the position of control. He or she has the power to make order out of chaos, form out of confusion. Finding that form can be deeply satisfying because the resources in oneself account for the source of inspiration and the tangible result.

Sensory Stimulation

When presenters enter the institution carrying the various colors and textures of their art materials, they bring another kind of exposure to institutional inhabitants: sensory stimulation. Institutions are built for security—in some cases, for punishment—but with few exceptions low-cost construction and easy maintenance are fundamental to their structure. Thus, color, softness and explorative nooks and crannies have little place when such priorities are maintained.

Institutions have made great strides toward improving the atmosphere of their rooms and public spaces, but the early writings of Goffman, Mehrabian and others speak to the subtle sensory deprivations that are hard to completely overcome. Goffman (1961) notes the lack of sensory stimulation with regard to sleeping, recreation, work, eating and most daily activities. The norm is to sleep, play and work in different places with different people and without a precise plan. In institutions this changes radically to doing everything in the same place with the same people and with a prescribed plan (Goffman, 1961, 5–6). (An example of such a prescribed daily routine is the Jail Routine, Insert 4.1, Chapter 4.)

The following passage (Mehrabian, 1976, 197–198) effectively describes the absence of sensory stimulation and personal space in routine institutional life and some effects on behavior:

> Most prisons are extremely drab, unrousing environments. Usually they are painted gray, have almost no visual perspectives; what can be seen, even in the yards, consists mostly of sky, gray walls and physical and human symbols eliciting submissiveness. Prison life is usually extremely regimented. Inmates make almost no decisions about working, eating, sleeping, or recreation, and have almost no options in relation to a myriad of domestic tasks—what clothes to wear, what hairstyles to choose, how to arrange and decorate one's room, how to entertain oneself—which most of us take for granted. Such a simple and utterly predictable environment produces extremely low levels of arousal . . . Many of the problems common to modern prisons—corruption, assault, drug abuse, violent homosexual cliques, strong arm hierarchies, racial tension—are in part, behavioral responses to environments that create prolonged and uncomfortably low levels of arousal . . . [There are no] territories that are exclusively [one's] own. There is no place in the prison that cannot be visited by guards and thoroughly inspected.

When the art workshops are in session, there is color, texture and movement, a hubbub of activity in sight, sound, touch and smells. The workshops, although performed in the same place at a designated time and with a prescribed plan, bring new stimuli in the form of materials, ideas and people.

Self-identity

The participant is made the nucleus of the art workshop from the outset as he or she works with the art materials and exchanges conversation with a presenter. The sense of self-identity that emerges naturally through the creative, self-directed activity is in contrast to the breakdown of self-identity that often occurs in the institutional setting. Goffman writes:

> On arrival in an institution an inmate is often stripped of his self-identity apparatus such as particular hair style, distinctive clothing, personal possessions; he is given regimented life style rules to follow and assigned this or that to meet needs ascertained by the institution. He is thus shaped and coded into an object that can be fed into the administrative machinery of the establishment.
>
> Goffman, 1961, 16

As individuals create art with presenters in an informal social atmosphere, they resume touch with the personal dynamics of life. At the same time, staff members see individual qualities of their charges as personalities emerge through the art activities and social interaction, qualities which are not so apparent within institutional routines.

That the experience is temporal and occasional does not negate its impact, for all experience is temporal and life's most memorable events are occasions. An early project to build on self-identity is Name Tags. Participants are instructed to create a picture including your first name and a picture of something to go with it to help people get to know you.

Figure 5.1 Name tags can be anything that pleases you. Student Sanna Lamenti chose this plump bug to show off her name

Figure 5.2 A nature scene of a mountain range is created by student Kimberly Sella

Figure 5.3 A name tag on a necktie is a new idea by student Kimberly D. Faber

Personal Space

The need for participants to have some private space within the public arena in which they spend every waking and sleeping hour is satisfied through the space that art activity can provide. Private space is integral to growth, allowing one to stand apart and assimilate experience and external stimulation, free from the observation of other people (Proshansky, 1976, 206–217). In artistic activity there is the opportunity to create one's own environment both while working and by producing products of one's creation.

Even in a large group, a sense of personal space and privacy can be generated by artistic activity. The creative work is done in a personal space on paper or other material, whether alone or in a crowded room. Art activity, combined with the chance to talk about it with someone else making art, affords a sense of privacy within a crowd, of space within confinement. Privacy is not simply being alone in a room, for being alone can be loneliness, alienation or, as in solitary confinement, inflicted psychological punishment. Privacy, in contrast, can be a state of deep sensory stimulation, whether alone or in close rapport with someone else.

Responsiveness to the Needs of the Service Agencies

Regimentation and Depersonalization

Goffman wrote his classic book on institutions long ago and both physical resources and attitudes in modern life have changed and improved, but the essential elements of institutional life persist and it helps to understand them. An institution, by the very meaning of its name, is regimented, its routines "institutionalized," the apathy and disillusionment of full-time line staff, and the mortifying depersonalization that comes with sharing facilities, protectors and lifestyles with strangers. He gives examples of personal mortification: exposure of the physical self in rooms or cells for others to look in on when they wish; the humiliation of having to beg for small things that one would normally provide oneself such as cigarettes or matches; and the revelation of one's dossier for others' inspection, which is a violation of one's informational preserve regarding self. When individuals are forced into the institutional setting against their will as in the jails, inmates can feel "totally exiled from living" while doing their time. (Goffman, 1961, 22–24)

Security

The sense of security that clients often feel inside their institutions, sometimes so clutching that they either refuse to leave or return in a short period of time, is an unnatural meld of fear of the outside world, relief at not having to make any decisions on their own and abdication of responsibilities for their actions. Responsible administrators recognize that the configuration of their buildings, the atmosphere, routines and isolation from community are negative, not positive influences on the clients they serve. But available resources and the constraints of time and numbers limit them to meeting only the most basic and overt needs. In so doing, they *institutionalize* the problems.

Sharing Institutional Goals without Conflict

For all the above reasons the institution may recognize that the purpose, approach and methods of the art and social interaction program are compatible with their objectives and welcome them, whether or not it has ever considered inaugurating creative activities. Chapter 20 includes some of these individual responses from site administrators.

The workshops, though they may not share the institution's goals, as in the case of the jail, must not be in conflict with them; for example, security is the reason for the jail's existence and the program must in no way jeopardize this. In all cases the institution is a more or less permanent facility offering full-time service to its constituency. The art workshops are at best an impermanent adjunct to that service. Realistically understanding both the value and place of the program in the total context of the institution's needs and characteristics is essential to its success. Bottom line: if the institution does not view the series as compatible, it will refuse it initially or remove it later if it appears to be in conflict. Fortunately, this has not happened in the program's history.

References

Goffman, E. *Asylums*. Garden City, New York: Doubleday and Co., 1961.

Mehrabian, A. *Public Places and Private Spaces*. New York: Basic Books, 1976.

Proshansky, H. et al. *Environmental Psychology: People and their Physical Settings* (2nd ed.). New York: Holt Rinehart and Winston, 1976.

Chapter 6

Barriers in Instituting the Series

It bears noticing that despite genuine reservations about bringing outside community into closed institutions, creative activities of one kind or another have become visible in the social services offered in virtually all sites mentioned in this book. Three barriers to be expected in inaugurating the art and social interaction program, with ways to counter them, are described in this section: initial admittance, acceptance of presenters and acceptance of the art activities.

Initial Admittance: The Jail Example

Barriers faced in getting through jail bureaucracy apply in more moderate form to other institutions.

Personnel

Personnel involved in jail routines are not there to nurture, cure or reform but to maintain security. The guards must be kept secure from inmate assault; the inmates must be kept secure from assault from one another; the institution must be kept secure from attempted escape. Services are provided only to the extent that the public is assured that standards and security are maintained. Certainly, the delivery and use of art materials could be a threat to security and is of no advantage to the institution. The loophole exists in the area of public relations.

The county sheriff, who has jurisdiction in the matter of jail programing, is an elected official. Publicity about good programs can rightly distinguish his reputation as one active in correctional reform and he may welcome the program. Officers working on the front lines are not concerned with public relations but with the practical aspects of maintaining security. Their attitude toward members of the outside community entering the jails, ignorant of jail hazards, equipped with bright ideas and a variety of implements and materials that are unfamiliar to them, will likely be one of suspicion and even contempt. The presenters may, in fact, be regarded as more rogues to watch over.

DOI: 10.4324/9781003592693-9

The dissatisfaction that staff may feel about their jobs, their superiors and their duties may be fueled by the command from above to allow the art program in. In that case, a climate distinctly unfriendly to presenters may follow. Many ways may then be devised to make presenters uncomfortable as they try to conduct the workshops. They may be mocked as idealistic but ignorant of the conning and cunning ways of the people to whom they are giving "recreation"; they may be kept waiting for long periods and then given only a few remaining minutes to provide the workshop; they may arrive to find conflicting activities scheduled, such as gym, and then told the inmates were not interested in the art, preferring gym; and they may be made, on very rare occasions, to endure embarrassing personal searches. Thus, continuing the art workshops when the resentment of staff is high can be a test in perseverance.

A Wedge in the Barrier

Although it may not be easy to convince jail officials and guards of the need the art program fulfills in the lives of inmates, the regularity, dependability and persistence of the workshop series continuing as scheduled can result in the program being accepted and ultimately respected. As guards and officials observe the concerned involvement of presenters with inmates during the sessions, they are likely at first to indulge them in their dubious efforts, then grudgingly welcome them. Then too, they may observe some worthy art productions by the inmates which they admire and alter their skepticism; a recognizably good (realistic) product can serve as a measure of worthiness to people unfamiliar with art processes.

Keeping the Wedge in Place

A problem which tends to repeat itself is that as presenters develop cordial relationships with inmates they may begin spiritually siding with their new friends "against the world." It then might not be easy to convince presenters of reasons for rules and the need for absolute adherence to them. Good advice to presenters at the outset and often repeated is to simply follow the rules without understanding their basis. Such conformity can serve as one's first taste of institutional reality.

As part of their understanding, presenters should be shown the other side of the coin: how inmates make weapons from such unthreatening items as a plastic toothbrush melted to receive a scrap of found metal sharpened on a cement walk; the vulnerability of guards who must work without weapons for their own security carrying only a nightstick while surrounded by hostile men who outnumber them by an impressive ratio; the hierarchy of command, as in the military where orders are given and taken without question; and finally, that if the art program interferes with any part of the complex security system which must function successfully for everyone's safety, it will be removed and with greater dispatch than that by which it was initiated.

Accepting Presenters

A second obstacle which must be faced is whether participants will welcome the presenters and what they offer.

Disturbing the Institutional Atmosphere

When the community is brought into an institution in the form of any outside person or group, the door is open to a brisk new energy that may jar the lethargy and routine of institutional life. The disturbance is felt as much by participants as by staff because the institution is often felt to be a refuge from the perils of the community or "real life." But the community is where the institutionalized came from and where many will return, thereby playing an integral part in everyone's past, future and present. They must also live with the community of others within the institution. When participants welcome the presenters, their materials and informal friendship, their lives are not only broadened to include those members of the outside world, but their expectations of future success in that world are increased.

The Transition from Apathy to Responsiveness

Among the Frail Elderly

Rousing the frail elderly to become interested in a new program takes a mobilization of resources to counter a combination of disparate problems. This may be fatigue combined with physical pain; arthritic immobility of arms and hands exacerbating the risk of fumbling; embarrassment at not "getting it right" and looking incompetent. All this making it easier to skip it and stay in the room. The frail elderly are forced continually to recognize new failings and develop cautiousness in their approach to new experiences just as they do in their approach to new walkways. Any movement from the safety of the chair is likely to be a cautious one.

On the positive side, if presenters make sincere and intelligent efforts toward personal contact with the residents, their enthusiasm will be returned because the residents need and want this contact. A circle of energy may then begin to flow, the art activity in its vortex. Because the contrast between past performance and present predicament is so great in the frail elderly, presenters may be a less threatening social presence than sons, daughters, grandchildren and others who knew them when they were strong. That factor and the known impermanence of the "friendship" may help to reduce the consequences of potential failure in the eyes of residents. Presenters are able to provide friendship without judgment, share new ideas and old stories, and receive residents not as they were, but as they are.

Elders of today, familiar as many are with internet services, email and texting, may have "no time" for projects in art. Rather than prodding them to join a group suggest that they watch, perhaps photograph others at work for sending to relatives. They can be asked to suggest titles for finished work, stretching the theme of a project, find illustrations on the internet of art by masters to share with the group. Engagement in the session via discussion if not physical participation can be effective in new ways.

Among Psychiatric Patients

In psychiatric facilities, medication combines with the chronic unresponsiveness of mental illness and the bleakness of the institution to create lethargy. Here, as in the nursing home, presenters do not make demands on patients in the way that professional staff who work with them daily must do; they keep no records on patient behavior, nor do they confer with others in a way that can affect rewards and punishments. Yet presenters encourage productivity, and because patients tend to like the presenters and the good things they bring, they develop the incentive to produce as the sessions continue.

Among Jail Inmates

Remarkably little transition from apathy to responsiveness appears among male jail inmates where presenters seem to be accepted almost immediately. The responsiveness of jail inmates to outside people and programs may be tactical in nature to obtain the perceived advantages of cooperation, tactics so ingrained as to be inseparable from personalities. (Yochelson and Samenow, 1976, pp. 484–528). Yet, despite this possibility, enthusiasm and productivity tend to characterize the sessions. In contrast, slower responsiveness seems to characterize the performance of female jail inmates, at least at the start. This improves as the sessions go on when lively conversations mix with the art to create an atmosphere of animation. The different reactions between male and female inmates to the program might be interesting for future research.

Among Youth

Youth populations also demonstrate little transition from apathy to responsivity for different reasons. Here it is a matter of redirecting rather than reviving energies. Except for teen-age youth with special problems whose external "toughness in attitude" forms an initial barrier to the projects, there seems little defensive responses among youth. Here, presenters have the opportunity to be in a genuine position of influence, serving sometimes as role models, sometimes as de facto counselors and, occasionally, even as proxy parents.

Among People with Physical and Intellectual Disabilities

Individuals here are challenged, of course, in diverse ways, but they share a remarkable history of overcoming adversity and are used to challenges which would stop many in their tracks. This ability places such individuals in an excellent position for the discoveries and challenges inherent in making art and generally take little coaxing for them to venture forth. The capabilities in diverse ways among the physically and intellectually disabled usually make the workshops particularly rewarding for presenters.

Adapting the art materials, techniques and approach to particular disabilities in the group is key to the success of the program. Among the hesitant, presenters should encourage a can-do approach, whatever the individual disability, as the necessary first step toward their summoning personal resourcefulness to explore the venture.

The Issue of Trust

In all the groups cited above, the ingredient of trust is essential in accepting presenters. But trust must not be confused with intimacy nor dependency nor with the professional relationship of client and therapist. Barriers of defensiveness have been built to protect marginalized individuals from people and events which might cause them more hurt. Presenters do not break through such defenses but rather build something else alongside. Participants then can reach out and take in what they need when and if they are ready.

Another reason presenters should not try to break through defenses is that they are untrained to follow through should the floodgates open. The issue of trust relates to acceptance of the presenter, and only on terms participants feel comfortable with. Remember this crucial caveat: *accepting the presenters' arrival brings with it the issue of accepting their departure when the series is over*. The issue of leave-taking and approaches for handling that difficult area is discussed in Chapter 16.

Accepting Visual Art Activity

A third barrier is participant (and staff) reticence to participate in creative visual art expression. This realm, a delightful venture in human experience, appears largely to have been excluded from most adult lives, although in childhood it was a natural and essential ingredient in mental growth and emotional health. As a result, most adults begin the creative art experience either by feeling incapable of doing it or by dismissing it as childish.

Attitudes and Associations

One reason to explain the American adult barrier to artistic expression (evidenced most forcefully in the nursing home) might be found in the strong work ethic of our society which relegates non-utilitarian activities to frivolity. A second reason for the barrier is the childishness associated with art activities: Children make pictures and things out of clay; grownups take on the serious pursuits of life.

There are, in truth, legitimate connections between play and its connection with making art: play and the fun of exploring; play and challenging yourself; play and free time to use as you please; play and making your own rules. But art as original vision, as shared communication and as a means to express human values is a serious, often profound pursuit highly valued in our society. Informal presentations of artists' work to illustrate the above might be helpful at some time after projects are explored.

A third less than positive adult association with artmaking is society's penchant for product-oriented goods and services. Creative visual activity, although producing objects, does not mass-produce and is generally just as concerned with the *process* of creating a piece as in the piece itself.

A fourth negative association with artmaking may be the fear of breaking through defense systems, which shield an untapped emotional world: the nearly impenetrable defenses of the severely mentally ill and the less overt defenses of the elderly against failure. The intricate defenses that make for rationalized criminal behavior is particularly complex (described well in the extensive work of Yochelson and Samenow). It would appear from the literature that the criminal has put no small effort into the defense of deviant attitudes. Perhaps that is why images of devils and other horned creatures often appear in their pictorial content (see Chapter 25).

Feelings of self-denigration, unfortunately perceived often in participants, do not make a good climate for personal expression of any kind, and that failing is a fifth barrier in the acceptance of art activity. Personal expression is the voice of the inner life as it reports upon all that is seen in the inner and outer worlds. To reject self is to reject the validity of those perceptions, and therefore to have nothing to say.

Conclusions and Partial Solutions

Presenters should begin with the hypothesis that engaging in creative art activity can be beneficial to adults in spite of the barriers described above. The effort is neither to be discouraged nor disillusioned by the attitudes described, which surely will be encountered; instead, to trust in the validity of the program and the projects and try to project that sense of validity. It is reassuring to acknowledge that if bringing free art and friendly socialization into confined environments were easy, it would have been done long before. Presenters are, in a very real sense, helping to break new ground.

Convey the Value of Independent Decision-making

Among the confined populations served in the program, art may be a relatively new experience in self-direction. Many participants, particularly in the jails and in the mental health facilities, are more used to taking orders than to making order in their own lives. Because they are so often out of control in their own situations, it may often be difficult for them to become sufficiently organized and authoritarian to make decisions in their artwork. Yet decisions must be made and made quickly in art as, for example, when materials become either dry, runny or non-blending at different stages in the course of their manipulation and the problem must be solved.

The selection process itself is a difficult process for people who do not make decisions easily; institutional life on the whole, generally programmed according to rigid plan, requires few independent choices. Thus, the opportunity to select materials, to make decisions as to what to create and how to do it, and to see these decisions through to completion can produce a revival of pleasure in one's capacity to make choices and to be independent.

Convey the Value of Sensory Stimulation

Stimulation through the introduction of new ideas and materials is built into art activity. This heightened stimulation of mind and senses may counter somewhat the blandness and lack of sensory stimulation that dominates institutional life as described in Chapter 5.

Moreover, the supplemental materials—photographs and magazines—used in the projects adds an additional element, that of cultural awareness, which can stimulate the senses.

Suggest an Application Process for Joining the Program Series

In some situations, most notably the jail, a measure of prestige can be added to the series by requiring interested participants to apply to join it. A simple Enrollment Questionnaire, Insert 6.1, filled out by those interested in what the series offers, gives importance to the project and if more people apply than can be accommodated, makes being selected a special privilege. There are few positive opportunities for being "special" in the institutional setting other than the customary displays of power which establish one's authority over others. Being called to attend a special weekly event, then bringing the products back to the room or cell to perhaps talk about what transpired, support the individual nature of the enterprise and the implication of talent that attends it.

Insert 6.1 Enrollment Questionnaire for Detainees

Name and Number______________________________ Age

1. Have you done any previous artwork in drawing, painting or sculpture as a hobby, or serious pursuit? If so, please describe.
2. How long do you expect to be detained in this facility?
3. What was your last level of formal education?
4. Why do you want to participate in the art workshop series?
5. Is there anything you wish to add pertaining to your participation in the art workshop program?

The questionnaire serves several purposes. In addition to providing some background information and indicating an inmate's expected length of stay in the facility—he or she should be prepared to attend about three-quarters of the series to be admitted—its formality itself is useful: Detainees must go to the trouble of filling it out and they must think about why they want to join the program. Applying indicates serious intentions, an attitude which can help the series begin on a proper note and at the same time raise the process of artmaking to a place of higher distinction than it might otherwise have, particularly in the eyes of the jail authorities.

Qualifications for admittance should be (a) sufficient length of detainment to attend most sessions; and (b) indications that the inmate is genuinely interested, as determined by comments on the application. Those inmates who cannot be admitted because of space allotment should be placed on a waiting list and admitted at any time during the series that someone drops out or does not attend. Such occurrences can be frequent in the jail where inmates may be moved to other facilities on short notice or punished for rule-infractions or for other reasons are not able to participate.

Figure 6.1 Student and female detainee drawing together

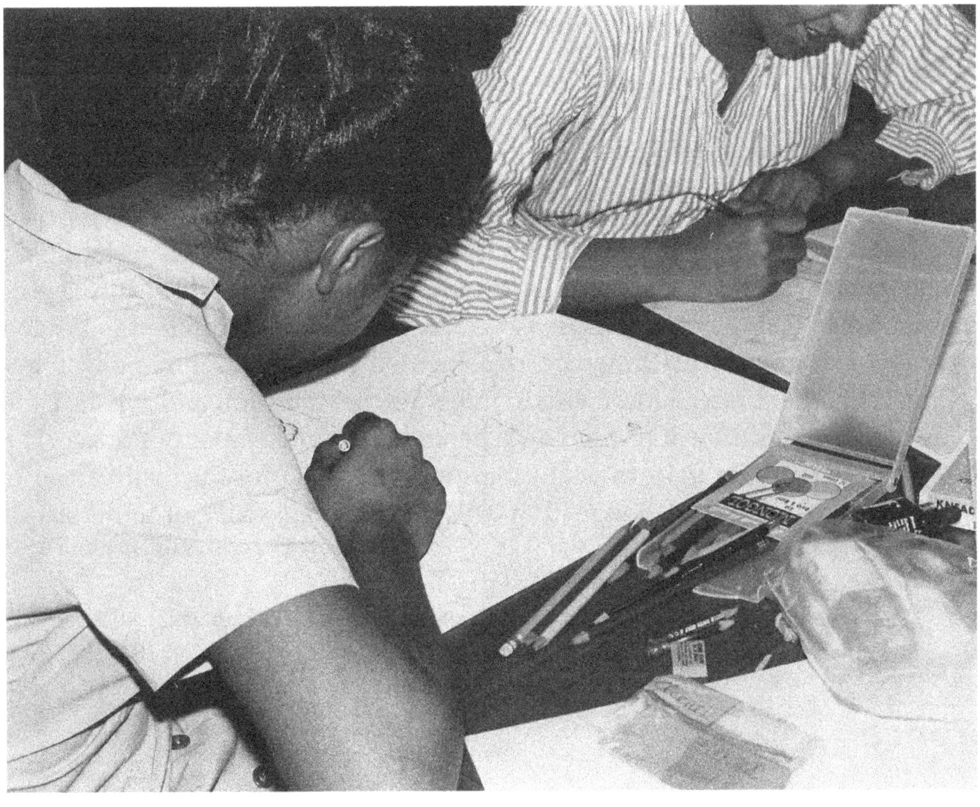

Figure 6.2 Female detainees drawing together

The time limitation of the series is also a factor that can work toward encouraging effort just as other "deadlines" do. There are only so many weeks to accomplish one's objectives: to improve; to have a chance to work with clay or paint or fabric or jewelry; to prepare an exhibition; and so on. The limitation of time and how best to use it should be a point of discussion throughout the series.

Reverse Persuasion

Reverse persuasion is a phrase that characterizes a situation in which presenters themselves begin to accept participant attitudes. It is not a remarkable phenomenon given the scenario of a newly organized small band of presenters confronting a large established institution. It is additionally unremarkable when one considers the limitations that are built into the program, most notably its limited contact hours leading presenters to feel that the program is too brief and too removed from participants' lives to genuinely affect them. This, we know, is true in part, but global judgments about the future (or past) of anyone's life are neither purposeful nor helpful. The duration and contact hours of the program could be adjusted, but if it is only weekly and for a limited span (customarily ten weeks), it is also a call to urgency to make the most of the opportunity, as in life itself.

Reverse persuasion can be illustrated by using this example: A presenter accepts that art processes are childish. She decides to present craft-oriented ventures that have utilitarian objectives, activities which she determines will be respected as more mature endeavors. Okay, but a better course of action is to include crafts but accompany it with fine art projects and the following argument: Although art may feel like play it is quite different, involving some of the finest resources humans possess: intelligence, imagination, a thoughtful perception of people, the world, and oneself. That, indeed, is not child's play.

Confronting Obstacles

Obstacles must be expected in any new venture. The challenge of the art and social interaction program is to confront them—to surmount them sometimes, to adapt to them at other times, but always to use them to reconsider the program's goals and function. The obstacles are there because of reasons, and those reasons must be understood. Therein lies the potential for learning and for growth. Presenters thrust into the new environment of an institution are challenged to try to understand it and to integrate their cultural and artistic experiences into it. Through conversation and discussion generated by the content of artwork, presenters have a rare opportunity to learn about the special concerns of the institutions and their inhabitants. With that new knowledge, they will expand their scope of understanding and their capacity to help.

Nothing will ever be attempted if all possible objections must first be overcome.

Samuel Johnson

Reference

Yochelson, S. and Samenow, S. E. *The Criminal Personality: A Profile for Change.* (Vol 1). New York: Jason Aronson, 1976.

Part Three

Preparing the Program as an Academic Fieldwork Course

Figure 3.0 Students Rick Larkin, Barbara Van Driel and Denise Colette bringing art supplies to county jail from the van which transported them from the college

DOI: 10.4324/9781003592693-10

Chapter 7

The Structure of College and Community Interaction

This chapter focuses on matters specifically related to the program as a college course. Readers will essentially be college administrators, faculty and students. Certain sections, however, pertaining to equipment, funding, budget and possibly site selection, will be of interest to activities personnel as well. Note that all chapters, before and after this chapter, include matters that pertain collectively to *any presenter* of the program.

Ways that College and Community can Support their Separate Goals

The college as an institution functioning in the community has a need to be accepted by the community. In sponsoring a program of experiential learning whereby college students actively use their academic studies serving community agencies, the college is furthering an image of involvement and concern about community problems.

In turn, the community is serving the college by providing an extension to the campus learning environment. When students work in local institutions and agencies, they are surrounded by a spectrum of human service activity involving medical and social services, public policy and administration, security systems, educational enrichment programs and more. Observing these functions at work offers perspective to students toward understanding the community as an environment of complex situations and problems. Such understanding is particularly significant for students who are interested in human service but who may approach community problems with idealistic and overly simple solutions.

DOI: 10.4324/9781003592693-11

Benefits of the Program to the College

To function effectively, the program must have the support of the college administration. As the program develops, the administration should be made aware of evaluations by institutional personnel. If the college administration is aware that the program is well received, it may strengthen its support.

The college provides faculty, instruction, direction and a portion of the equipment and supplies necessary for a successful program to the student body. The gains to the college in providing these services can be summarized as follows:

- The college retains the image of an institution involved and committed to the community. A positive relationship with the surrounding community is a universal concern of colleges. Sporadic incidents reported in the news sometimes place the college campus in a negative light from the standpoint of community residents. A responsible program of community service helps to counteract such negative impressions.
- The college has the opportunity to provide a unique educational opportunity for students beyond its classrooms. There is little doubt that community institutions with their diverse populations and resources, their special problems and solutions, and their direct contact with the professionals who serve their needs can provide the college with educational opportunities.
- The college has a chance to build relationships with elected and professional members of the community. The existence of a well-run community service program may count in the college's favor when issues arise such as physical expansion, bus service, road improvements and so on. A positive image of the college involved in community service may also assist in attracting guest speakers from the community on topics of concern.
- The college is engaged in developing an innovative program that has the potential to receive funding and recognition for the services it provides through grants in the arts, the humanities, education and health care, as well as grants earmarked for specific populations such as the physically disabled and the elderly. Grants awarded to the college strengthen its prestige and expand its program offerings.

Benefits of the Program to the Community

The community (site hosting the program) has much to gain in receiving the program's services. These gains may be summarized as follows:

- The potential to ease the workload of site personnel. Residents involved in the program may become easier to handle, requiring less attention from staff.

- Promotes individual and group behaviors already in place. These are improving sociability; accepting institutional regimen; expanding capabilities; increasing motivation to participate in other activities (observed and reported by past institutional evaluations). In agency settings where attendance is optional increased numbers are seen, extending institutional outreach.
- The institution succeeds in educating a portion of the public about social problems related to its constituency. As students are made aware of these problems, they often choose jobs or careers to continue their helping involvement. The program may attract media publicity, further extending the capacity of the institution to educate the public.
- The isolation of individuals within these sites is not helpful to their recovery nor to their ultimate return to the community. Half-way houses and other midway points designed to help formerly confined psychiatric patients join the mainstream are often poorly received by the community unaware of their special problems. The education of college students in seeing these individuals differently adds to an attitude of acceptance when these folks show up among them.
- The program helps to sensitize staff personnel to special qualities of their clients which may emerge through the art activities and interaction with students. Staff personnel are sometimes turned off to their clients because of regimens and routines that create stressful accommodation.
- The program may cause staff to be more open and enthusiastic about cooperating with outside groups. Outside groups are sometimes viewed as threats or encumbrances to routine duties. The art program, by adapting itself to routine while adding its rewarding ingredients, alleviates concern about outside group interference. Some staff are annoyed by the materials of art and respond negatively to the "messiness." Most institutional administrators, however, understand the need that people in their care have to feel a sense of *belonging* in the outside world. Community entering the wards in the form of responsible college students is one of the least encumbering ways of introducing that exposure.
- The program by its nature and its college sponsorship reassures the institution that the outside community does care about what it is doing. The jaded feelings to their clients that institutional personnel may fall prey to are somewhat due to the isolation of the institution from the "living" world, and the distressing notion that the outside world does not really care if those inside are "locked up" forever.

Relating the Program to the Liberal Arts Curriculum

Gaining Acceptance by the College

Notwithstanding the benefits described above, there can be in-house problems in establishing the program as a regularly scheduled course. The program fits into a social work course of study but requires art faculty with commitments to its own curriculum to teach it. Moreover, the concentration of required courses in social work does not permit many electives. Though it fits into an arts course of study, some fine arts departments are resistant to art education courses or those that involve the *use* of art rather than solely the process and product of art, choosing to concentrate on pure studio arts and art history. The pilot program, while not a pure studio art course and using art distinctly as a vehicle, was accepted because of the interdisciplinary and experiential nature of the proposed outcome for students: a personal exposure to contemporary people, problems and issues. Ramapo College of New Jersey, a state college just opening its doors at the time, was particularly interested in integrating academics and hands-on experience, a factor in the program's acceptance which could apply elsewhere. Colleges are recognizing the long-term impact of such learning and are open to opportunities to bring this into existing courses and internships.

For students, one of the rewards of learning is the excitement of seeing various subjects connect and come alive. Relevancy in academic studies is an objective for students as well as for their parents, and many colleges nationwide have responded to the call for less cloistered, more life-respondent curriculum opportunities. Ways in which the program can advance interdisciplinarity and relevancy in academic studies are suggested in this section.

Academic Courses Related to the Program, Insert 7.1, is provided to show academic relationships to some of the people, places and problems encountered in fieldwork. Titles were drawn primarily from art and the social sciences and will vary, of course, from college to college. Insert 7.2 that follows is a suggested memorandum announcing the program.

Interdisciplinary Faculty Involvement

To begin planning the correlation of academic studies, faculty from such areas as art, psychology, sociology, American studies, urban studies and education should be informed of the scope of the program. To do this, a memorandum describing the prospective course can be sent to all relevant departments. A sample is offered in the Introductory Inter-College Memorandum, Insert 7.2. The course syllabus (see Appendix 1.A) should then be made available for those faculty and students expressing interest, along with information supplied by institutions so that the relationship to other courses can be identified.

Guest Lectures and Team Teaching

Some faculty members may see the value of the program as an extension of their courses and seek to discuss ways in which the program could more closely relate to the content of their curriculum. If such interest is present, there is the additional prospect that those faculty members might appear as guest lecturers in the program to speak to various problems in depth. Faculty interest might extend to team-teaching of courses, which is an excellent way to advance the interdisciplinarity of the program.

Student Counseling

Another area of faculty participation is in counseling students, especially if and when emotionally charged situations occur. A faculty psychologist who is willing to become

Insert 7.1 Academic Courses Related to the Program

Life Cycle I and II
Social Theory
Scope and Methods of Sociology
Deviance and Social Control
Sociology of Work and Occupations
Societies and Sociocultural Evolution
Social Issues
Social and Cultural Ecology
Theory and Practice of Social Work
Social Reality and Law
Introduction to Social Work
Human Behavior and Social Environment
Child Welfare
Insanity and Society
Ethical and Legal Issues in Psychology
Group Dynamics
Social Psychology
American Medical Systems
Field Study in Community, Culture and Behavior
Human Ecology
Human Fulfillment and Human Destruction
Environmental Psychology
Psychology of Social Process
Scope and Methods of Psychology
Psychology of Learning
Psychology of Personality
Developmental Psychology
Death and Dying
Community Psychology
Abnormal Psychology
Educational Psychology—Learning and Learner
Psychology of Creativity
Art in the Psychological Environment
Basic Drawing
Basic Painting
Basic Sculpture
Printmaking
Basic Design
Introduction to Visual Arts
Basic Photography

Sources for listings were obtained from the Ramapo College of New Jersey Catalogue

Insert 7.2 Introductory Inter-college Memorandum

To: ____From:

____

Subject: Interdisciplinary Course, Offering: Art and Social Interaction Date:

The course, "Art and Social Interaction" includes instruction in drawing, painting and sculpture for fieldwork presentation in local community institutions and agencies. Sites may include a jail, psychiatric hospital, facility for the elderly, veterans' hospital, mental health center, substance abuse facility, youth home, shelter for domestic violence, after-school setting or facilities for the physically and intellectually disabled. The approach and projects are designed for the improvement of self-image and sense of personal accomplishment. Students have the opportunity to gain insight into themselves and the community through their encounters with individuals in sometimes unapproachable segments of society whom they may never otherwise meet. In doing so, students gain increased understanding of some of the major issues of our time: crime, old age, mental illness, child and spousal abuse, poverty, disability, substance abuse and war; and what our American institutions can and cannot do to help.
Course Content

1. In class: Instruction in art projects; methods of presentation; methods of evaluation; approaches for specific institutional groups, staff, situations and problems. Home assignments: readings, completion of written logs, papers and art projects.
2. Fieldwork—student teams are arranged according to their choice of field sites; approximately ten weekly sessions.
3. Campus visit by site representatives, possible full class field trips.

Credits: Day:
Time: ______
Instructor and Project Director: ____________

knowledgeable about the program can help students handle problems that arise by serving as program consultant and as informal advisor to students during regular office hours.

Planning a Related Course

A further suggestion for faculty participation albeit more involved is to plan a course geared for students in the program. Content in such a course could include such topics as:

- A survey of literature on related subjects: crime causality, child abuse, aging, etc.
- The goals and endemic problems of institutions in helping their constituents.
- The acquisition of observation and listening skills.
- Evaluation processes: short term and long term.

The list of potential course material is as long as there is faculty interested in an academic team-relationship with the program.

Granting Fieldwork Credit

Curriculum committees in the departments of psychology, social work, sociology, disability studies, law and society, and education should be made familiar with the goals and structure of the program with a view toward granting fieldwork credit. If credit toward a student's major is applied, a substantial gain is made not only for the student but for the institutions served, as more students then become attracted to community service and the helping professions.

Chapter 8

Pre-Registration Course Planning

Preparing Written Materials

Written materials needed for instituting this program as a college course are important, in order that college administrators, faculty leaders, students and site representatives all know what is being done and how. For this reason, samples of all such materials are offered in this text. Converting materials copied from the pilot program to new situations will be easier than faculty having to generate new documents.

Catalog Description

For space restrictions, the catalog description of the course must be concise, but the scope and personal commitment required by students must also be comprehensive. A sample course description for the catalog is offered in Insert 8.1.

Insert 8.1 Course Description for the College Catalog

Students learn specially designed projects in drawing, painting, sculpture and crafts which they present in small teams to the residents of selected institutions. The projects are designed to affect the self-esteem and motivation of individuals confined in difficult personal environments. The suggested fieldwork program of ten weeks consists of approximately four hours per week. Students select their sites from among participating institutions, including jails, psychiatric hospitals, nursing homes, drug rehab centers, domestic abuse shelters and facilities for youth with various needs. The approach, readings and creative arts learning are designed to further student understanding of the social issues of our time by direct exposure to those involved. Prior art experience is desirable but not required, however students should possess a high level of responsibility, interest in social institutions and a creative, well-balanced personality.

DOI: 10.4324/9781003592693-12

Summary of Pre-registration Written Materials

- Syllabus (a sample appears in Appendix 1.A).
- A listing of *Academic Courses Relevant to the Program* (Insert 7.1), sent to faculty and administrators involved in academic planning and made available to students.
- *Introductory Inter-College Memorandum* (Insert 7.2) introduces the course; a personal note might suggest relating the program to other courses.
- Course Description for College Catalog (Insert 8.1).
- Other written materials unrelated to registration are described in subsequent chapters listed below.
- Summary of Projected Line Staff Assistance (Insert 11.2—Chapter 11), a document needed to prepare institutions for their role as hosts to the program.
- Project Checklist of Materials and Amounts (Insert 14.2—Chapter 14), valuable for the expedient assembly of tools and materials for selected projects.
- Log Format and Log Cover Sheet for students (Appendix 1.B and 1.C), documents that guide students in their home assignments of site observations.

Planning Classroom Space, Equipment, Budget and Funding

Classroom Space

The college facility should have characteristics that serve multifaceted needs. A list of minimum requirements follows:

- A studio space with sufficient tables and chairs to use for producing artwork.
- A source of cold water.
- A wall for tacking and displaying artwork.
- Sufficient cabinets, shelves and countertops for storing art materials and student work.
- Sufficient floor space for storing large items such as clay, wood, fabric, materials and so on.
- A room for one-time accommodation of site representatives who will attend the orientation toward the beginning of class sessions (and the symposium toward the end of the term if that is scheduled).

- Appropriate lighting and electrical resources to accommodate art activity, including the possible use of a portable copper enamel kiln and other small pieces of equipment as desired. A list of Basic Equipment appears in Insert 8.2. The location of a kiln for firing clay works (optional) may or may not be in the same location, as special electrical and ventilation requirements are needed for this equipment.

Equipment

The kind of equipment that is most useful is modest in expense; many items can be eliminated without curtailing the program's ability to function. Most of the equipment would remain in the studio or classroom serving as the program's base of operation. Other items are of a portable nature and capable of being transported to field sites. Still others may be owned by institutions and made available for use. A list of suggested equipment is offered in Insert 8.2. No approximation of prices given due to the great variation in cost for these items.

Insert 8.2 Suggested Equipment (all optional)

Portable kiln for copper enamel jewelry
Paper cutter
Kiln for firing clay objects
Portable jigsaw
1/4-inch drill with sanding attachments

Budget

It is of course not possible to propose a complete budget until definitive factors are determined. The number of institutions and participants involved will influence expenditures as will the age and nature of participants; that is, inmates and other capable adults will require more sophisticated materials than young children. Nevertheless, a rough approximation of material costs for a given number of participants is offered in Insert 8.3 with a view toward providing a baseline for colleges and institutions to begin to consider the program a viable prospect.

Funding

In this section are suggested avenues for funding the art and social interaction program. Most of these sources will already be familiar to college administrators and faculty, such as grants' opportunities on the local, state and national level for social services related to specific constituencies.

Funding Sources Through the College

An allotment for basic expendable supplies and standard equipment should come from the sponsoring college department(s). Since a portion of program supplies and all equipment is used for direct student use in learning the project methods, the program is justified in receiving budgetary assistance consistent with the funding of other courses.

Insert 8.3 Approximate Budget for Expendable Supplies

The supplies and approximated rough budget for use by 15 participants and three presenters in a ten-session series in 4–5 institutions is offered below. Note that many of the supplies listed are not expendable and can be used with multiple groups. Since prices vary greatly in place and time, the budget should be used only as a rudimentary starting point in preliminary planning. Projects can be eliminated to save expenses, such as jewelry with copper enameling.

Drawing paper reams, varying in quality and size	$150.00
Watercolor paper, colored paper, Bristol board, paper rolls	$250.00
Pencils, felt tipped markers, oil pastels, crayons	$200.00
Inks (water based)	$125.00
Watercolor paints, acrylic paints	$400.00
Brushes (for watercolor and acrylic)	$200.00
Palette knives, wood sticks, disposable palettes	$100.00
Jewelry supplies (copper shapes, enamel colors, tools)	$300.00
Hammers, pliers, staple gun, nails, misc. hardware	$200.00
Colored tissue	$300.00
Solvents, glue, glue sticks, spray paints	$150.00
Scissors, shears	$150.00
Staplers, staples, tape, clips, wire, cord, etc.	$150.00
Clay	$200.00
Clay tools	$300.00
Plaster of Paris	$125.00
Plaster wrap	$300.00
Foil, stuffing, waxed paper, paper towels, cups and plates	$125.00
Mixing bowls, containers	$100.00
Sundry items	$150.00
Total	$3975.00

Grant Applications

Most colleges and many institutions have offices that specialize in obtaining funds for worthwhile projects from outside sources. The art and social interaction program has potential for obtaining grant funding in the broad areas of education and the humanities, with a special focus on community service. Grants designated for service to specific *groups* such as youth, the aged, incarcerated men and women, disabled, intellectually challenged and other special populations should be pursued, as well as grants focusing on the *kind* of service such as educational enrichment or art instruction. Grants' administrators should be consulted to determine where, when and how grant applications are best made.

Corporate and Local Business Contributions

In addition to pursuing grant funding, corporations and local businesses could be contacted for monetary and material contributions to help support the program. The institution is in a better position than faculty; however, some presenters might feel comfortable approaching

Figure 8.1 Students Ellen Ziegler, Jill Doyle and others draw their separate images on either side of a long strip of paper to create a mural

local businesses whose material products they think would benefit the program such as paper supplies, for example. (A letter of acknowledgment for this assistance should be dispatched by faculty for businesses to use for public relations and potential tax credit.)

If done through the college, an account should be set up through the business office in the name of the art and social interaction program so that ongoing contributions can readily be made and acknowledged. Expenditures could then be made from the account as needed following procedures designated by the college business office.

Contributions by the Institutions

Institutions can be asked to contribute a nominal sum to assist with the purchase of materials for their constituents. Participating in this tangible way has more than monetary value; it reinforces the value placed on the workshop series and consequently reinforces the commitment of the institution. That commitment may then be reflected in other support services such as staff assistance during workshops, better space allocations, closer contact with the presenters, etc. The funding may be allocated as an allowance with which presenters purchase supplies and submit receipts, or for direct purchases. Note: it is best not to pursue this endeavor until the program has been well established in the institution.

Chapter 9

Curriculum Content

Art and Social Interaction as a fieldwork course has two major spheres of operation which might be categorized as (a) what occurs as classwork, and (b) what takes place in fieldwork, the two areas creating an integrated whole. The approach and methods for use in fieldwork are acquired during class time to prepare students for their work in the sites; the events that occur in fieldwork prepare students for wide-ranging issues surrounding the people they meet, the institutions and the art activity generated, all of which are examined in class.

The field component is a series of ten weekly sessions in one facility over the course of the semester. Two sessions in another facility are added to give students additional exposure. Two different sites served over the ten-week series is ideal but often difficult for student work and class schedules. The fieldwork arrangement will be decided by the faculty leader depending on the time and credits allotted to the course.

A great deal of subject matter must be included in each class session before and after the series is underway, strategically planned in timing and content and well organized to fulfill both student needs and the complex needs of the institutions. The art activity is the vehicle between classwork and fieldwork and is a subject described fully in Part Five.

The subchapters in this section contain the full spectrum of course content, which would be included in an ideal situation. It is recognized that limited time factors will necessitate restrictions and adjustments.

Overview: Time Frame, Fieldwork, Site Selection, Art Projects, Logs

The Semester Time Frame

Curriculum content, while broadly based in order to fulfill the goals of the program, must still be tailored to fit within the stringent time limitations imposed by the college semester. This tailoring is one of the major challenges for faculty leadership. The usual college

DOI: 10.4324/9781003592693-13

semester runs approximately 15 weeks and, in general, classes meet once or twice per week for a total of four hours. This text will use a 15-week semester as a format. Classes will likely meet twice a week. The syllabus indicates what is included for the *week*. A sample syllabus appears in Appendix 1.A which includes the suggested content of class sessions and home assignments. Class time can be adjusted by reducing or expanding the number of projects. The content is ambitious but workable.

Fieldwork Planning

Student teams plan for their weekly sessions on site in class. Time is allocated for this. Team members discuss projects they've done in class and select the one they want to bring. The team decides which member will gather the supplies and bring them, who will introduce the project and describe in general how to proceed, who will collect supplies and return them, and so on. Bringing a selection of finished products to the site is always a good idea (making sure it is not just one or two which might signal the way a finished product is supposed to look).

One of the keys to successful fieldwork is the cohesiveness of the student teams; this is more likely to occur when students make the time to share ideas concerning the special needs of their participants and then equitably plan their tasks for the session. Nevertheless, often one student leader emerges from the team and because the leader is conscientious, much of the planning and sometimes presentation relegates to him or her. This situation is not only unfair to that leader but unfortunate for members of the group who let it happen because the organizational skills of planning and presentation is an experience to be gained in the program.

Student Site Selection

Students select their site or sites serving one per week or two (determined by the faculty teaching the course) early in the semester. The process for selecting sites is described in Chapter 12: Orientations. Students work throughout the term at the same site (or two sites) conducting one (or two workshops) each week for the ten weeks. The number of workshops is determined by faculty in connection with credit hours allotted, size of student enrollment, institutional needs and other factors. In general, the time spent at each site is between 2 and 2.5 hours including set-up, session, art display with discussion of work, clean-up and 15- or 20-minute post-session talk with the liaison or other staff.

Art Projects

Art projects are introduced and worked on in class and completed at home. Part Five, The Creative Art Projects, includes a broad selection of projects together with full descriptions about how to create them. Each project is grouped according to medium and includes suggestions for use in various sites. The "Suggested Content of Class Sessions" (Syllabus, Appendix 1.A) includes home assignments in art, organized to prepare students for introducing the projects sequentially in their field sites.

There may neither be time nor interest in using all of the projects described in this text. The intent is rather for faculty and students to select from those that are described and to generate other projects as interests are perceived. New projects suggested by students are encouraged but must be carefully examined and approved by faculty for their appropriateness in specific sites. A student, for example, thought colorful tissue collage over a bottle would make a lovely project for women inmates to brighten up their sleeping quarters, not considering that the bottle's broken glass creates a weapon.

Logs

The major class assignment is composing logs after each fieldwork session. The logs are the focus of anecdotal observations—the raw material of evaluation—and a major academic exercise. Because the log is so integral to the program, students must be given a clear idea of (a) why it is important and (b) what it should contain. For this reason, a Log Cover Sheet (Appendix 1.B) and Log Format (Appendix 1.C) are offered to assist students in recording the events of the session. The log is integral to the program for several reasons:

- The logs direct student observations to participant behavior. By knowing what to look for students can make more valid observations about the success of the projects and note specific improvement in areas of artistic activity and socialization.
- By having to record significant conversations, students may listen more closely to what participants are saying. Conversations which appear mundane may be significant in the context of other events that occur during the session or in earlier or later sessions.
- The logs help students become "professional" in their evaluation of the session and its participants by recording their observations in organized and coherent form.
- Finally, the logs provide faculty leadership with an account of what has gone on in each session. After reading several different student logs from the same session, the faculty leader should have a reasonably good impression of the spirit and content of the event.

The Log Format

The Log Format (Appendix 1.C) should be distributed to students and discussed point by point prior to the first fieldwork session. Periodically and with student permission, logs that are particularly insightful or comprehensive might be read aloud so that students are inspired to give their logs the attention that is needed.

Reading the logs is time-consuming, of course, and may deter some faculty from becoming involved at all; however, this writer has found no substitute for the input contained in the logs. Actual attendance by the faculty leader during fieldwork sessions—the only other way to obtain direct input—is a poor substitute, as sessions change when an outsider is present, especially the students' instructor. Although visits must periodically be made for supervisory reasons, the intimacy that has grown between participant groups and student teams is altered when the faculty *official* appears on the scene.

Critiques

Class sessions early on should include informal "critiques" of each other's artwork. Such post-project discussions are a vital ingredient in every fieldwork session, giving participants a way to "shine" among their peers. A good procedure for accomplishing the critique is this:

- Students mount work on the classroom wall.
- Students then come forward voluntarily, one at a time, to select one or two works; they comment on each, discussing style, color arrangement, subject matter of interest, and what they like about it or what works well. Then they encourage comment from the group.
- Discussion can expand on the selection of colors in relation to the season, the components of design as elements are repeated or made to stand out, interesting aspects of composition and how the viewer's eye is directed to move through it and, finally, the events and scenes in the picture and what the artist might have been thinking about in producing it, at which point he or she is called upon. The intent of the critique is to make the artist stand out in a crowd. The suggested content is to help the one talking find the words.
- An alternate conduct of the *critique* is to have individual participants come forward to talk about another participant's work they especially like. They then call on that person to talk about his or her own work, who then chooses another participant to do the same until all have had a chance.

Oral Book Report

Whether there is time for this will depend on factors determined as the semester progresses. A book is chosen by each student, and a brief summary of it presented to the class. A citation and short description is prepared. The faculty leader is informed in advance to monitor its significance and prevent duplicated reports. The oral presentations are best reserved for one or two classes (depending on class size) late in the semester, the time length for each depending on the number of students presenting. The purpose of the oral presentations is threefold: (a) to benefit the student; (b) to benefit the class; (c) to add to the program's bibliographic references. After the report is presented, students seek questions and comments from their audience.

The presentations should introduce the class to salient topics related to sites and constituents. As the bibliographical resources of the program are enriched, new students entering the program each semester can be referred to titles related to their choice of site. The books or passages from them may also be useful to give to participants related to conversations transpiring in the workshops.

In-class Enrichment

Several areas of enrichment have the potential to add depth and perspective to the program. These are guest appearances, film and video showings, internet sources, readings and a supplemental seminar. A description of the guest lectures, film and seminar is included in this section. A required or recommended reading list, as previously noted, is left to faculty leadership according to his or her discipline and direction. Suggested readings are included in the Syllabus (Appendix 1.A). The Annotated Bibliography contains citations from which readings might be selected.

The time frame in which the program must function constitutes the main constraint on the use of class supplements. If the recommended seminar described below accompanies the program, considerably more opportunity will be available to explore outside sources.

Guest Lectures

The most appropriate subject matter for guest lectures would concern institutions and their constituencies and the social problems they represent. (Topics affording background material for students in their work at the sites are listed in Insert 3.1 Suggested Site Information to Provide Presenters) Professionals who work in fields related to the program—such as psychologists, art therapists, social workers, agency directors, lawyers, prosecutors and judges—simply talking about their workday can influence student performance in fieldwork and affect career goals as well.

Group Guest Visits

Two formal opportunities are designated for several guests to appear at once: one is the *orientation*, held approximately three weeks after the semester has begun when students have learned the approach to fieldwork and completed several art projects; the other is the optional *symposium* conducted as the final class of the semester.

The Orientation

At the orientation (described in Chapter 12), institutional representatives present background information about their sites: the kind of clientele served, the problems dealt with and any other specific information they wish to convey. Following each presentation, the representatives sit at tables prepared for them with pad and pen to talk informally with students and answer questions. Schedules are set for the art sessions. Students then sign up with the representatives for the day and time designated and teams are thereby set which will work at the sites throughout the semester.

The Symposium

A symposium scheduled at the end of the program is an opportunity to provide a roundtable opportunity for feedback about the strengths and weaknesses of the program. (Unfortunately, busy schedules among the site representatives often prevent this valuable experience from happening.) In it, the guest representatives are invited to recount what went well in the workshops and what might need improving. Students are free to introduce their perspective on such things as participant involvement, participant/staff relationships, institutional assistance and so on. The symposium should be an experience culminating the learning that has taken place throughout the semester and should offer fresh insights to those attending.

Digital Supplements

Insightful, well-chosen material, in addition to enriching the program, can inspire reading and research in other courses students are taking. Appendix 2.B references a 9-minute clip of the art and interaction program in action.

Out-of-class Enrichment

Faculty/Student Conferences

Periodic individual conferences between the faculty leader and students are helpful for everyone. Such conferences might be held shortly after the first class, another at mid-semester and a final one at the end of the semester. The first conference would help students understand various aspects of the course and guide them in relating the course to other studies. The mid-semester conference could be used to help students strengthen work within their team and in their field site as noted by reading their logs. That meeting could also guide students to prepare for leave-taking discussions at their sites.

The end-semester conference could be used to give students ideas for their participants to use to continue being creative after sessions are over and to help them cope with their own leave-taking experience. Some students might feel a profound sense of guilt because of what they perceive as "dropping" the individuals they have worked with over the course of the semester. A private conference with the faculty leader might help to put those feelings in perspective. The conference would also give students an opportunity to voice their feelings about the program: its effect on their attitudes, values, education or career plans. These private conferences can take place during class while students work on art projects.

Planning a Related Seminar

Ideally, though understandably difficult to come by given the constraints of course load and economics, a two-credit seminar might be added to the program taught by a faculty member academically related to the program. This opportunity would permit more complete discussion of issues raised in the field sites, logs, lectures and readings. The curriculum as structured above exposes students to a broad range of subject matter. Their enrichment would certainly be enhanced by an opportunity for deeper learning and discussion.

Part Four

Community Field Sites for the Art and Social Interaction Program

Figure 4.0 Child painting with watercolors at the housing project day care. Clay sculptures made earlier are on the table

DOI: 10.4324/9781003592693-14

Chapter 10

Determining Community Field Sites

This section pertains to the faculty leader who will decide which facilities to contact to host the art and social interaction program. The procedures are therefore addressed to the college situation. Social workers and activities personnel already working for or within their institutions should adapt this section to their needs as they would with other sections of the text. Volunteers working independently or through a community agency might also be selecting sites and should take what they can from this information.

Program Criteria for Selecting Appropriate Sites

Selection of sites for the program should be made according to a need for the service and the ability for site personnel to provide assistance. That assistance should include support during the sessions and commitment to the full course of the series. The type of help will vary according to the nature, size and clientele of the institution, but certain categories of support are basic to smooth functioning. Insert 10.1, Criteria for Selecting Sites, lists the factors to be considered.

A letter stating what is required from the institution for the program to begin should be prepared in advance so that personnel can be made cognizant of their role. A sample letter appears in Insert 10.2 at the end of the chapter: Advisement Letter to Institutions. Other factors that the faculty want to include in the document can be extrapolated from material in this section. Details and modifications can be worked out between presenters and staff at the site.

Insert 10.1 Criteria for Selecting Sites

The site should have no similar program or service already in existence.

The site, by its cultural or sociological significance, should provide a learning experience for presenters.

The site should be able to provide a representative to serve as liaison to assist presenters in understanding the institution and its constituency.

DOI: 10.4324/9781003592693-15

The site should provide staff to arrange the logistics of space and furnishings, bring participants to and from the workshops and be on hand throughout the sessions.
The site should have sufficient space and facilities to meet the needs of the program.
The site should be located with geographic proximity to presenters for ease in travel.
The site requirements for students to serve should not be overly difficult, understanding that procedures such as fingerprinting, background checks and notifications regarding communicable diseases such as COVID-19 and TB are necessary.

Locating and Visiting Sites

1. Make preliminary telephone calls to members of the community familiar with the kinds of facilities that would benefit from the art and social interaction program.
2. From the list of contacts, select which to further investigate. Reaching the right person in each site is important as only those with the vision to be interested in the unique aspects of the program and have the authority to institute it (or refer it forward) can be of help. Initial contacts which do not work out lead to others which do.
3. If there is positive response to the idea of the program, arrange a meeting.
4. At the meeting explain the concept of the program in as much detail as possible. The explanation might provide a visual overview through whatever photographs, evaluations or sample artwork is available. A 9-minute video on YouTube can be sent via attachment and link in advance (Appendix 2.B). An informational handout is useful, such as a printed photo essay, flier or brochure briefly describing the goals, approach and methods of the program (see flyer Figure 10.1). This book might also be left for administrative perusal. Request a tour of the site, an introduction to relevant staff and, if possible, some of the participants expected to join the workshops.
5. Write a follow-up letter to each institution clarifying the general agreements reached in the discussions and request a return acknowledgment. A sample, Advisement Letter to Institutions, Insert 10.2 is provided.

Faculty may be unfamiliar with some of the institutions described in these pages and therefore hesitant to approach them. This is understandable as most are customarily not visited by outsiders other than relatives. Nevertheless, lack of familiarity should not be a deterrent, as once the series is underway, the "distance" of strangeness will be removed. If a responsible person is reached who sees the program as helpful, your efforts and initiative are well spent; if this fails to occur, it may signify that the site personnel or constituency is not ready for the program. Perhaps they will be open to it the next time it is offered.

Figure 10.1 A sample flyer to introduce Art and Social Interaction, Ramapo College of New Jersey

Presenters' Criteria for Selecting Sites to Serve

Because presenters may know little about the institutions they are preparing to serve, information should be provided at the start of the term. This can be accomplished in several ways, any or all of which might be used:

- This text.
- A short video tape of the program (see Appendix 2.B).
- Descriptions provided by the faculty leader who has selected the sites.
- Literature provided by the participating sites.
- A representative attending the college-based Orientation (which occurs after about three class sessions).
- Staff at the site orientation and tour (which is expected to occur at or before the first workshop session).

Depending on how the faculty leader sets up the college course with regard to credit hours, presenters will be serving either one site or two for their ten weeks of fieldwork and will choose which to serve at the campus orientation. The choice might be made for interest alone or to augment an academic major or to pursue a career goal. In all instances, the opportunity to observe individual clients, the professionals who work with them and the institution itself are opportunities to take advantage of:

- If enrolled in a specific course of study, for example gerontology, the nursing home or adult day-care center or veterans' hospital would be good fieldwork sites.
- If enrolled in a broad course of study, for example American institutions, the jail, drug treatment facility or psychiatric center would be good fieldwork sites.
- If interested in issue-related studies, for example the relationship of poverty to delinquency or the effects of domestic violence on children, the urban after school facility or domestic abuse shelter would be good fieldwork selections.
- If close to a career determination, such as working with individuals with physical and intellectual disabilities, a facility serving such disabilities would be a good fieldwork choice.

Insert 10.2 Advisement Letter to Institutions

College Letterhead

Site Heading

It was a pleasure to meet with you recently to discuss the art and social interaction series that we are planning to begin in your institution. I would like to review with you at this time the arrangements we have discussed and the areas of support that are needed for smooth functioning of the program.

The workshops are expected to be conducted weekly for .... weeks commencing .... and ending........ It is expected that approximately ...... presenters will lead....... participants in the series.

The support that is needed is as follows:

1. A liaison appointed from your institution who will be the contact person for the presenters. The liaison, if possible, should be present during the sessions or look in on them periodically.
2. Attendance and brief presentation by you or a liaison describing your facility and its clientele at a campus orientation, tentatively scheduled for.......... .... at... o'clock in room ....
3. An orientation at your institution for presenters who will be conducting the series. Ideally, they should see the area in which they will be working, possibly meet with some of the staff and participants, be given an introduction to the purpose and general routines of the institution and the rules governing conduct and safety. A time for this event should be set at the campus orientation.
4. Set-up of a consistently available time period each week along with facilities to accommodate the number of participants expected to attend the sessions.
5. Ensuring that at least one attendant will be present throughout the sessions. Ideally, the individual will be consistently the same though it is understood this may not always be possible.

6. Planning for a brief but regularly scheduled discussion period of 15–20 minutes with the presenters after each session by you or knowledgeable staff. It is at such meetings that questions can be asked and suggestions for improvement voiced. It is to everyone's advantage that these sessions take place, however, briefly.
7. Evaluation of the program's effectiveness is important. Therefore, we need your help in determining any positive effects the program might be having on the participants in your facility.

We realize that therapy, medication, outside influences and other programs make evaluation difficult, but any observations that you or other staff are able to make relating client behavior to the program will be appreciated. Toward the end of the series, you will be given a short form to assist you in this consisting of questions and some observations to look for.

Please acknowledge your support of this letter as soon as possible. We are pleased to be part of the responsible and creditable work that you are doing and look forward to a mutually productive experience ahead.

Sincerely yours,
Name
Title

Chapter 11

Site Responsibilities, Personnel and Support

The support that institutions and agencies agree to supply to participate in the art and social interaction series can be categorized under three headings: responsibility for physical facilities and logistical support; responsibility for recruitment of participants and assistance during the sessions; responsibility for providing information and cultural awareness post sessions to students.

Physical Facilities and Logistical Support

The physical facilities offered in institutional sites will likely be less than ideal for an art program. Institutions that have good facilities often have good programs already in place, a factor which would negate a need for including the site. The space and furnishings allotted for the series need not be generous, merely adequate and reliably available when the workshops are scheduled. The space required will vary according to the type of group and numbers participating, but listed in Basic Facilities Required for the Sessions, Insert 11.1 are suggestions for *all* groups.

Additional Facilities for Special Groups

The frail elderly:

- Space for wheelchairs to maneuver to and from the tables or in and out of the room while the sessions are still in progress.
- Enough chairs, floor and table space to enable presenters to intersperse themselves to work or to help while still leaving room for wheelchairs.
- Good lighting to offer maximum advantage to those clients with poor vision.

Youth:

- Clean floor space for spreading out while drawing, painting, working on clay or making constructions.

DOI: 10.4324/9781003592693-16

Psychiatric patients:

- Well-ventilated or separate area for smoking.
- Close by seating area for patients willing to watch but not ready to participate.

Insert 11.1 Basic Facilities Required for the Sessions

Enough floor room for tables and chairs to accommodate the expected group.

Tables with enough surface area to accommodate each participant with up to 12″ × 18″in space. Tabletops should be smooth for drawing and painting and at a comfortable working height in relation to the chairs, stools or wheelchairs.

Chairs that can be arranged around the table without taking more room than necessary and seating that accommodates the display and discussion of artwork at the end of the session.

A source of water that is accessible, at least to presenters and staff.

Absence of conflicting entertainment, such as TV, digital devises, pool, ping-pong.

A moderate amount of storage area for holding unfinished work.

Temporary wall space on which to display finished drawings and paintings, space which need not be in the same room as the workshops.

Sufficient clean-up equipment and waste baskets so that participants can help presenters clean up if they wish to.

Staff Responsibilities in Recruitment, Assistance and Supervision

Most often, staff members attending the workshops are not the liaison to the program. Staff may consist of orderlies, counselors, childcare workers, guards, attendants, volunteers—in short, a wide variety of persons who because of frequent job turnover, alternate duties and other factors will be unfamiliar with the goals and methods of the program.

The Liaison

The most significant institutional responsibility is the designation of a liaison to the program, one person who can:

- Act as the spokesperson for the facility in matters that relate to the program.
- Assign staff attendance at the sessions and oversee participation.

- Be available for periodic advice and consultations with the presenters.
- Be knowledgeable about the institution and its constituency and supply the educational enrichment to presenters in the post-session dialogues. (Line staff assistance is described in Insert 11.2).

Insert 11.2 Summary of Projected Line Staff Assistance

Staff assistance before the session:

Prepare tables, chairs and space.
Prepare or assign wall space for display of work.
Assemble participants and assist them in seating.

Staff assistance during the session:

Encourage participation.
Attend to physical needs, as necessary.
Attend to discipline and safety concerns, as necessary.
Help presenters obtain materials, water, etc.
Inspect materials when necessary.
Help presenters identify participants' names.
Help to hang artwork.

Staff assistance after the session:

Return participants to wards, cells or rooms.
Return tables and chairs to original positions.
Preserve participant artwork where applicable.

Attending Staff

Without support by responsible attending staff, the program will function but not as well nor as easily. It may occur, not infrequently, that line staff feel inconvenienced by the change of routine that accompanies the program. The staff may then follow administrative directives only grudgingly. With a discouraged attitude, there is little chance that the project activities and goals will advance beyond the duration of each session and as a result, gains made may not survive the presenters' departure. Therefore, staff regularly attending the workshops should be educated in advance about the program's direct benefits to the clients in their care. Afterwards, any elements of the program that might be causing conflicts should be modified to address staff concerns.

The Conflict Between Routine and Disruption

The duties that line staff undertake in assisting the program take place before, during and after the session. Insert 11.2, Summary of Line Staff Assistance, summarizes those duties and is followed by a brief analysis as to how presenters and staff might cooperate to minimize disruption. Before beginning, it must be noted that routine is not necessarily good—it can deaden both clients and staff—and disruption is not necessarily bad; it can enliven clients and staff. Routine is easier for custodians than change as it requires less thought, less flexibility, less challenges. Custodians providing day-to-day care of institutionalized people in a frequently unpleasant environment may see disruption, however well received by clients, as only added interference. It is a livable balance between routine and disruption that is sought. A clear notion of what is expected of staff can help to structure *disruption* so that it itself can become routine.

The list of duties is not extensive and when their charges are engaged in the activities life is often easier for staff, not more difficult as participants may be less demanding, may act more agreeably with one another and may behave, generally, in a more constructive manner.

The Importance of Notification and Assembly

In the simplest situations, the sessions are announced over a loud speaker and participants are asked to assemble at a designated time. More often, however, participants must be "mobilized" from bedrooms, TV rooms, cell blocks or wards. Advance announcement is important, not only to ensure the presence of participants but to generate a sense of importance about the event: The announcement implies that a scheduled weekly event is dependably about to take place for the group participants; that presenters have returned specifically to be with them; and that fresh new ideas and materials are on hand to be used individually by them. All these elements work together to produce a positive climate for the actual event. In contrast, when the program is not adequately announced in advance, haphazard arrivals, departures, attendances and absences can create a climate not only of confusion but of insignificance.

The Importance of Staff Presence Throughout the Sessions

Although presenters conduct the sessions and are responsible for administering the services of the program, they are not trained in the discipline, counseling, health care or psychological/social needs of their groups. Problems can be expected to arise such as aggressive or bizarre behavior, arguments and fights, begging illicit favors and so on. Only staff regularly familiar with the group can deal with this effectively.

Participants quickly recognize the unfamiliarity of presenters to their personal ways and to institutional regulations and might play upon this naiveté by testing, provoking and in other ways upsetting the session. They are aware that presenters are there only temporarily and can have no effect on administering discipline or granting privileges and thus take advantage of acting-out opportunities. Youth, and adults as well, might use disruptive or bizarre actions to demonstrate to peers and to themselves their power over those "in charge." Chronically ill psychiatric patients ritualistically wedded to rewards such as cigarettes for good (meaning docile) behavior, might ignore the presenters entirely unless the custodian of those rewards is present.

The reasons for discussing at length this aspect of staff responsibility, which may appear so rudimentary to the reader, is because it is that which may become one of the most likely sources of problems. If the series is well-organized in meeting its requirements, it will run smoothly in the institution. If the staff begin to use it as a time to go off to do other things, problems will begin. Affected will be adverse behaviors that divert creative energy from the program, such as the continued "testing" of presenters for their toleration of disruption. Equally important will be an undermining of the program's importance as a significant institutional activity.

Staff Participation in Projects

Staff is encouraged to creatively participate, not only to reinforce the validity of the art activities but to acquire personal experience in the use of the ideas and materials. By becoming familiar with the methods, the staff can introduce the projects between and even beyond the sessions, thereby furthering the impact of the program.

Respect for the Regularity of Participation

Hopefully, staff and administrators will place value on the regularity of weekly attendance at the sessions. Participants might take time to develop courage in the art processes and self-confidence in their social interaction with presenters. This means that staff should never use the weekly sessions as a disciplinary tool: for example, punishing inmates or youth by not allowing them to attend the sessions. Nor should other events be scheduled at the time of the workshops, for example, movies, gym, field trips or other treats making choices difficult. Necessary commitments can often be alternatively scheduled so as not to conflict with the weekly workshops, once the value of consistent attendance is recognized.

The emphasis in concluding this section is that a sense of freedom is offered within the confining atmospheres of the sites that are served, a defining element of the program: the freedom to make art; the freedom to engage with people without judgment. It is essential to maintain a structured support system of responsibilities so that freedom can be permitted to flourish without chaos and with consistent opportunities for discovery.

Staff Contribution to the Education of Presenters

Communication between presenters and the liaison is needed for all parties concerned; a predetermined, regularly set-aside time for this interchange should be established at the outset. The best time is directly after the sessions to allow for feedback on the session and the exchange of questions and answers about participant responsiveness. Offering specific background information can be helpful at this time to help presenters understand the failure or success of their efforts. While records are usually confidential, other information can be offered to give presenters a better understanding of the connections between the problems and the performance of certain individuals. Without these connections, presenters may often be working in the dark or at best focusing their efforts in the gray area of group rather than individual responsiveness.

The Post-session Dialogues

The post-session dialogues between liaison and presenters need not be lengthy nor confined to a set amount of time. A relatively problem-free discussion might last ten minutes while other discussions might require twenty. The liaison can further the success of the sessions, explaining specific client needs and changing situations. For example, explaining that a disturbed patient saw his close relatives the day before, and this has upset him and possibly accounts for his withdrawn persona.

Feedback should work both ways, always respecting the divergent goals of each. For example, the liaison might ask presenters to mount an exhibit of the best work of participants for a forthcoming visit from the State. Since neither competitive selection nor creating impressive products are intended in the workshops, presenters could comply with a project that would impress by the color and texture of its materials, such as tissue collage, mounting a display of unique finished pieces. Similarly, presenters might ask the institution to permit a project they might have been doubtful about, such as clay modeling considered too messy or otherwise undesirable. In each case, flexibility and accommodation are possible with the opportunity for dialogue.

Chapter 12

Orientations

The home-based orientation held on the college campus is designed to bring a representative of each site scheduled for the program to the college to introduce their facility. It should be held in a building not hard to locate on campus and a meeting room suitable to accommodate the representatives, faculty and students engaged. (This chapter, because it is a college campus event, will refer to the presenters as "students" throughout.)

The Home-based Orientation

Time Frame

The home-based orientation is attended by representatives from all participating sites, each of whom describes in as much detail as possible within about an approximate 10–15-minute time frame each, their facility and the constituents represented. The speakers should include the best day and time for the weekly sessions to be conducted as well as the topics suggested below. The intent of this overview is to help presenters make their site selections for the series.

The orientation should occur early enough in the semester to allow for at least ten full weeks of continuing field sessions to follow, but late enough for students to have absorbed sufficient background in class on the approach and projects of the program. In class also, the faculty leader, in describing the various site possibilities, should informally poll students to determine their range of interests. Disinterest or unexpected aversions to certain populations could appear in spite of prior discussions in those areas. Adjustments might then have to be made in the range or number of specific sites planned and alter the list of invited representatives accordingly.

Preparations

A representative from each site is invited to attend. Each is notified via email about the purpose of the orientation and the date, time and place. A suitable arrangement is made

DOI: 10.4324/9781003592693-17

to receive responses and follow-up calls are made as necessary. Preceding the orientation, students may sign up to bring refreshments. This responsibility may not be necessary if there is modest funding to be had for a coffee service, breads, cheese, crackers, dips, juice, utensils and such.

The faculty leader may want to invite appropriate college administrators to stop in and meet the site representatives at the start of the orientation before individual presentations get underway. This allows administrators to see for themselves the community outreach that occurs and may ease the way for financial support. Faculty might also want to video tape the proceedings for future use.

Presentation Topics

During the preliminary refreshment period, everyone present meets informally. After this, each site representative is introduced by the faculty leader and each makes a presentation about his or her facility. Topics addressed should include:

- The best days and time proposed for the workshop series.
- The size and scope of the institution; the range and disciplines of staff, for example, physicians, psychologists, social workers, therapists, counselors, custodians, guards.
- The range of individuals served and the composition of various wards or units.
- The type of problems faced by individuals with whom students will be working.
- The kinds of problems faced by staff members in serving their constituents.
- What special admonitions they would offer, both to protect students and ensure the well-being of those served.

Students should be encouraged to ask questions during and after the presentations.

Arrangement Formulations

Following the presentation, each site representative is assigned a seat at a table in the room; there they answer further questions and begin formulating the schedule of workshops. As deliberations regarding choice of site, available days, best times and travel logistics are made, student teams are formed and a tentative list made. Students may go to several tables before determining their sites.

On the representative's list should be written the site's name, address and telephone number, and the liaison's mobile number and e-mail. Each list will include the day and time of the fieldwork session. Under these headings, students who have decided to serve those sites write their names, e-mail addresses and mobile phone numbers. A copy of each completed list is taken by the faculty leader and a Master Chart created (see Insert 12.1).

Organizing the teams, generally comprised of three to five students for each site, sometimes takes manipulation and trade-off to ensure no overflow of students at one site and no liaison "goes home empty" at another. Surprisingly, these circumstances are infrequent.

Day and Time Factors

A factor which will have significant bearing on the choice of sites is the projected day and time for the sessions since students will have school and work obligations that limit their time. Institutions also will have preferred times for the workshops. This will vary but certain educated generalities hold true:

- All institutions schedule events around meals. Therefore, 12:00 to 1:00 and 5:00 to 6:00 are generally unavailable hours.
- Many residents in the psychiatric hospital and nursing home are "better" in the afternoon and in addition, routines such as physical therapy may be reserved for the morning hours; therefore, the preferred time would generally be between 1:30 and 3:30.
- Youth facilities will usually have educational scheduling during the day and therefore the preferred time would be "after school" between 3:00 and 5:00 or 6:00 and 8:00; however, preschool sessions could be held earlier in the day.
- Jails may have work routines during the day. Therefore, the preferred time would be in the early evening between 7:30 and 9:00 except during visiting evenings. Progressive jails using the program educationally like classes for the GED (high school equivalency) and similar activities might prefer a regular time period, possibly in the morning, 9:00–10:00 a.m.
- Outpatient mental health facilities and day programs for the physically disabled might have various times in the day and evening when sessions are best scheduled, depending on the therapy or work obligations of their constituents. The art sessions might be included as an aspect of regularly scheduled activity or offered as a new service entirely.

Organizing Successful Student Teams

If (a) the type of institution and (b) the days and times of scheduling are resolvable and there are still opportunities for choice, the following factors might be considered to form the most cohesive and potentially successful teams:

- Variety of expertise: (students already familiar with fine art media are in a position to expand the artistic opportunity for participants.)
- Variety of personality: some students may be more outgoing or have more leadership capabilities than others, qualities which can add to the tenor of the workshops.
- Variety in age: students have the potential of becoming role models and age relationships are often a factor in such alliances. Also, mature individuals can inspire younger ones and vice versa.
- Variety in ethnic background: students may customarily form social relationships with those of similar ethnic backgrounds. Students have an opportunity in forming teams to acquire fresh new views of those with different backgrounds, therefore, a mix is desirable.
- Gender is also a factor for several reasons. In the housing project and urban afterschool situation, fathers are often absent and thus a male student may have special importance for youth. In the jail, female students working with male inmates in the engaging climate of the art sessions may promote meaningful conversations as opposed to conditioned responses relating to sexual conquest. Inmates may discover different aspects of women through some of the discussion topics of the session—such as in art, music, academic studies, work routines, friends—and develop new values in their future gender relationships.

Finally, however, the most important factor in the success of student teams is the cohesiveness of the group including:

- Support of one another in a shared purpose.
- Flexibility in helping when needed.
- Willingness to meet and discuss plans and problems.
- Commitment to the high degree of personal responsibility that is necessary in working in an institutional setting.
- Readiness to share the responsibilities of the sessions.

The Master Chart

Eventually, choices are made, and scheduling conflicts are worked out by various adjustments across the board. As stated, sometimes the leader may have to encourage alternative site selections when too many individuals sign up for certain sites and not enough for others. It is rare for a site not to be served at all if students were poled in class as to their interests in specific site populations.

When site selection is finalized, a "Master Chart" is formulated from the lists which the faculty leader took from each table of the orientation. The list is brought to class for simple corrections that might be needed in contact information and session times.

A sample Master Chart appears in Insert 12.1. When the Master Chart is finalized, it is then run off and copies are distributed to each student and e-mailed or given to site representatives. The Master Chart is an indispensable aid to the smooth running of sessions. Because it contains full names and phone numbers, the chart should be kept in a safe place and not brought into the sessions or carelessly left behind. (The title "Student" or "Presenter" is interchangeable depending on the program originating in the college or an outside organization.)

On-site Orientations

During the campus, home-based orientation, site representatives arrange a time during the week when they will be available to introduce students to the actual site in which they will be working. The purpose of the on-site orientation is to:

- Provide information about the facility and if possible, a tour.
- Show students the participants with whom they will be working.
- Introduce students to appropriate administrators and line staff.
- Advise students about the institution's routines, regulations, security measures and prohibitions.

Insert 12.1 Sample Master Chart Format (duplicate as needed)

<table>
<tr><td colspan="6">ART AND SOCIAL INTERACTION
Semester/Date</td></tr>
<tr><td colspan="3">SPONSORING COLLEGE
Address
Phone
E-mail</td><td colspan="3">FACULTY/PROJECT DIRECTOR
Title
Direct
E-mail</td></tr>
<tr><td colspan="3"></td><td colspan="3"></td></tr>
<tr><td colspan="3">SITE:
Address
Phone
Name of Representative
Mobile phone
E-mail
Day and Time of Sessions</td><td colspan="3">SITE:
Address
Phone
Name of Representative
Mobile phone
E-mail
Day and Time of Session</td></tr>
<tr><td>Presenter's name</td><td>Mobile Phone</td><td>E-mail</td><td>Presenter's name</td><td>Mobile Phone</td><td>E-mail</td></tr>
<tr><td>____________</td><td>__________</td><td>_____</td><td>____________</td><td>__________</td><td>_____</td></tr>
<tr><td>____________</td><td>__________</td><td>_____</td><td>____________</td><td>__________</td><td>_____</td></tr>
<tr><td>____________</td><td>__________</td><td>_____</td><td>____________</td><td>__________</td><td>_____</td></tr>
<tr><td>____________</td><td>__________</td><td>_____</td><td>____________</td><td>__________</td><td>_____</td></tr>
<tr><td colspan="3">SITE:
Address
Phone
Name of Representative
Mobile phone
E-mail
Day and Time of Session</td><td colspan="3">SITE:
Address
Phone
Name of Representative
Mobile phone
E-mail
Day and Time of Session</td></tr>
<tr><td>Presenter's name</td><td>Mobile Phone</td><td>E-mail</td><td>Presenter's name</td><td>Mobile Phone</td><td>E-mail</td></tr>
<tr><td>____________</td><td>__________</td><td>_____</td><td>____________</td><td>__________</td><td>_____</td></tr>
<tr><td>____________</td><td>__________</td><td>_____</td><td>____________</td><td>__________</td><td>_____</td></tr>
<tr><td>____________</td><td>__________</td><td>_____</td><td>____________</td><td>__________</td><td>_____</td></tr>
<tr><td>____________</td><td>__________</td><td>_____</td><td>____________</td><td>__________</td><td>_____</td></tr>
</table>

The on-site orientation is not only important for the content suggested above. It also gives students the only opportunity they are likely to have of seeing participants outside of the controlled workshop setting which they themselves are going to provide. All presenters sometimes get a distorted view of the predicament of the people with whom they work when they see them only during the sessions. They may wonder why such benign, normal, controlled and adequate individuals are institutionalized at all, without fully comprehending that the workshop may create a benign, normal, controlled environment to which they are relating.

Students may attend more than one orientation. However, their decisions regarding site selection are made during the home-based orientation, and the purpose of the on-site orientation is essentially to prepare them for their forthcoming weekly presentations.

Preparatory Duties or Requirements

Increasingly, agencies and institutions require preparation of various kinds for "interns," even for the limited ten-week time frame of the art workshops. Such requirements may include background checks, TB testing, physical examination, proof that certain shots or vaccines having been obtained. Another requirement done either by the facility or independent arrangement might include finger printing.

To work in some facilities, an affiliation agreement might be required between the college and the site before the program can be instituted. In other instances, students might be required to physically attend a lengthy orientation to the site covering privacy rules and other issues required by State or Federal mandates governing volunteer service.

Such demands, albeit deemed necessary by the institution for everyone's protection, can sometimes make a facility which could benefit greatly from the art and social interaction program too difficult to serve because of the time and effort required. Those obligations can clearly dull enthusiasm for getting things underway, but the good news is most can be readily accomplished once pathways for undertaking them are understood and become routine.

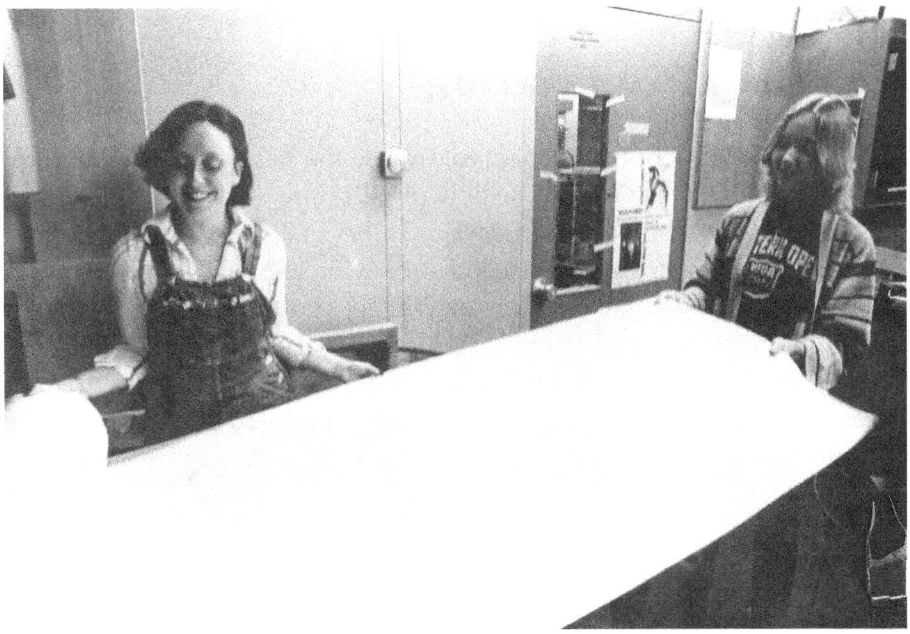

Figure 12.1 Students Donna Schmaydey and Jill Doyle unroll paper to bring to their site for a mural project

Chapter 13

Logistics of the Art and Social Interaction Sessions

Preparing the Weekly Sessions

Preparing *each* fieldwork session includes:

- Selecting projects
- Gathering project materials
- Coordinating transportation
- Notifying others of absence or lateness
- Setting up table arrangements and seating
- Distributing supplies
- Helping participants
- Handling distractions

Pre-workshop Preparation

Before each class ends, student teams meet to discuss the projects they plan to present that week. Their selections may result from the new project done that day in class or ideas taken from the Project Checklist: Chart of Art Materials, Insert 14.2, or suggestions made by faculty or other students or by participants themselves in previous sessions. Choice must sometimes be made from the supplies available if they are still *out* at other sites.

Discussion should include the planned approach—will one person explain the process to all, or will presenters lead small groups at separate tables? Will there be a theme connected with the project (need not be) and if so, what? It can be helpful to devise a tentative (and flexible) calendar of planned projects (though often not easy with supply chain problems and inconsistent participant attendance.

Gathering Project Materials

It is less chaotic if one person is designated to assemble supplies for his or her group. That individual makes a list of the assembled supplies. A class volunteer (recruited early in the term and

DOI: 10.4324/9781003592693-18

functioning throughout) records the site, date, student in charge and the listed items. The team member taking the supplies signs the list. This procedure makes it possible to keep track of supplies which might otherwise remain in someone's possession for weeks or even after the series has ended. *Students are cautioned to return supplies in timely fashion to enable others to use them.*

The Emergency Kit

In addition to the art materials collected each week, an "emergency kit" is purchased by each student and brought along to permit a session to take place if a supply mix-up occurs. This might occur when students have supplies in their cars and then have car trouble or are late or incapacitated for other reasons. With a modest emergency kit consisting of the following materials several projects in drawing, painting, collage and art/writing improvisations can be offered without any additional supplies on hand:

One small- or medium-size sketch pad (Xerox paper is also usually available on site)
One set of colored markers
Ten pencils with erasers
One watercolor set with brush
Roll of masking tape
Five glue sticks
Small pair of scissors

Basic Materials Supplied by the Facility

Some sites will have the budget and the willingness to purchase basic supplies and make them available throughout the series. This kind of support substantially eases the process of

Insert 13.1 Basic Art Materials Recommended for Purchase by Sites

(Estimated for 12 participants and 3 presenters: total 15 people)
10 thin-tipped black felt markers (Sharpies or other brand)
5 sets of colored felt markers or equivalent number, sets include 8
5 sets of colored pencils (sharpened), sets include 12
15 double trays of watercolors
15 watercolor brushes
5 plastic palettes (pads) for mixing colors
5 sets of cray-pas (oil pastels)
15 pencils #2 with erasers, sharpened (or 1 set of 30)
1 ream of paper: medium-weight bond, size 9″ × 12″
12 pads of watercolor paper, size 9″ × 12″ (will be cut into smaller units)
12 newsprint sketch pads 9″ × 12″ (opt.)
6 pads of charcoal paper (opt.)
6 rolls of 1/2″ masking tape
12 pairs of scissors blunt-tipped
3 rolls of double stick tape, 12 glue sticks,12 packages assorted colored construction paper

materials collection. Unfortunately, many institutions, some of which were chosen because of the absence of available resources, will not be able to provide support of that nature.

Basic Art Materials Recommended for Purchase by Sites, Insert 13.1, lists these, should facilities have the budget to provide them. The materials can be purchased directly or bought by presenters, providing receipts for reimbursement.

Transportation and Arrival

Students will be commuting to their field sites from home and school by a variety of means, public and private. Many will be living on campus without access to cars and travel may become a priority in selecting sites. In general, student teams arrange among themselves how they get to their sites: students picking up others without cars, taking turns driving, sharing expenses and so on.

Absence or Lateness and the Negative Implications

On some occasions, students will be late or even fail to get to their sites. A major obligation in such eventualities is timely notification to fellow teammates and to the institutional representatives. Students may not be aware of the serious implications that attend lateness or absence in the context of the program. The simplest of these is the excess work and responsibility placed on other team members; the pressure would be felt by both presenters and participants.

More subtle are other negative results. (1) If absence or lateness causes the cancellation of a session, continuity is lost and the momentum of creative involvement slows. (2) Presenters might begin to be considered unreliable by institutional representatives. (3) Participants might believe that presenters do not really care about them after all and the sense of trust that had been slowly developing might waver. Participants are more likely, in their lack of self-confidence, to accept some failure of their own—something they said or did—to cause the absence.

Finally, presenters may not be aware of the degree of attachment formed and the anticipation of their arrival. Notification can do much to alleviate the problem of lateness and absence by providing advance warning, explanations and time for others to adjust the session.

Set-up at the Sessions

Seating Arrangements

The way tables and chairs are arranged for the art workshops is significant; it can encourage or discourage participation. Moreover, the best arrangement for one group may not work as well for another. In addition, certain changes in format may be desirable at different times within the same group. A few examples of various seating arrangements are given below to show common situations that may be encountered:

The Long Table

This is often the only arrangement that can be provided by the institution. It is not the most conducive set-up for conversations and the social interchanges related to the process of creating art. It is, however, often preferred by some adult residents and patients, especially in the beginning, allowing fewer people to see their work. As the sessions progress, smaller tables may be accepted which will permit easier socialization to take place.

The long table might also work well with youth where less person-to-person eye contact causes less distractions and more focus on art activities. Also, with more examples of art-work spread around the table, children might be less inclined to assume that one particular example is how the artwork is supposed to look.

In all situations, presenters should try to seat themselves on either side or opposite participants.

Smaller Tables

Here, participants are seated on all four sides with a presenter, and this tends to be more conducive to verbal interaction.

The Floor

All work does not have to be done at the tables. The floor is also an area that may be used for working, certainly with children.

Figure 13.1 Students drawing with children on the floor at the housing project day-care center

Figure 13.2 Children model clay with students on the floor of the Paterson housing project day care

Chairs Alone Without Tables

Chairs can be moved to other areas of the room for private conversations while drawing on sketchpads.

Presenters may be able to request permission to change table and chair arrangements to fit different situations that occur. As the sessions continue, what works best will become apparent.

Helping Participants

Presenters should always try to be seated in the best position possible to oversee and assist operations, remembering that you yourself are being seen as you work on the selected project. In general, you should sit apart from other presenters, not grouped together. Ideally, there should be a participant on either side of you and one seated across to encourage verbal communication. One presenter might also circulate to make sure that everyone is engaged, and materials are available. Individually, you should be prepared to move to help should a presenter seem overwhelmed and need assistance.

Distributing Supplies

Supplies ideally should be placed within easy reach and available for all to use, but, of course, this depends on the situation. In psychiatric centers, all materials would need to be carefully dispensed. In the jail, every item requires controls, including those as benign in appearance as pencils, everything carefully counted in advance to be counted by officers on arrival; the amounts also must be meticulously retrieved on leaving. In all sites, supplies that might be characterized as dangerous such as scissors and other sharp tools need to be placed under wraps and only dispensed as needed.

Keeping an eye on materials and their accessibility is an important task throughout each session to maintain enthusiasm for the project and avoid problems: the frail elderly have difficulty reaching because of arthritis and failing eyesight. Children who can easily reach and see can easily spill what is in their path. If a tool is squirreled away undetected, in any of the sites served, the program itself risks being suspended.

If you are already seated at the start of the session, distributing supplies can serve as an introductory period in which familiar greetings take place and an air of expectancy about the project begins to build. Some participants are eager to help distribute supplies and some like helping with clean-up. If there are no institutional reasons to the contrary, this activity should be encouraged as there is a positive sense of power and authority in taking on the role of a presenter.

Introducing the Project

In some situations, the sessions are best begun by having one presenter explain the project to the total assembled group. Following this, further explanation and assistance as needed can be provided by the others. Another method is to have each presenter provide leadership for his or her own small group from the start. Explaining the project and helping along is always needed for the project to evolve successfully even with the "join in" approach as you create your artwork alongside. You further your teaching and leading skills by this practice here and in future endeavors.

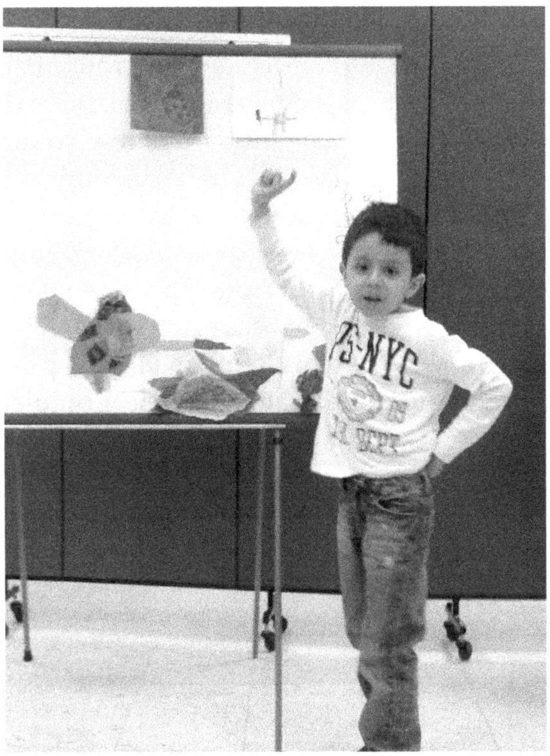

Figure 13.3 Child talks to the group about his picture at a Father Joseph afterschool program

The "Join In" Experience

The art and social interaction workshop has a "join in" spirit, meaning that presenters and participants work side by side on their individual projects. Your emerging pictures and ones nearby should inspire comments. For example: "that tree could use a tire on it for kids to swing on . . . I love those kind of flowers, what kind are they?" The pictures become a safe and engaging way to share a small part of someone else's life.

Handling Distractions

Radios, digital devises and TV are the most common distractions to the workshops, limiting conversations and also changing them in nature. Intimate discussions about family or one's hopes and dreams cannot be shouted across the table over amplified voices and music or to a head dipped into a cell phone. Instead, personal statements are likely to be squelched in favor of small talk. Silence, on the other hand, particularly while working creatively with trusted others, breeds reflective comment. Presenters should not bring smart phones into the sessions and try to ensure they are not used by others.

Tact, Discretion and Solutions

Participants understandably might feel somewhat invaded when music or TV is turned off by "outsiders." Therefore, tact and patience must be brought to bear to try to resolve the situation. Making a statement at the outset to the assembled group that sessions work best without external devices kept on and asking for cooperation will help. If there appears to be no friendly accommodation to that request, a compromise of low volume could be reached as pertains to music. TV and other digital devices should be discouraged unless cancellation of the sessions is threatened. That may be the case in some institutions where one recreation room is used for everything and the TV stays on from sunrise to lights-out. Cell phone devices, if permitted at all, will be difficult to eject from the session. Perhaps presenters can find clever ways to use them creatively when that occurs.

Other distractions may interfere with the workshops such as ping-pong or pool, visitors entering, patients removed for therapy or medication, physical problems on the premises such as electrical failures and flooding, security alerts and any number of other events. Occasionally, there may also be long waits before the sessions are permitted to start due to the external obligations of guards or custodians. Presenters in all situations should try to remove avoidable distractions and cope with unavoidable ones.

Part Five

The Creative Art Projects

Figure 5.0 Puppets L-R by Kevin Brennan, Beth Caruso and Marie-Noelle Cariddi

DOI: 10.4324/9781003592693-19

Chapter 14

Presenting Creative Art Projects

Presenting creative art projects is the core of the art and social interaction program. For consistently successful workshops, presenters must understand the special approach, methods, materials and processes uniquely designed for this program. The information is organized under the following headings:

Approach: guidelines for presenting the projects.
Introductory Remarks to Presenters: suggestions for planning.
Preparing Supplies and End Products: notations related to materials used in the art projects, safety concerns, site security.
Project Checklist: Chart of Materials and Amounts: an itemized listing of art projects in chart form including the materials and amounts needed for an average size group of 15 people (12 participants and 3 presenters) (see Insert 14.2).
Art Project Description and Processes: a full description and methodology for producing the projects offered in the program. The numbers listed in the art projects described in Chapter 15 and in the Project Checklist (Insert 14.2) are the same to permit easy cross-reference. The art activities are described under the following headings:
Drawing and Design
Collage
Painting
Sculpture
Fabric Projects
Puppets
Jewelry Projects
Innovations and Variations

DOI: 10.4324/9781003592693-20

Approach

Because of the dual goals of art productivity and social interaction, the workshops need to be structured in organization to minimize frustrations in the art process but informal in their presentation to encourage social interchange.

The approach is not one of direct instruction; instead, presenters offer the materials for the project and encourage participants to join with them to explore the materials in artistic ways. It is easy to slip into a purely instructional mode whereby the presenter is perceived as a teacher and the participant a learner, an arrangement that alters and inhibits the social atmosphere.

Determining "Success"

There should be no standards of right and wrong in determining the success of the productions. Rather, success is marked by the individual's self-satisfaction in being able to produce from the inventiveness and inner vision of mind and imagination. Efforts to abandon cliché images such as hearts, letters in a name and stick figures, and instead find new and personally relevant images, are encouraged. Artistic "accidents" can help to accomplish this, and the reader may recognize methods for producing such accidents in most of the project descriptions described.

Encouraging an attitude of openness with respect to image-making is often one of the most difficult tasks in the beginning of the series. That is because many of us do not honor our personal vision as to what is beautiful and honest, valuing solely the "professional" sight of those expected to know, fed through the written and oral media of the times or fleeting and provocative social media posts. These external concepts must be balanced by the validation of our own perceptions. What and how we see is intimately related to our personalities, insights, wisdom, wit and sensitivities. Our experiences are loaded with themes for artistic expression and tapping that source is essential. Through the unique design of the projects in their focus and spontaneity of process, participants have a chance to discover imagery that is both original and honest. The presenter's task is to encourage the individuals they are working with to be open to this.

An attitude of openness is also necessary for those observing and evaluating what is produced. Presenters must try not to validate a work from the limited viewpoint of their own aesthetic awareness or their personal compatibility with an artistic production, particularly in the artistically primitive or unfamiliar environments dealt with in this program. Accepting new ways of seeing can be a vital link in communication.

The discussion above should not be construed to mean that aesthetic considerations have no place. Among some participants it is and should be a goal. The emphasis here is that aesthetics alone should not be the criterion for judging the success of a project. More important is what occurs in the *process* of creation: the effort put into it, the sensual exploration of materials, the discovery of new capabilities, the activation of thoughts, feelings, memories and fantasies.

Motivation

Some stimulation is frequently needed to motivate institutionalized individuals who are lulled into lethargic states, or their medication dulls energy. An element of freshness, surprise or a sense of new adventure provides such stimulation, and this can be done via the projects and materials. Surprise is in the change of colors as paints mix or the blend of wet-on-wet watercolors or in the emergence of shapes from clay or in the color formations of wet tissue papers overlaid one upon the other. These elements of change give a sense of power or, at the very least, control to participants as they master the materials and guide the events that follow.

Spontaneity

Projects which encourage spontaneity are useful in the beginning of the series when participants are unfamiliar with art materials and fearful of "making mistakes" on the clear white paper offered to them. To some, the blank paper surface can be threatening in its invitation to failure. Fears of ruining the page, spoiling the materials, making a mess or wasting someone's time may accompany initial reaction to the art experience. The workshops are intended to support and bolster feelings of confidence, not supply new justifications for incompetence. Thus, a process should be in place, particularly in the early sessions, whereby participants are rewarded with interesting results despite predetermined attitudes of inadequacy which they may have.

One such process is "free form drawing" (Project I.A). The project emanates from a scribble. Though the scribble is sometimes used in art therapy as an aid in eliciting symbolic projections for analytic purposes—not the intent here—it excels as a warm-up to *discover* images as opposed to producing them. The word "scribble" tends to have pejorative connotations because of its association with childish behavior, so for the purposes of the program is better entitled "free form drawing."

The project is an excellent opening for the first sessions because it is easier for participants to *select* from the many lines and designs produced by the scribble than to *decide* what to put down on the paper. Other processes such as wet-on-wet watercolors (Project III.A), colored ink pictures (Project I.C) and tissue collage (Project II.A) are similarly designed as processes which may help participants attempt new things with less fear of risk.

Control

As participants become more comfortable with the art processes, they will hopefully be able to produce images representing the thoughts, feelings, experiences, memories and fears that occupy their lives. Encouraging their confidence to do this is an objective of the art workshops, the ability to portray what they want in the way that they want without risk: in effect, feeling that they are *in control*.

Freedom in the Context of Art

Physical, mental and emotional freedom is frequently denied to those who participate in the program because of a variety of reasons: confinement connected with potential harm to self and others; physical, mental or emotional incapacities; or economic immobility. Yet freedom is inherent in the artistic process—freedom to choose color, line, design and texture; freedom to move forms through space; freedom to select and produce from one's inner resources or outer reality. Developing the potential to liberate sensual, emotional and intellectual responses and to direct those responses toward artistic production is an objective of the workshops because in using that freedom to make artistic decisions, one is exercising the capacity to make personal decisions. Moreover, strengthening self-image by completing an art project strengthens the courage to tackle other decisions.

Introductory Remarks to Presenters

Keep in mind as you read this entire chapter, **Presenting Creative Art Projects**, that it is specifically for you, a man or woman who is preparing an experience for others as well as yourself. Use the projects to release your own creativity. The information should be like a memory backpack carried with you as you prepare for each workshop, so that you can extract the most from each activity and guide others.

- Plan your project in advance with these considerations:
    - The appropriate project for the age and competency of participants.
    - The supplies and materials needed.
    - The approach you will use to introduce the project.
    - The kind of assistance you will provide.
    - How you will conduct the end-session critique.
    - Ideas for extending the impact of the session.
- Present each project with a minimum of instructional advice, making yourself available to offer assistance as it is needed. Some specific technical information will of course be necessary and you will quickly get a sense of those areas. Generally, people are not interested in solutions until they have the problems. That is especially so with people of limited patience or those with small reservoirs of self-confidence who need encouragement and success more than they need challenges. The more overt instruction given, the more necessary it may seem to "get it right" and consequently the participants may become more vulnerable to failure.
- Right and wrong is the first challenge you must attack. Personal artistic expression as encouraged in these projects has no right and wrong. That concept is one that may not easily be accepted by people who have spent much of their lives taking orders or lived with a feeling of inadequacy in accomplishing tasks successfully. Once it is accepted (and it can be if you endorse and convey this), you may encounter the beginning of some exciting productivity.
- Your own experience with the medium will be invaluable in helping you become sensitive to those areas which might present difficulties in mastery. Guidelines as to how to proceed in presenting the projects are included in the text, but judgments will have to be made continually as you adapt the projects for individuals with different capabilities.
- It is sometimes helpful to bring in several samples of finished work when doing the more complex projects such as foil figures, puppets and clay sculpture to give participants incentive to stay with the process. The samples should have variety to demonstrate that there is no one "right" way and to deter copying.

- Drawing on someone else's picture is generally not advisable; however, there may be times when this is appropriate and even helpful. Always ask first if the individual would like you to participate in his or her picture and only after ascertaining with certainty what the picture is about. Then what you add should not be alterations but enhancements of the individual's picture concept, for example, a ground line, stems to flowers, leaves, a companion person, a similar design, etc.
- Some participants may request, perhaps insist, that you draw the picture or a component of the picture for them. That act may have more significance than the simple execution of a drawing. It can connote gift-giving or manipulation of you as an authority figure or the establishment of a bond with you or game-playing or a reinforcement of the individual's own inadequacy to do the job. Therefore, you must try to understand the nature of the need that is expressed and react in such a way as to make the experience positive rather than negative. Remember too that a "gift" to one person, particularly to a child, may be interpreted as denial and rejection to another. It is generally most productive when work emanates purely from the individual, but as in other "shared" drawings, there are circumstances when additional support can be beneficial.
- In order for you to adequately guide, encourage, elicit responsiveness and solve problems you must try to be comfortable with your role as an enabler and with the informal "join-in" approach of project presentation. In addition, you may often be working with some individuals or groups, such as jail inmates, energetic youth or older senior citizens, who want a deeper artistic experience than the informal "join-in" approach permits, so that they can execute more complicated ideas. Ideally, therefore, you should feel confident enough with the materials and procedures to take the project further or to introduce a related but more substantial project. You do not have to be an expert; in fact, your personal excellence in accomplishing an artistic work may be discouraging rather than stimulating to participants. You merely have to feel secure that your own experience with the project is thorough enough to be shared. In some cases, you may be able to refer a participant to another presenter who has more technical ability than you in a given area or decide to bring in reference material, such as pictures from a magazine, when special assistance seems to be needed.

In sum, explore the processes, become familiar with the materials, and understand the concepts and approach. Become a person with knowledge, practical information, and feeling for artistic form and expressive possibility. Then the person of sensitivity and caring, which you already are if you entered this program, can function effectively.

Preparing Supplies and End Products

Inserts 14.1 and 14.2 will help you prepare the supplies and materials for your weekly sessions.

Insert 14.1 Preparation and Care of Supplies and End Products

Prepare an exact list of hard supplies, such as scissors, pencils, pens, masking tape, brushes, markers, staplers, paints, glue, etc. Count these items for proper tabulation before leaving the college and again before leaving the site.

Containers for water should not look like drinking cups, as some participants confuse paint liquid with juices.

Cut two or three different paper sizes to encourage choice and decision-making.

Bring paper towels and other paper goods as needed. Do not depend on finding them at the site.

Check to make sure brushes are usable and clean. Wash immediately after use. Pack brush-side up.

Check to make sure paint lids are closed tightly before packing and transporting. Wipe the lips of tubes before capping to avoid sticking.

Arrive early to set up.

Arrange tables for maximum comfort, interaction and access to you and to dispensing materials. Arrange with other presenters to sit in dispersed fashion among participants rather than together.

Distribute supplies in ways to avoid cramped seating. Supervise the storage of unused supplies for security reasons.

Consider mounting completed two-dimensional work for display, as is or on heavier weight black paper. Use double stick tape for this purpose (listed in the Project Checklist as optional).

If sufficient supplies are available and only if institutions permit, have participants sign out for such things as oil pastels, colored pencils, markers and sketch pads for use between sessions.

Transport finished work carefully. Bring boxes if clay sculpture is to be transported for firing. Store finished work at the site if possible.

Bring paper and pencils to each session for use as a warm-up before the designated project begins and for those who finish quickly or prefer to draw rather than do the project.

Sharp Objects and Materials of Concern

The following materials may be acceptable at some sites but not permitted at others where security concerns overrule their use. A complete list of all materials, in any case, should be made and presented to appropriate site personnel before each session. This is *required* in the jail and psychiatric setting but still advisable for all sites.

Sharp materials of concern are the following:

Scissors, point-tipped
Scissors, blunt-tipped
Staplers
Pins

Nails
Knives
Wire
Needles
Pointed wood sticks

Other materials of concern might be:

Glue in any form including Elmer's glue, glue sticks
Scented markers
Tape of various kinds
Printing inks

Use your judgment and do not be offended if what you consider a benign material is not permitted entry. There is a reason for this.

Insert 14.2 Project Checklist: Chart of Art Materials (for 15 people total)

I. Drawing and Design

A. Free Form Drawing
30 sheets plain white paper 8.5 × 11
15 pencils
5 packs, set of 8, thin-colored markers
12 colored pencils
15 sheets black and colored construction paper 9 × 12
3 rolls double stick tape for mounting finished work
B. Designs in Oil Pastels
8 boxes (sets) oil pastels
15 sheets white charcoal or watercolor paper 9 × 12 cut in half and quarters
15 sheets black and colored construction paper, cut on site for projects and mounting work
1 roll double stick tape and 3 glue sticks
C. Colored Ink Pictures
15 sheets watercolor paper 9 × 12 cut in half and thirds
Small assortment water-based colored inks
8 pens with nibs
8 regular black pens fine-tipped
15 straws or paint pipettes (opt.)
1 roll paper towels
D. Theme Drawings
30 sheets white drawing paper 8.5 × 11
15 pencils with erasers
5 sets colored pencils
5 sets crayons or markers

E. Picture Drawings with People
15 newsprint sketchpads or stack of Xerox paper
15 pencils with erasers
5 boxes (sets) colored markers
5 boxes (sets) crayons or oil pastels
15 sheets black and colored construction paper
1 roll double stick tape and 3 glue sticks

II. Collage

A. Tissue Collage
15 sheets white card stock, assorted sizes
5 packs colored tissue different colors
1 quart white glue
15 brushes, approximately 1″
8 containers to hold watered-down glue or decoupage
B. Photo Collage
5 magazines with pictures*
15 dispensers white glue
15 sheets cardboard
15 brushes 1″
15 scissors
15 glue sticks
*consider pre-cutting out pictures
C. Strip Paper Collage
1 box cut paper strips, assorted sizes & colors or
6 rolls pre-glued colored tape
15 sheets card stock
1 roll masking tape
8 jars white glue or 15 glue sticks
1 roll paper towels
1 roll double stick tape

III. Painting

A. Watercolor
30 sheets watercolor paper 9 × 12 cut in half or thirds
8 trays watercolor paints
15 sectioned trays for mixing colors (opt.)
15 watercolor brushes, assorted sizes
4 rolls 1/2″ masking tape
5 small sponges
8 containers for water

1 roll paper towels

B. Watercolor and Tape Pictures

All of the above (III.A)
2 rolls 1/4″ and 3/4″ masking tape

C. Watercolor and Rubber Cement Pictures

All of the above (III.A)
1 pint or quart rubber cement
15 3-oz paper cups
15 rubber cement peelers

D. Watercolor on Plaster Plates

All of the above (III.A) no paper
15 plastic coated paper plates lunch size*
10 lb plaster of Paris
1 roll aluminum wire to cut in "u" shapes as hooks
1 large plastic bowl for mixing plaster
5 5-oz paper cups
5 3″ pointed wood for incising decorations (opt.)
1 can polyurethane spray (opt.)
** Plates will be filled with plaster and hooks in advance, solid and ready for painting*

E. Acrylic

15 sheets watercolor paper cut 4.5 × 6 or 5 × 7, a good beginning working size
15 acrylic brushes, assorted sizes
1 pkg. disposable paper palettes
12 tubes acrylic paints, assorted colors or jars
8 containers for water
1 roll paper towels; rags
15 table easels with stiff cardboards for backing and clips to fasten board to easel (all opt.)
8 palette knives
15 pencils/sketch paper

F. Gesso Pictures in Color

All of the above (III.E)
1 pint or quart Gesso
15 sheets heavy white paper or smooth cardboard or thin wood
6 jars tempera paints, various colors
15 wooden craft sticks or palette knives
15 brushes, basic quality, assorted sizes

G.H.I. Theme Painting in Acrylics, Murals and Special Projects

Items in III.E as needed
Several magazines and greeting cards to inspire themes
1 roll white paper for murals & dinner party project
1 scissors, Thumb tacks or tape for murals
Paper, glass, Plexiglas, cardboard or wood as desired for special projects

IV. Sculpture

A. Clay Sculpture
15 cardboards or thin wood bases
50 lb clay (See Clay chapter for type)
15 clay tools
15 small wood blocks
15 plastic storage bags and ties
1 covered dish for slip
7 rags
3 sturdy boxes or trays

B. Strip Paper Sculpture
15 cardboards squares/rectangles
1 bag of plain or colored paper strips (cut & collected from magazines & scraps)
5 jars white glue or 10 glue sticks
2 doz. paper fasteners
6 prs. scissors (opt.)
5 rolls masking tape
5 cub size hand held staplers

C. Foil and Paris Craft Sculptures
1 roll standard aluminum foil
1 roll toilet tissue, or
1 bag cotton balls, or
1 bag fiberfill stuffing
5 cub size staplers/staples (opt.)
15 scissors*
1 box straight pins (opt.)
4 rolls Pariscraft, called plaster wrap if ordering from Amazon
8 containers for water

For mounting figures:
8 sheets cardboard or
15 thin wood bases, assorted sizes
2 doz. 3″ brads (nails without heads)
3 hammers
1 can flat black spray enamel
1 roll thin gauge wire
**Pariscraft strips can be cut in advance to avoid cutting on site*
1 can black spray enamel

D. Plaster Carving
10 lb bag plaster of Paris
15 containers for filling plaster, e.g., plastic bags/milk cartons, cups, etc.
1 mixing bowl
15 sandbags or bean bags

15 paring knives
15 files
2 wire brushes, assorted wet/dry sanding paper

E. Plaster Relief Sculpture

1 roll waxed paper
5 lb bag plaster of Paris
1 mixing bowl
25 5-oz paper cups
15 wood coffee sticks
1 pointed tool
Assorted wet/dry carborundum paper
1 pint shellac, opt.
1 pint alcohol, opt.
1 set 5-minute epoxy
15 thin wood bases, assorted grit sandpaper
1 tin dark brown shoe paste, or
1 can black spray enamel
1 can polyurethane (opt.)

V. Fabric Pictures

15 thin wood, Masonite or cardboard bases
1 bag fabric scraps
8 jars white glue
15 scissors
15 wood sticks
3 yards cotton muslin (opt. for group wall piece)
1 roll picture wire
3 doz. screw eyes

VI. Puppets

15 toilet paper rolls
1 bag fabric & trimmings
7 jars white glue
1 bag fiberfill stuffing
1 box buttons, assorted
1 bag discarded nylon hose
4 rolls wool—black, yellow, brown and red
7 cub size staplers with staples
7 scissors
1 card needles
1 box thread, assorted colors

1 roll thin wire (opt.)
1 roll white mural paper (opt. for creating scenery for puppet play
4 boxes (sets) colored markers (opt for play)
1 roll 1/2″ masking tape

VII. Jewelry-Making

A. Copper Enamel **main items may be bought as a set*
1 small kiln with cord
8 jars glass powders, assorted colors
1 box assorted glass stones
1 box assorted glass threads
40 copper shapes
3 pcs. medium grit sandpaper (cut into 20 small squares)
15 sifters
15 tweezers
15 spatulas
1 jar detergent
1 jar Agar gum solution
4 grates
4 fireproof pads
1 hole punch
assorted copper findings
1 set 5-minute epoxy
B. Found Object Jewelry
(all items optional)
1 box assorted small objects
1 wire cutters or shears
1 jeweler's hack saw
4 soldering irons
2 tubes solder & flux
1 roll cord or string
2 sets 5-minute epoxy
1 roll wire
2 metal files
C. Plaster Formed Jewelry
Selected items in IV.E
7 sets watercolor/tempera paints
15 brushes
7 water containers
30 pin-backs
3 yards thin leather cord

Figure 14.1 "Palm Tree at Sunrise," collage in fabric by student Renee Charles

Figure 14.2 Sculpture created with foil and plaster wrap then painted in acrylics of a couple walking together by student Melissa Denneau

Chapter 15

Art Projects

Descriptions and Processes

Most project illustrations are available to view in color online at www.routledge.com/9781032972008.

I Drawing and Design

A Free Form Drawing

Description: The free form drawing is useful as a first exposure to creative visual arts methods because it is a process of selecting lines and images from random markings as opposed to producing a drawing "from scratch" on a blank piece of paper. This is not only less threatening to non-artists but an artistic engagement in the discovery of new forms from what appears on the paper.

Free form drawing is potentially suitable for all populations.

Process:

1 Use light-weight white newsprint or Xerox paper. Make a free form scribble with a standard #2 pencil, utilizing as much of the page and as many strokes as desired. Swing the hand freely without planning how and where the strokes will go. Simply watch and enjoy the markings that appear on the paper.
2 Following this, try any or all of the following procedures:
   a Discover images in the lines and bring them out by darkening.
   b Create shapes by enclosing lines to form masses and shade in various ways.
   c Add new lines suggested by images found in the scribble.
3 Add color with felt markers, oil pastels or colored pencils.

Illustration: Figures 15.1 and 15.2 are examples of free form drawings begun as a scribble in pencil then added to with thin-tipped colored markers.

DOI: 10.4324/9781003592693-21

Figure 15.1 A scribble added to with thin-tipped sharpie, student Anna Willis

Figure 15.2 A scribble added to with pen and felt-tipped markers

B Designs in Oil Pastels

Description: This project encourages the exploration of color through broad application and overlay of one color on another. Because oil pastels are easy to use, non-staining and versatile, the medium is popular among both youth and adults, can be introduced early on and is safe for incarcerated or otherwise confined populations.

Illustration: Figure 15.3 is an example of a design in oil pastel.

Figure 15.3 A butterfly and a rose drawn in colorful oil pastels, student William Dorsett

Process:

1 Use medium-weight white charcoal or watercolor paper which has a somewhat rough texture. 9 × 12 paper can be cut in half or thirds for economy or smaller compositions.
2 Create designs using either the tip or the side of the oil pastels, peeling away the wrapping. Break the sticks for more control.
3 Overlay and blend colors on the paper.

Designs can be created stylistically abstract or representational.

C Colored Ink Pictures

Description: Inks are brilliant in color and free flowing. By their fluidity, inks lend themselves to exploration. The project is useful to encourage bold applications of media. Use only water-based ink so as not to stain clothes if spilled. The project is best suited to competent adults; also not suited to children who might not be able to resist splashing the ink. The straw-blown aspect of the project is successful aesthetically but should not be used with confused individuals who might misinterpret the use of the straw and suck in rather than out. It is doubtful the project would be allowed among inmates but worth asking.

Process:

1 Straw-blown method: Use colored inks, heavy-weight watercolor paper, and plastic straws or paint pipettes. Dip the straw or pipette into the ink bottle and gently blow the ink onto the paper mingling the lines to create designs and images.
2 Or squeeze a drop of ink onto the paper with an eyedropper, then tip the paper to weave the ink into patterns; or propel it with a craft stick. If too much ink is applied, try pressing another paper onto the page, remove and produce a monoprint (a single print from the drawing).
3 Draw with pen nibs in the traditional way, dipping pen in ink and applying. Apply lines with varying widths; encourage participants to experiment with a second ink drawing using a different method than on their first.
4 Create a title for the piece and suggest others do so as well for abstract pictures in the "critique" at the end of the workshop.

Illustration: Figures 15.4, 15.5 and 15.6 are examples of fluid ink pictures.

Figure 15.4 Example of a picture with black ink drawn with pen nibs, student Steve Vermenlo

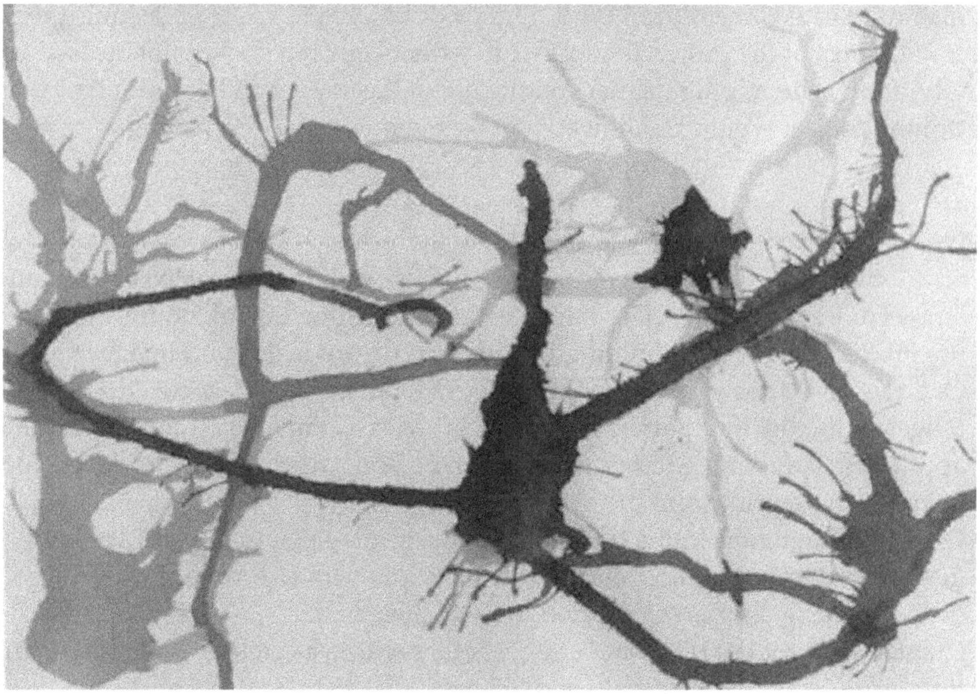

Figure 15.5 Example of a picture tipping lines of black and gray ink

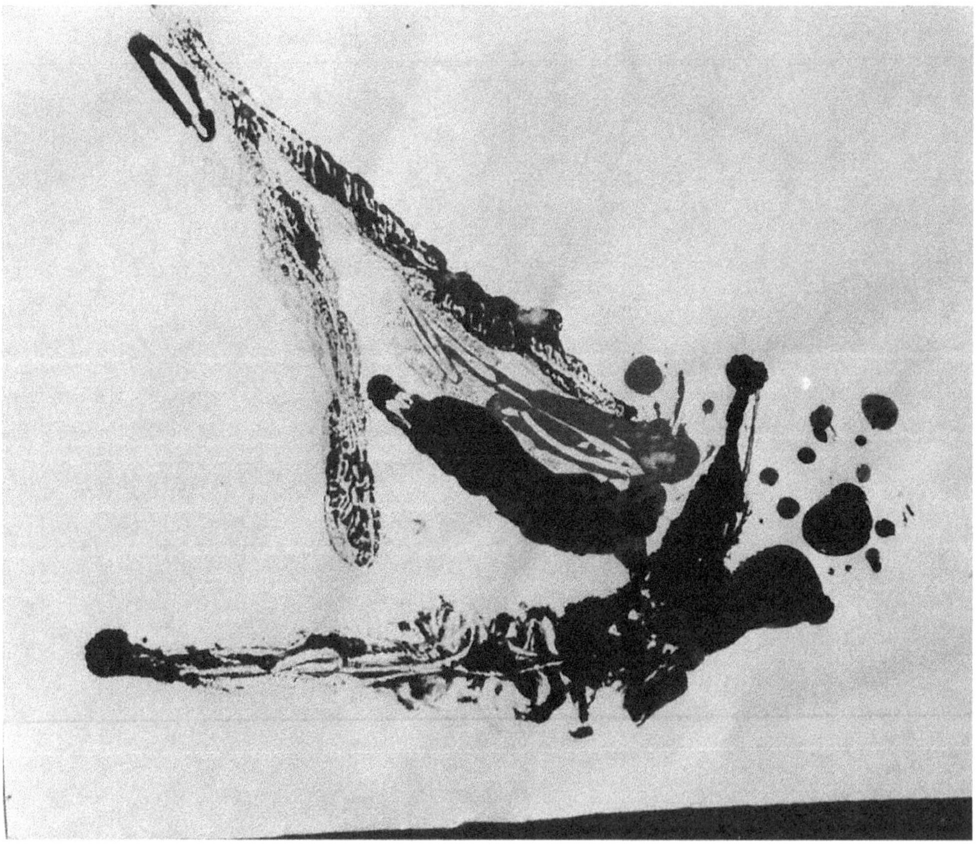

Figure 15.6 Example of a picture with straw-blown colored inks

D Theme Drawings in Pencil

Description: Individuals new to visual arts expression are often as uncomfortable with notions of what to draw as how to draw. Presenting thematic ideas may stimulate memories, experiences and perceptions and consequently expand creative thinking. Theme drawing works well with adults, as they have many experiences to draw upon but tend to feel more awkward than youth about drawing a picture with no subject in mind. The project presents an opportunity with youth and with jail and prison inmates to select themes of an inspiring nature or one where projecting their personal feelings might be helpful.

Process:

1. Use regular white drawing paper or a sketch pad. Draw in pencil according to a broad theme. Suggested themes: vacations real or imagined, seasons, drawings inspired by old photographs, animals, insects, nature, holidays, food, family and relatives, friends, your home outside or inside, your neighborhood, your childhood, your self-portrait (how you think you appear to others; how you feel to yourself).
2. Add color to the theme drawings using markers, colored pencils, crayons or oil pastels.
3. Regardless of the group theme, participants should always be free to draw what they wish. It is wise to have pencils, paper and color in one form or another on hand at all sessions for those who are either uninterested in the project or have a personal theme in mind which they wish to develop.

Illustration: Figure 15.7 is a provocative example of a theme drawing in pencil, in this case, a portrait of how one feels to oneself.

Figure 15.7 A drawing showing eyes peering out from a mask with many horns. Done by a student who had served time in prison

E Picture Drawings with People

Description: Projects which include representing the human figure are valuable for several reasons. For one, the project encourages participants to observe and think about characteristics of the body and facial features—their own and others—the tactile as well as the visual impressions of what they observe. For another, the project provides an opportunity to portray oneself and others in the personal environment of home, work or recreation. The project can be done purely from imagination or from "life," asking someone to voluntarily "model."

Presenters should be familiar with their groups before introducing this project, and group members should feel comfortable with one another and have shared several previous projects together. It is therefore a project that is best done toward the end of the workshop series. The task can be eased by simply asking participants to "Make a picture showing one or more people *doing* something." The project is further simplified by using cutouts from magazines to make the picture. (Presenter teams should prepare and bring lots of cutouts from home in advance including a variety of both people and environments, home furniture, sports milieus, shops, etc.) The project is potentially suitable and safe for all clientele.

Process:

1. Use a newsprint sketch pad and pencil with eraser. Present several thematic ideas, trying to draw on a participant's experience and interests. If stick figures (discouraged) are the only method agreed to, require they be embellished with distinguishing features, clothing and an environment produced around them.
2. Using the same materials, ask someone to pose. After drawing, require the figure in the picture be given an action and setting suggested by the pose, for example, shopping in a supermarket, hanging clothes, waiting for a bus, washing at the sink and so on.
3. Color the picture with markers or crayons.
4. For an alternative method use markers or crayons at the outset. The model in this case only poses briefly to generate ideas, after which pictures are made from the imagination.

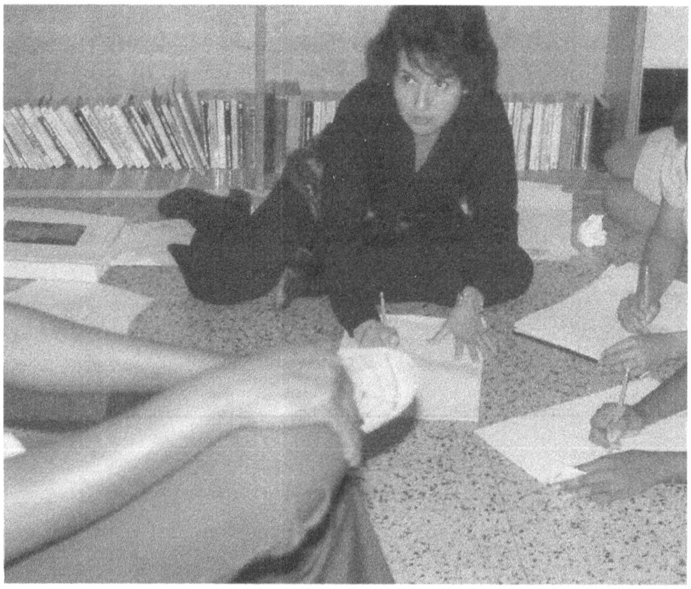

Figure 15.8 The author draws with female detainees at the jail as another female poses

Figure 15.9 A drawing of a woman standing by a car dressed in a shirt and skirt under a bright sun, Rockland Psychiatric Center, Orangeburg, NY

Figure 15.10 Theme drawing—An inmate painting a picture of a judge and jury above a defendant going up in flames, Essex County Jail, Newark, NJ

II Collage

A Tissue Collage

Description: Colored tissue when torn and brushed onto paper with watered-down white glue has a vivid painterly quality. Accomplished results may appear without the deliberate strokes and small motor movements of painting techniques. Also, the process of selecting colors and shapes and applying the tissue is easy and fun for individuals new to the artistic experience, less challenging than creating new lines and color patterns with brush strokes on a bare surface. Because the project is usually unfamiliar to participants, there are fewer preconceptions to overcome than in drawing or painting; for example, one is not likely to say, "*I* can't draw," or "*I* can't paint," when approached with this project.

Tissue collage is particularly well suited to the frail elderly or to participants with physical disabilities in which hand control may be difficult to maintain and failing eyesight may make drawing and painting frustrating. Tissue collage also lends itself to the creation of useful items, such as note cards, in which case the *object* produced may provide additional satisfactions. Tissue collage takes relatively little explanation. It is a good project to use early in the workshop series and is suitable for all populations with certain caveats. The elderly may find its potential messiness disturbing, so good preparation is important, a good idea is to roll up sleeves in advance. Plastic gloves can be helpful as hands can be temporarily stained though washing with soap and water removes this. The project uses watered-down Elmers glue (about half and half). Liquid glue of any kind might not be allowed in prison institutions. Bringing in examples of the exciting finished work produced in tissue collage may circumvent these reservations.

Process:

1 Prepare the work surface with newspaper, as the wet colored tissue can stain. It washes off with soap and water if it stains hands. Use white cardboard of a selected size. It is often less threatening and more successful to start with a modest rectangular size of about 9 by 7. Tear off a piece of colored tissue and place it on the paper surface, then brush over it with diluted white glue or with decoupage, which is a similar premixed substance. Brushes should be about ½" or 1" wide, the quality not important, and washed well after use.
2 Continue adding torn tissue to form a design or a picture.
3 Overlay tissues in different colors to see the hues change.
4 Other flat surfaces besides paper and cardboard can be used, such as wood.
5 Tissue collage can be applied over three-dimensional objects such as boxes, vases, bottles and cans. One must, of course, be certain that any surface or form is not dangerous or prohibited in the institution, such as glass or metal.

Figures 15.11 and 15.11a are examples of tissue collage on paper. Figure 15.12 is an example of tissue collage on a plastic bottle.

Figure 15.11 Tissue collage on heavy paper—sunset, student Peter Holzman

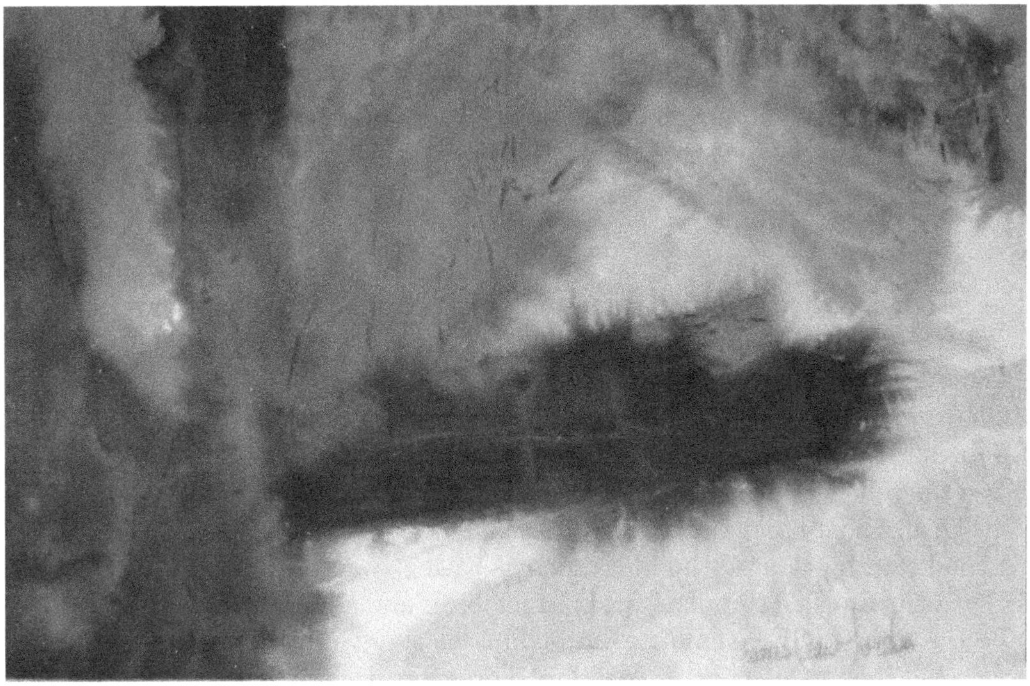

Figure 15.11a Tissue Collage abstract, student James Crawford

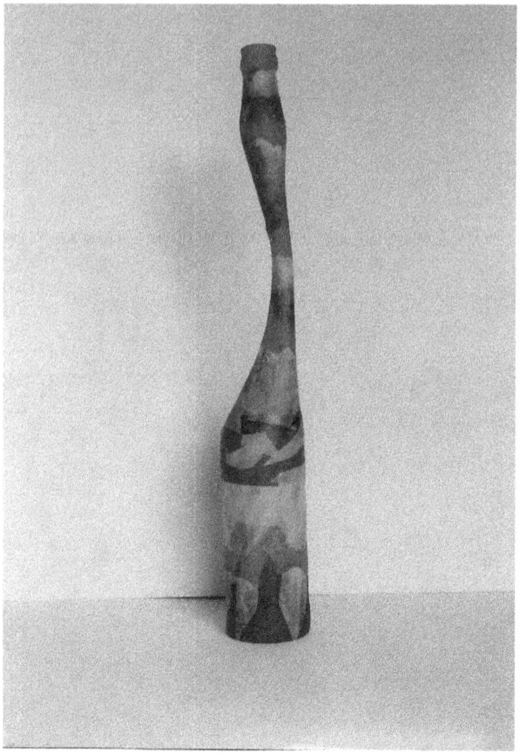

Figure 15.12 Tissue collage wrapped around a plastic bottle

B Photo Collage

Description: Photo collage affords the opportunity to select and arrange images according to personal interests and aesthetic judgments. It is a method of organizing a limited space, creating a limited environment, focusing on a limited world. As such, the project affords a sense of control and yet can be executed by groups with wide-ranging mental, emotional and physical proficiencies. With physically disabled patients, presenters can do much of the mechanical work of cutting and pasting without diminishing the selection and placement process required of the creator. Glue sticks work fine if liquid glue is either not feasible or not allowed in the setting.

Process:

1 Use white cardboard or other substantial material. Apply selected magazine photos or fragments of photos with diluted white glue or decoupage or glue sticks to form an integrated picture.
2 The picture can be design-oriented, using color, line and space relationships in an abstract formation.
3 Or the collage can be theme-oriented. The themes offered in "Theme Drawing" (I.D) also adapt to photo collage. Other themes are:
   Food relating to family holidays such as Easter, Thanksgiving or Christmas. These pictures often stimulate specific memories and associations.
   Furniture: This may stimulate future thinking about how to decorate one's home, or the memory of a home in childhood or before residing in the institution. Selecting furniture to clip may also provide a sense of owning and arranging the items.

Houses and landscape: The choice and arrangement of house and landscape components offers an opportunity to demonstrate taste, ideas of comfort and enjoyment, and fantasy visions of an ideal living space.

4 Encourage capable individuals to integrate spatial and color relationships in their pictures and recognize success in such efforts in the post-session critiques.
5 Brush over the collage with diluted white glue or decoupage when it is complete. Magazines useful for the project: *House and Garden*, *Ladies Home Journal*, *Architectural Digest*, *House Beautiful*, art magazines, department store ad publications, food advertisements and so on.

Illustration: Figure 15.13 is an example of a photo collage.

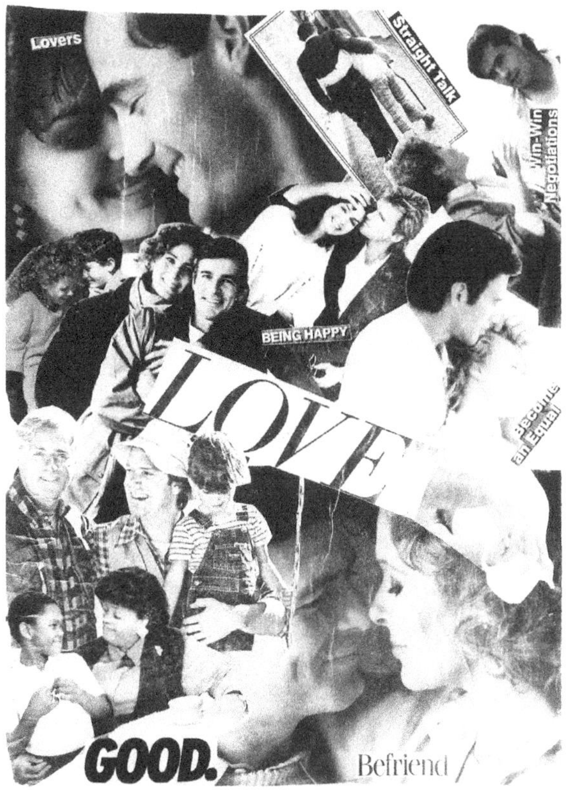

Figure 15.13 A photo collage picture of smiling people with the word "Love" at the center

C Strip Paper Collage

Description: Paper strips in multiple colors are often available as the trimmed scraps from work orders in the graphics department of the college and in large offices. These trimmings can be used to create two-dimensional collages hung on the wall or twisted into shapes to create three-dimensional sculptures stapled onto cardboard bases. The variety of geometric shapes forms the basis for both projects.

The shapes can generate thematic ideas. Themes for two-dimensional collages are: landscapes, seascapes, back yards, outer space, homes (exterior or interior view). Try creating a fanciful interpretation of a house, not a realistic one.

Suggested three-dimensional paper sculpture themes are: a playground, a carnival, a rocket launching, trees and flowers, the natural landscape or imaginative abstractions in space.

Strip papers in different sizes can inspire a relatively quick collage, which makes it a good project for impatient or hyperactive children. Because of the inventiveness required and trial and error process in assembling the shapes, the project lends itself to commenting on one another's creations, talk conducive to building trust. In contrast to some other projects, the material is neat and clean and does not require spreading-out space. As such, it can be adapted to most populations.

Process:

1 Use pre-cut colored strips of paper or cut colored construction paper into strips.
2 For two-dimensional pictures, cut or tear the strips into desired lengths and paste with white glue or glue sticks onto heavy paper.
3 Add drawing lines in pencil or ink if desired; however, the simplicity of the geometric shapes should not be obscured with too much mixed media.
4 For situations when extremely easy applications are needed, use ready-made rolls of pre-glued colored tape. These require only wetting with a damp cloth or paper towel after tearing and are useful for young children or disabled adults with creative eyes but limited dexterity. The rolls, however, do not have the size diversity of the cut strips and tend to produce less exciting results.

Illustration: Figures 15.14 and 15.15 are examples of two-dimensional strip picture collages.

Figure 15.14 A strip paper collage showing trees, a bumble bee, flowers and sun rays shining on everything, student Elissa Regina

Figure 15.15 A strip paper collage showing a palm tree, ocean waves and clouds half covering the sun, student Don DeVries

III Painting

A Watercolor

Description: Watercolors are versatile in capturing impressions of nature once you learn to go with the flow of paint on paper, working with the medium. The quality of paper is an essential ingredient in successful productions. Therefore, use watercolor paper (heavy paper with some tooth). Painting on small squares of watercolor paper cut to size from pages on the pad is an unthreatening way to begin. Watercolor painting is suited to all populations without exceptions. Use the project often, at any time from the beginning of the series on. Note: acrylic paints can be used with this same procedure, with two distinctions: colors can be overlaid one on another; paints are soluble when wet, turning hard when dry. Mix colors on your palette rather than applying directly from the tube or jar.

Process:

1 Cut the paper, into relatively small squares or rectangles, approximately postcard size. Then with ½″ masking tape, tape all four edges to the table surface, keeping

even borders on the inside edges of the page (to become the picture frame). Masking serves two purposes: (1) it prevents the paper from curling when wet and (2) it provides an attractive border when the painting is complete and the tape removed when dry.

2 Wetting the paper is a decisive factor in the painting process. There are three basic methods of using water and paint. Begin with wet-on-wet:
   a **Wet-on-wet**: After taping the edges of the paper down with ½" masking tape evenly on all four sides, wet the paper with a brush or sponge. Proceed to paint by wetting the brush and dipping into pigment. In wet-on-wet painting, the object is to *go with the flow!* Take direction from the medium to discover what you never knew could appear beneath your hand.
   b **Wet-on-dry**: Dip the brush in water, then in pigment and paint fluidly on dry paper.
   c **Moist-on-dry**: Moisten the brush enough to pick up pigment and paint on dry paper.

3 Experimentation is necessary to discover:
   a How colors change, first when they are mixed together and then after they are applied to the paper.
   b How the addition of water affects the translucent or opaque quality of the colors.
   c How colors run together to give a variety of effects, and how to control this with your brush—or rag or sponge.
   d How drying affects the edges of forms, the colors and the overlay of one color on another.
   e How using different size brushes and other paint tips can create interesting detail.
   f How scenes, moods, memories, nature, fantasy and experiences, even in fragmentary form, can be conveyed in the painted picture.

Illustration: Figures 15.16, 15.17 and 15.18 are examples of watercolor painting using the three techniques.

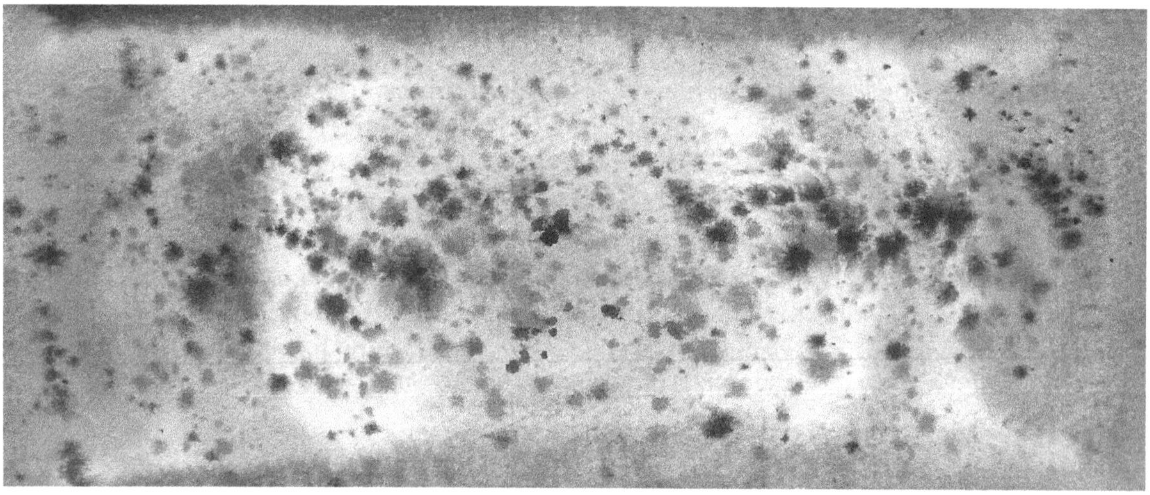

Figure 15.16 An abstract watercolor painted with droplets and a wet-on-wet technique, student Raul Bernal

Figure 15.17 Watercolor of flowers painted with a wet-on-dry technique, student Jeanine Diehler

Figure 15.18 Watercolor of multicolored flowers painted with a moist-on-dry technique, student Tanya Doram

B Watercolor and Tape Pictures

Description: This project provides another opportunity to organize a limited space artistically. Create the divisions either purely aesthetically considering only space and design; or like a patchwork quilt consisting of decorative patterns; or content-oriented divisions relating to an issue, such as stages in life or seasons of the year—any concept that works with sequential or grouped images. The project is suited to all populations and could be done any time after the first few sessions. Seek permission for the tape among incarcerated populations.

Process:

1. Apply masking tape not only to the borders as in the last project but in a pattern on the paper:
   a. Irregular patterns.
   b. Square, rectangular or other geometric organizations.
   c. Grid patterns.
2. Proceed to paint using the experimental processes described in "Watercolor Painting" (III.A). The paint is prevented from adhering to the masked portions of the paper.
3. When the paint has dried, carefully remove the tape. Alternatively, clean the tape with a damp rag and leave it on the picture.

Illustration: Figures 15.19 and 15.20 are examples of watercolor and tape pictures with the tape removed after painting.

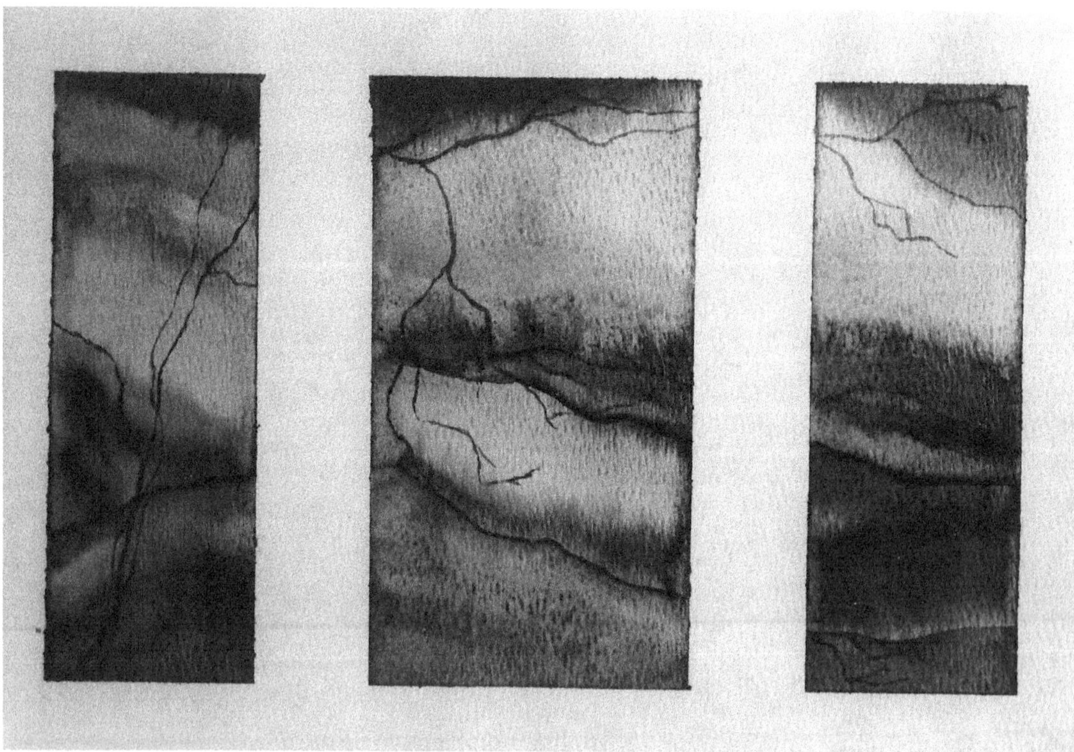

Figure 15. 19 Watercolor and tape picture with the tape removed when dry

Figure 15.20 Strips of tape attached to this watercolor and made integral to the picture's design, student D. Weinich.

C Watercolor and Rubber Cement Pictures

Description: Rubber cement can be poured to flow in free-swirling patterns. When dry, it masks off the areas on which it was poured and watercolors will not flow into those areas. The project encourages fresh new lines and forms to emerge and as such, extends the ideas conveyed in "Free Form Drawing" (I.A). As a health hazard, rubber cement should not be inhaled or handled excessively; for that reason, the project is not recommended for children. When used with adults, keep containers covered and remove them as soon as the picture design has been poured. The spirit of the project makes it particularly suitable for adults who have been restricted in their ability to be creative, as both the process and product can be surprisingly rewarding. Liquid adhesive of any kind would be prohibited in incarcerated situations. Note that ordinary Elmer's glue can be substituted by guiding the glue to flow in patterns. It will take longer to dry so offer another project while waiting.

Process:

1 Rubber cement, dispensed into small, flexible squeeze bottles (or paper cups if there is no danger of ingestion), is trickled onto the paper in a free flowing design. Control the pour to deliver thin or thick lines, broad sweeping lines, slender curves, squiggles, shapes, dots or any manner of formations.
2 Allow the rubber cement to dry for approximately one-half hour. (A separate watercolor painting might be done during this interlude.)

3 Tape the paper with an even border to the table surface and proceed to paint as described in "Watercolor Painting".
4 When dry, carefully peel off the rubber cement to reveal the pattern. Alternatively, the rubber cement patterns may be left on the paper without peeling.

Illustration: Figure 15.21 is an example of a watercolor and rubber cement painting with the rubber cement left on.

Figure 15.21 A watercolor painting in which rubber cement was swirled on in a pattern before painting and left to remain. Rubber cement can remain or be removed.

D Painting on Plaster Plates

Description: This project is as artistic as painting on paper but because plaster is solid, it features the advantage of being potentially useful as a trivet or wall hanging. The plaster can be decoratively incised to add an element of sophistication. The project is well suited for older adults who value useful products. Others, including youth living in residences and after school programs, will enjoy being able to present the plates as gifts. The project won't be accepted, of course, in incarcerated populations because of the material.

Process:

1 Prepare the plates (ideally by two people working together in advance of the session) in the following manner:
   a On a flat surface lay out plastic-coated plates—lunch or dinner size according to preference.
   b Cut 2″ pieces of aluminum wire for hanging; bend these into U shapes and set aside.
   c Shake plaster of Paris by hand into a pail or bowl half-filled with water. (A 3-quart bowl half-filled will produce approximately ten plates.) Do not dump in the plaster, but working swiftly, close to the bowl spread the plaster evenly.
   d When the plaster rests without sinking in a small mound just above the water's surface, stir the mix by hand, squeezing out any lumps. Stirring must be efficient but smoothly done. Setting time is approximately three minutes. Agitate the mix as little as possible while stirring to avoid forming air bubbles.
   e Working quickly, pour the plaster first into paper cups for helpers to distribute (optional) and then into the waiting paper plates.
   f Jiggle the plates to spread the mix across the entire surface.
   g Insert the wire for future hanging near one end of the plates before the mix has set.
   h If the mix begins to set before all the plates have been poured, use the remaining plaster in cups to carve shapes (see Sculpture IV.D and E, "Plaster Carvings" and "Plaster Reliefs").
   i Later when the plates are fully set, pack them carefully in a box for transporting leaving them in their plastic plate "molds."
   j When ready to paint, lift out the plaster plate and invert to use the smooth side for painting.
2 The plates can either be decoratively incised with any pointed tool and then painted with watercolors or painted directly without incising.
3 As the plaster absorbs the paint, a pleasing "fresco" appearance is created. The paints can be left muted in this way or sprayed with polyurethane in satin or gloss finish. An equal mix of shellac and alcohol can be used in place of polyurethane for a gloss finish.

Illustration: Figure 15.22 is an example of watercolor on a plaster plate. Figure 15.22a is an example of acrylic on a plaster plate.

Figure 15.22 Colorful patterns painted in watercolor on a plaster plate, student Kim Faber

Figure 15.22a A red flower painted in acrylic on a plaster plate, student Grace Helbig

E Acrylic Painting

Description: Acrylics have the advantage of being water soluble when wet but waterproof when dry. They are quickly drying as opposed to oil paints which may take days to dry and are not used in the program. The qualities of acrylic paint make it a permanent but flexible medium for exploring color, tone, contrast and texture.

It is not recommended that you make a sketch before beginning to paint. A preliminary drawing imposes limitations by perpetuating preconceptions such as, for example, that the paint is supposed to "fill in" the drawn spaces. Indeed, it may, but the concept that paint creates space is a more expansive way to proceed, a way that invites innovation. As in watercolor painting, explore the materials to discover what they can do in partnership with your ideas. See Watercolor Painting III.A to use the wet-on-wet technique, first putting masking tape down along the edges before wetting the paper and painting.

Some individuals still may feel a need to plan their pictures in pencil before risking the painting process and only through such deliberation gain the courage to paint. Accordingly, bring pencils and paper along for working out those ideas. Participants need not be discouraged from processes that feel safe and comfortable, but suggestions can be made to help them acquire the courage to explore.

Process:

1 Use heavy-weight paper with some tooth, such as watercolor paper or canvas board. Place the paper flat on the table surface or clip it to a board and prop it against something stable or a portable table easel (if these are supplied).
2 Paints can be diluted with water or mixed with acrylic medium to change their consistency and intensity.
3 Mix the colors to create more subtle hues, rather than using paints directly from the tube or jar. Use a disposable palette (available in pads) for mixing colors.
4 Have a variety of brush sizes, a palette knife and rags available for both expanding your horizons and controlling your medium. Wash brushes immediately after use and periodically while in use to keep them flexible.

Illustration: Figure 15.23 is an example of acrylic painting.

Figure 15.23 Acrylic painting—a moon's reflection on the water

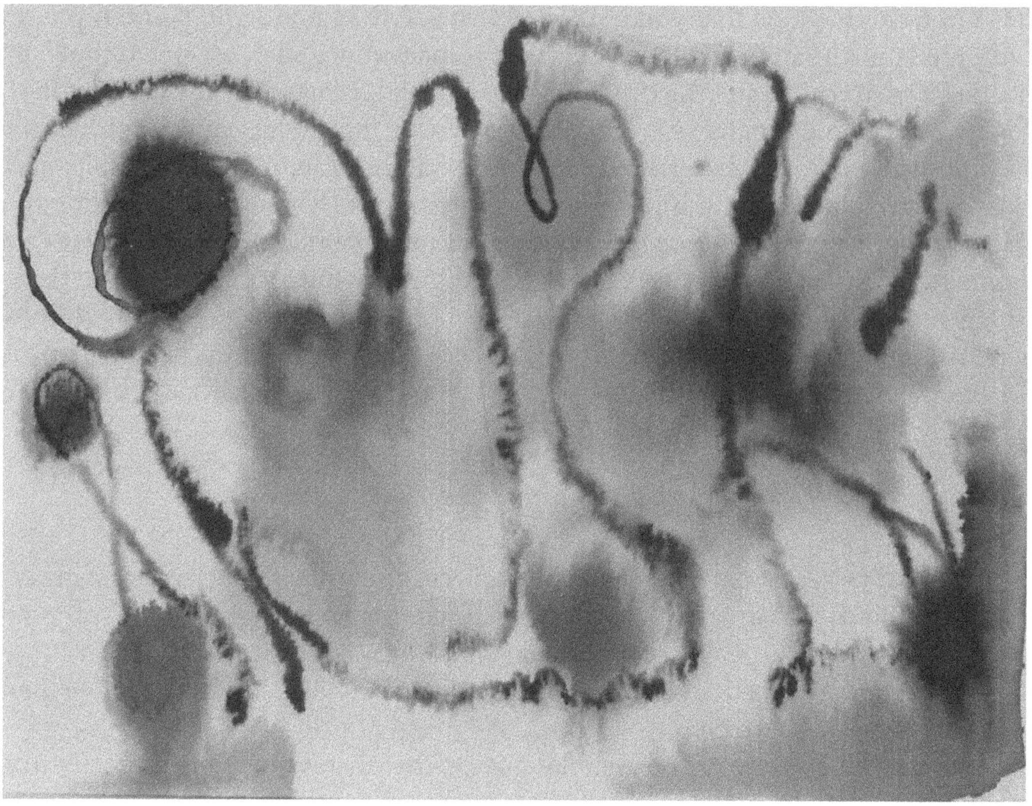

Figure 15.24 Gesso applied on thin wood as a base for painting with tempura or other medium

F Gesso Pictures in Color

Description: Gesso is a prepared white plaster product that spreads easily and can provide an interesting textured surface for painting. The material, when used as a base for painting, as in this project, can introduce participants to the artistic possibilities of texture as a change from the very smooth surfaces they may feel wedded to.

Process:

1 Spread gesso onto a surface of cardboard or thin wood. Create pictures with tempura paint or other painting medium while the gesso is wet.
2 Use brushes and palette knives or wood craft sticks as drawing instruments. Brushes must be washed frequently because gesso becomes hard when dry.
3 Letting the gesso dry before applying color will produce different effects.

G Theme Painting in Acrylic

Description: It is often helpful in generating ideas for painting to establish a group theme for the painting. A list of specific themes is offered in "Drawing and Design" (I.D). A broad theme that lends itself to painterly expression if the outdoors is visible is "A Look out the

Window." Ideas might percolate about cityscape; people doing things; architectural shapes and designs; the infinite variations in nature.

1 Ideas can also be generated by looking at selected magazines. Pictures should not be regarded for copying purposes, but for the purpose of generating ideas—ideas relating to one's associations with people, places and nature; culture and ethnicity; current events; and images of fantasy. Useful magazines in this connection are: National Geographic, Life, Look, magazines on sports, photography, natural history and travel.
2 Art books generate aesthetic responses as well as thematic ideas. Postcards, prints and images of artwork might also be shown and discussed.

H Murals

Description: A mural is created in acrylic paint or other medium, such as felt-tipped markers or even crayons, with a group of individuals participating. There are several advantages to the mural project beyond its creative potential: The mural encourages socializing as individuals work closely together creating their picture. The project works well with all populations and because of its social nature, it is helpful in easing relationships among people confined for long periods.

Prepare to paint or draw with people working in their own designated space, either on one theme or themes relating to each other, such as sequences in a single theme:
   a Tape or tack the paper to the wall or lay it flat upon the table or floor.
   b If people are working on both sides of the paper, draw a line along the length of the paper before starting and cut when the mural is complete. In this way, the images will all face in one direction when the mural is hung.
   c Because the mural is a *group* project, an individual may find it a comfortable *hiding place* while exploring his or her creative ideas.
   d The discussion (or critique that follows every art project) should include things that the group talked about, as well as the artistic results, to generate more socializing opportunities.

2 Themes for the mural should be provocative ideas that are personally interesting but stimulating for group participation. Suggested themes:
   a Where do you want to be in ten years? This theme should be used only in sites where the concept is heartening and not potentially depressing, as it would be with the aged.
   b What do you want to be or do or have in ten years? Youth may represent the fame they hope to have, jobs, careers, families, dwelling places or cars they hope to own.
   c Places you want to travel to.

3 The theme should ideally serve as a kind of bond among all those present, as individuals show aspects of their desires in one shared space. Hopefully, during and after the painting or drawing process elements of the hopes, dreams and plans projected in the mural will be verbalized.

Illustration: Figure 15.25 shows a mural project being created on the floor.

Figure 15.25 Mural being created by students Barbara Van Driel, Ellen Ziegler and others on the floor, later cut lengthwise to hang properly

Figure 15.25a Mural being created on the wall by students Cindy Klein, Arlene Beckman and others.

The Dinner Party

Description: A specific group project called **The Dinner Party Project** is valuable for the interaction it affords. Everyone enjoys getting an invitation to dinner. Like the mural project, it presents an excellent socializing opportunity and is suitable for all populations.

1. Invite the participant group to "a dinner party." People should sit opposite one another and side by side, as they would while dining.
2. Set up for the dinner party by spreading a sheet of mural paper out on a long table, masking down the edges. Alternatively, large papers can be placed individually, as place mats.
3. Use a dinner size paper plate, a lunch size plate and a paper glass to draw the outline of these on the flat paper.
4. Invite "guests" to draw whatever they would like to eat on their plate—whatever pleases them.
5. Add drinks, coffee, tea; add cutlery and napkins, decorate the plates.
6. Invite those who finish early to draw flowers and candles for the table.
7. Note that cut-outs from magazines can be prepared in advance and applied by individuals, when drawing seems daunting.

Illustration: Figure 15.26 is an example of a dinner platter created as a collage with cutout food and beverages.

Figure 15.26 Cutouts of plates of food pasted on paper for the dinner party project, student Melissa Johnson

Illustration: Figure 15.27 is an example of a complete dinner with beverage, desert and silverware drawn on a place mat.

Figure 15.27 The dinner party project drawn with pencil and crayons by student Michelle Osciak

I Other Special Projects

Description: Acrylic painting lends itself to different projects by using diverse painting surfaces. Just ensure that the surface to be painted cannot potentially be harmful to oneself or others.

Although some material usefulness may occur, keep in mind that the use is secondary to the artistic process. Some examples of special projects include:

- a Note paper pictures, also using watercolor, ink, colored pencils or markers. This could encourage written communications to other residents or to friends and family.
- b Painting on plastics. Ordinary containers for deli products are suitable. Lids work well on their own. Translucent effects can be achieved, in which case productions could be hung on a window.
- c Painting on wood.
- d Painting of artifacts and found objects for either decorative or utilitarian productions.

Process:

Just make sure the object to be painted is clean, dry and unbroken and able to take the painting medium. As in "Painting in Acrylic" (III.E), encourage the mixing of color and consistency to obtain subtle hues and tones.

Illustration: Figure 15.28 shows examples of deli containers and lids painted in acrylics.

Figure 15.28 Deli containers and lids painted in acrylics, students Jessica Cullari, Karen Beir, Jessi Zalme and Melissa Johnson

IV Sculpture

(Most of the projects included below, together with other sculpture projects, are described more fully in the author's text *Sculpture as Experience*; see Annotated Bibliography.)

A Clay Sculpture

Description: Clay is pliable and versatile, soft when moist and hard and permanent when baked in a kiln. It is easily pushed, pulled, pounded, poked and pressed into shape, but the limits of its endurance must be understood and appreciated. Clay sculpture is an excellent project for youth and adults of all ages. Some elderly participants might be reluctant to manipulate clay as it is messy, but a simple demonstration showing that it readily washes off may alleviate this concern.

Process:

1 The type of clay sculpture described below is intended for kiln firing. [Note: Where no kiln is available, use self-hardening or oven firing clay. Children's colored modeling clay is also fine to use and readily available. It does not harden and can be used again and again.]
2 Dispense an adequate amount of clay. Wedging eliminates air bubbles; a simplified wedging process is to repeatedly throw the clay on its ends and sides, thereby compressing its masses. Stand for leverage as you throw the clay against the table. There is a joyous freedom in this action which almost everyone seems to enjoy.
3 A good way to begin the sculpture is to throw the clay mound into a shape that you like. Then press the form onto a board for easy turning and place this at eye level to be able to see it clearly as you work. Use a small wood block to make initial shapes, using both the surface and edges of the block to press, pat, indent and cut. Concentrate on the major forms and their relationships, rather than on details.
4 Add additional clay to the form as you wish but press it on well; do not merely "stick it on."
5 Use wood blocks and clay wedges to support forms as needed.
6 Turn the form frequently and look at it from a distance from time to time to see it clearly. The forms are hard to see when you are on top of them.
7 Manipulating the clay will often suggest ideas as accidental shapes are prospects for seeing new things. Offer suggestions to prevent rejected efforts from being abandoned or destroyed by their creators. Here are constructive ideas to do this:
   a A flat pancake shape, a common production of young children, might evolve into a face or an animal.
   b Shapeless masses can suggest food by painting the shapes after firing. Bugs, spiders, worms may also show up.
   c Square shapes or mounds can be rescued by making furniture: tables, chairs or sofas. Once the furniture is there, imagine placing people on the chairs around a table or seated on a sofa. Once the people are on the sofa, the TV set might be envisioned not so far away. Furniture and furnishings in clay are good suggestions to make for long-term institutionalized patients who have no substantial personal possessions.
8 Participants may often consider a smooth texture the only proper way to finish a piece; however, the result is usually not smooth but bumpy, having a slick surface like that of an unlevelled road topped with a thin coat of tar. Therefore, show participants how to obtain "smooth" using a wire tool with a serrated edge followed by one with a flat edge; or how to apply clay without rubbing away the marks to achieve interesting textured surfaces.
9 If a part cracks or falls off the form when the clay is no longer very soft, replace it with slip. Make slip by mixing a small amount of clay and water together to the consistency of cream. Crosshatch the area with a wood tool; put slip in between the two parts; and press the sides firmly together. Pinch the edges together and add extra clay at the joints as needed.

10 If not completed during the session and becoming dry, cover the form with a damp rag, and then securely cover over that with a good plastic bag. If the form is still wet, only the plastic is needed.
11 When almost complete, hollow out the form from the bottom to allow for shrinkage during firing. A guide in hollowing is to maintain approximately 1″ thickness of solid clay all around.
12 After hollowing, air-dry the piece thoroughly. To transport to a kiln, pack work carefully in boxes. Touch up any damaged areas on arrival and place to dry on open slats of wood allowing air to circulate underneath.
13 If the work breaks in the kiln or just prior to firing, it can often be repaired after firing by: (a) first file off fine particles from the bottom of the piece; (b) then press the parts together with quick setting (5-minute epoxy); (c) add the fine particles to cover the seam while still wet using a thin wooden stick or plastic glove.
14 A good patina for fired clay sculpture is dark brown Kiwi shoe polish (paste wax) mixed with a little turpentine for easy spreading. Work can also be painted but the addition of color will change the impact of the sculptural form; therefore, give careful thought to the end result desired.

Illustration: Figure 15.29 is an example of sculpture in earthenware clay.

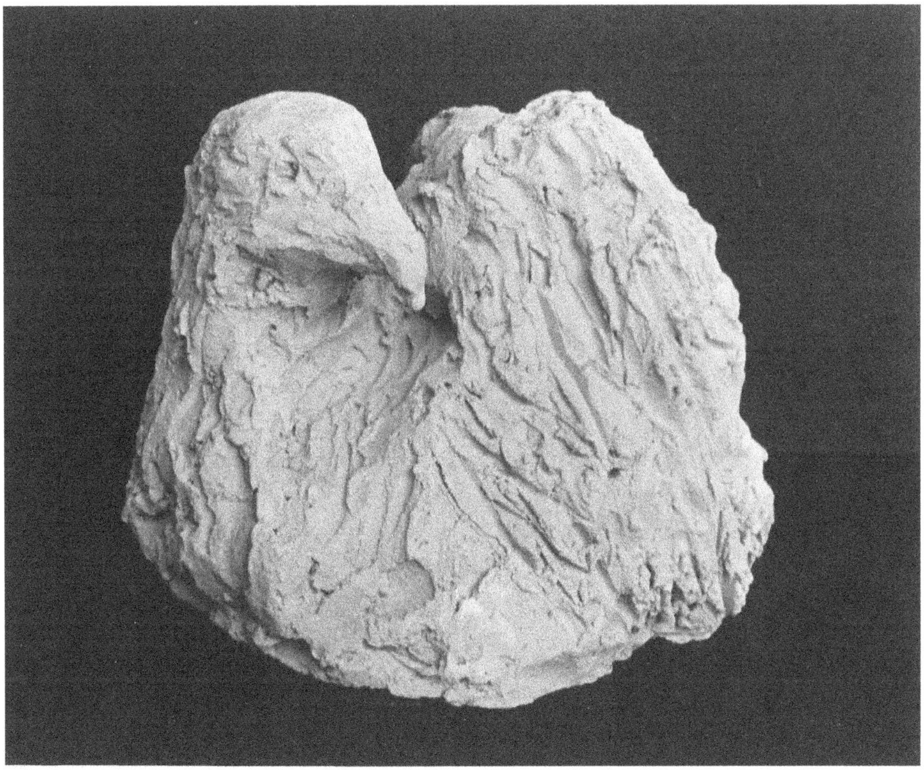

Figure 15.29 Clay sculpture of a bird

Illustration: Figure 15.30 shows examples of small sculptures in self-hardening colored clay.

Figure 15.30 Small sculptures of animals in colored clay, students Jessi Zalme, Lisa LaMontagne, Peter Scarola and Juliette Betancourt

B Strip Paper Sculptures

Description: This project is simple and inventive and suitable for youth and adults. Glue sticks, masking tape and staples may or may not be used in jailed settings. It is fun and challenging to imagine the paper structures as models for architectural installations.

Process:

1. Use cut strips (as in project II.C). Using white glue, glue sticks, staples and/or masking tape, adhere the strips to each other and to a wooden or cardboard base as a three-dimensional structure.
2. Fabricate a design, landscape, abstraction, etc., letting the simplicity of the strips inspire you.
3. When finished, paint the construction via spray-paint (outside) one color throughout to integrate the colors, textures and forms, or leave each of the colors as is.
4. The sculpture can appear to be a scale model for something much larger fabricated in metal or marble or wood or fiberglass.

Illustration: Figures 15.31, 15.32 and 15.32a are examples of strip paper sculpture.

Figure 15.31 Strip paper sculpture mounted on poster board, student Carole Finkelstein

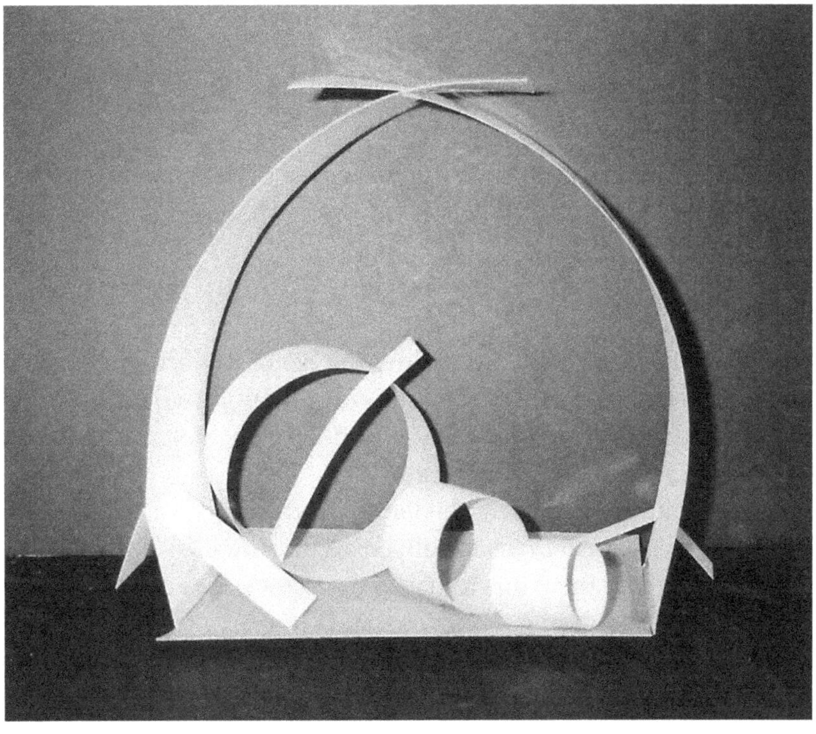

Figure 15.32 Paper sculpture created with thin circular strips by student Ilana Houton

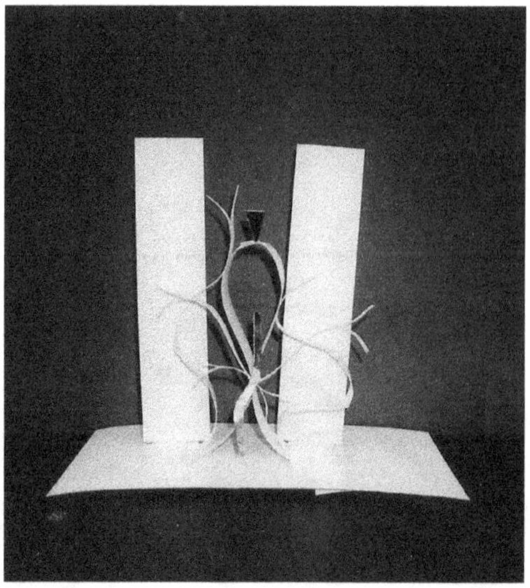

Figure 15.32a Strip paper sculpture of two upright rectangles, student Kaitlyn Ferguson

C Foil and Plaster Wrap Sculptures

Description: This project allows for three-dimensional creation of figures in action. A lone figure can be created but two figures in some relationship is recommended. The procedure is easily followed requiring no formal training to create a human figure and no large preparation of sculptural materials. Because this project is especially popular and psychologically expressive, detailed process and illustrations are provided. It is suitable for all populations. Note: More detailed information about this project appears in the author's book *Sculpture as Experience* (see Annotated Bibliography).

Process:

1 Dispense foil into square sheets.
2 Wrap a small amount of stuffing into one corner of the square for a head using one cotton ball, or two squares of toilet tissue, or one-half of a facial tissue—proportions for an adult head.
3 Tear the opposite corner of the square half-way toward the center and squeeze the divided sections into two (uneven) legs.
4 Tear the arcs that extend outward (below the head) inward one-third of the way toward the center and squeeze them individually into two (uneven) arms.
5 Make hands and feet by folding back a portion of each of the four extremities so that they become symmetrical in length.
6 Squeeze the remaining foil along the length of the body; or form it into a skirt; or stuff it with tissue to form breasts, belly, hips or buttocks.
7 Bend the figure *only* at the joints to try a variety of poses or actions: standing, running, sitting, kneeling, falling, lying, etc. and choose one.
8 Add foil accessories as desired, for example, clothing, sports equipment, animals or objects by attaching additional foil with staples. Furniture can be added to the composition by folding cardboard into suitable shapes and stapling this onto the base.
9 A second figure should be made in similar fashion so that (a) the method can be practiced again and (b) two figures can be created in relationship to one another, a process that may have psychosocial value beyond the rewards of completing the project.

10 Optional if time allows: Wrap all parts of the figure(s), except for the supporting legs, with a single layer of plaster wrap which has been pre-cut into thin (1/4") strips then dipped lightly in water before applying. The plaster wrap dries in approximately 20 minutes.
11 Find or cut a wooden base for the figure composition in a size to fit the figures. A black pre-sprayed or painted base is suggested.
12 Hammer a long headless nail into the base to extend along one supporting leg of each figure. Wire the leg to the nail and add a final strip of plaster wrap to cover it.
13 The finished sculpture can be left white or subsequently painted with acrylics.

Because the project is easily done anywhere among most constituents (with exceptions) using materials that are safe and available and end results effective for personal expression, detailed illustrations are provided to ensure its success.

Illustration: Figures 15.33 to 15.38 show how to form a foil figure.

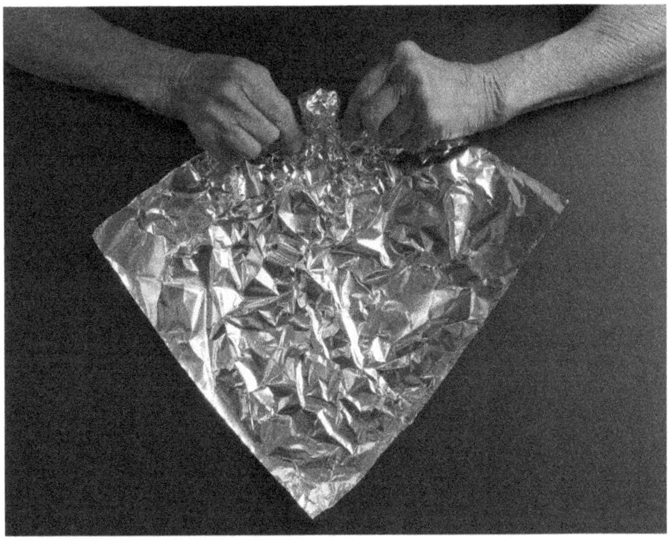

Figure 15.33 Squeeze under the head to form a neck (Nos. 1 and 2)

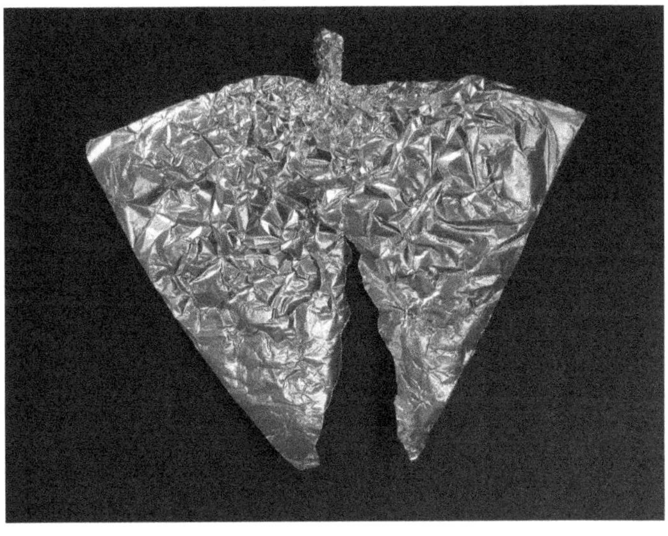

Figure 15.34 Tear midway up from the bottom, then squeeze to form two legs (No. 3)

Figure 15.35 Tear midway toward the middle on both sides then squeeze to form the arms (Nos. 4 and 5)

Figure 15.36 Squeeze the midsection to form the body and/or clothes; begin to bend the figure at the joints to get ideas for an action (Nos. 6 and 7)

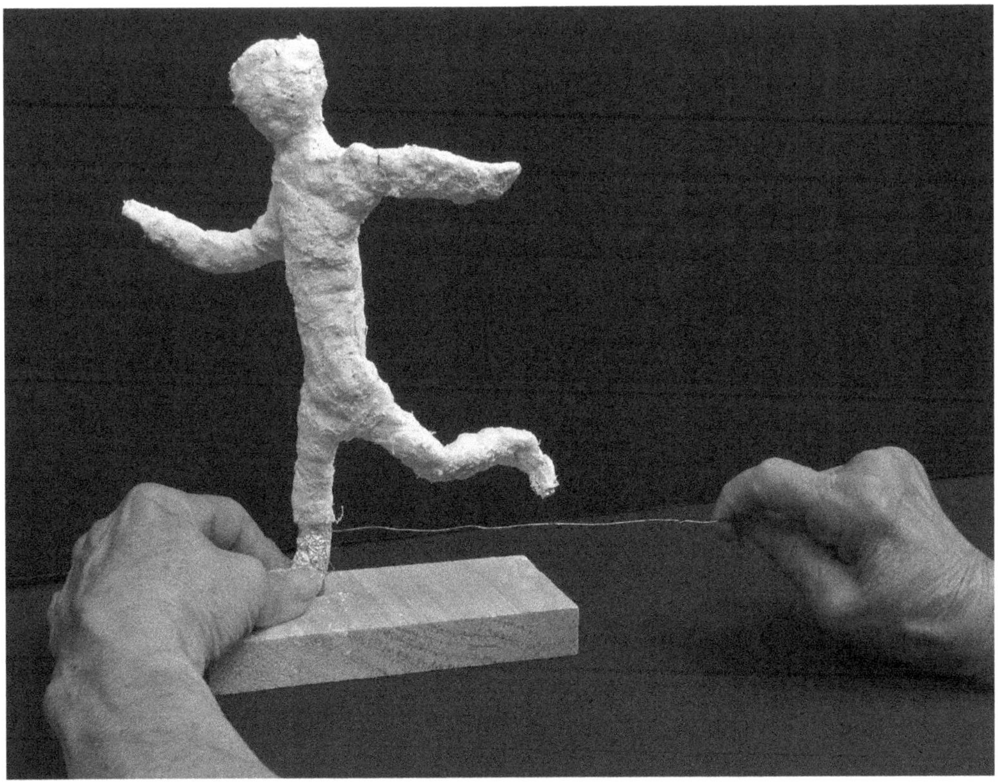

Figure 15.37 Optional: for permanence: wrap with thin strips of plaster wrap dipped in water around the figure's torso, arms and legs; let dry; insert a headless nail in a wood base; then secure one unwrapped leg of the figure to it with a wire (Nos.10, 11, 12)

Figure 15.38 A finished sculpture coated in plaster wrap, the figure's arms and legs are bent at the joints, torso leaning forward, wire added: a runner at the finish line, by student Paul Barbier (Nos. 10, 11, 12)

Illustration: Figures 15.39, 15.39a, 15.40 and 15.41 are examples of foil and plaster wrap figure compositions.

Figure 15.39 Clown with a balloon and happy child in foil and plaster wrap, student Donna Solimine (Nos. 8 and 9)

Figure 15.39a Family in foil, plaster wrap and acrylic paint, student LaFrancis Singletary (No.9)

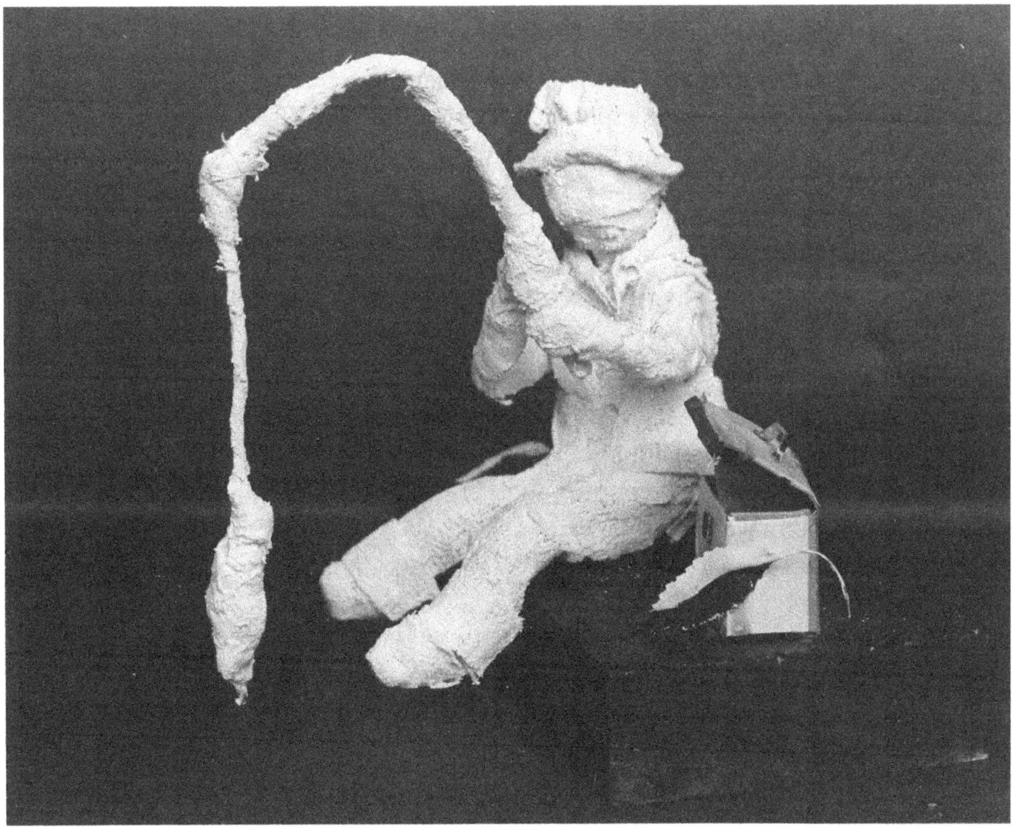

Figure 15.40 Fisherman, foil and plaster wrap composition (No. 8)

Figure 15.41 Dancing mother and daughter created in foil and plaster wrap by student Edna Dagan (No. 9)

D Plaster Shapes or Jewelry

Description: This project involves pouring wet plaster from a cup onto wax paper and then pushing the puddles into shapes as the plaster dries. The process produces shapes of a wild variety. Shapes need to be thick and not so fragile as to break. When dry they can be sanded, filed and painted as decorative objects or jewelry pins and pendants. The project would not be permitted in an incarcerated or psychiatric setting. See Figure 15.54 to see finished painted shapes.

Process:

1. For this project, prepare the plaster at the site (see Section III.D, Painting on Plaster Plates for mixing instructions).
2. Place a square of waxed paper for each participant on a flat table surface. Make sure the paper itself lies completely flat.
3. Pour the plaster into individual 5 oz. paper cups and give one to each participant to use immediately.
4. Fold the top of the cup into a pouring spout. Pour shapes onto the wax paper. The plaster thickens as it dries, so wait as needed as you pour.
   a. Use the wood stick to push the plaster into shapes and continue to manipulate the shapes as the plaster thickens.
   b. Form into simple geometric shapes, abstractions or a pattern for a wall hanging.
   c. Thin shapes are fragile and will break, so push the plaster into thick shapes and lines. Broken shapes can still be used, just file or sand the edges to shape them.
5. If you plan to hang the shape, press a hole into the plaster with a nail when plaster is firm or carefully later after it has set.
6. Do not move the wax sheet from the moment the plaster begins to set.
7. After setting, lift the shapes from the waxed paper.
8. Coat the shapes with equal parts of shellac and alcohol for an "antique" finish or spray the shapes with satin or gloss polyurethane.
9. The shapes can be painted when dry with acrylics and used for pendants or mounted as wall sculptures on prepared wood bases.

V Fabric Pictures

Description: Fabric is associated with clothes and other sewn goods and as such has associations that are not only materialistic which is good, but familiar, which is even better. Elderly women may try fabric projects more easily than paper projects which may connote insignificance to them. Children may also be impressed with the material significance of their work in fabric. There is a change of *surface*—from paper to fabric—but no change in the aesthetic objectives. Females more so than males will be attracted to the project.

Process:

1 Use a firm surface such as cardboard.
2 If possible, find a variety of scrap fabrics in various colors and patterns to encourage an imaginative selection process. Consider unusual materials such as felt and burlap in addition to those around the house.
3 Select a background fabric according to the picture concept: landscape, seascape, cityscape, residence (interior or exterior) or abstract composition. Use white glue to adhere the fabric to the surface.
4 Cut scraps of fabric into shapes to form the picture.
5 Consider a group wall hanging combining individually made pictures. A unifying theme can be suggested but fabric selection and picture ideas should be left to the individual.
6 People in fabric are fun to make too. Paper forms of people can be purchased in a stack from school art supply catalogs and decorated. Decorate with fabric clothes, accessories, hair and ribbons. Create faces with colored markers.

Illustration: Figures 15.42, 15.43, 15.44, 15.45 and 15.46 are examples of fabric pictures.

Figure 15.42 Fabric tree with button flowers and landscape, student Johanna O'Rourk

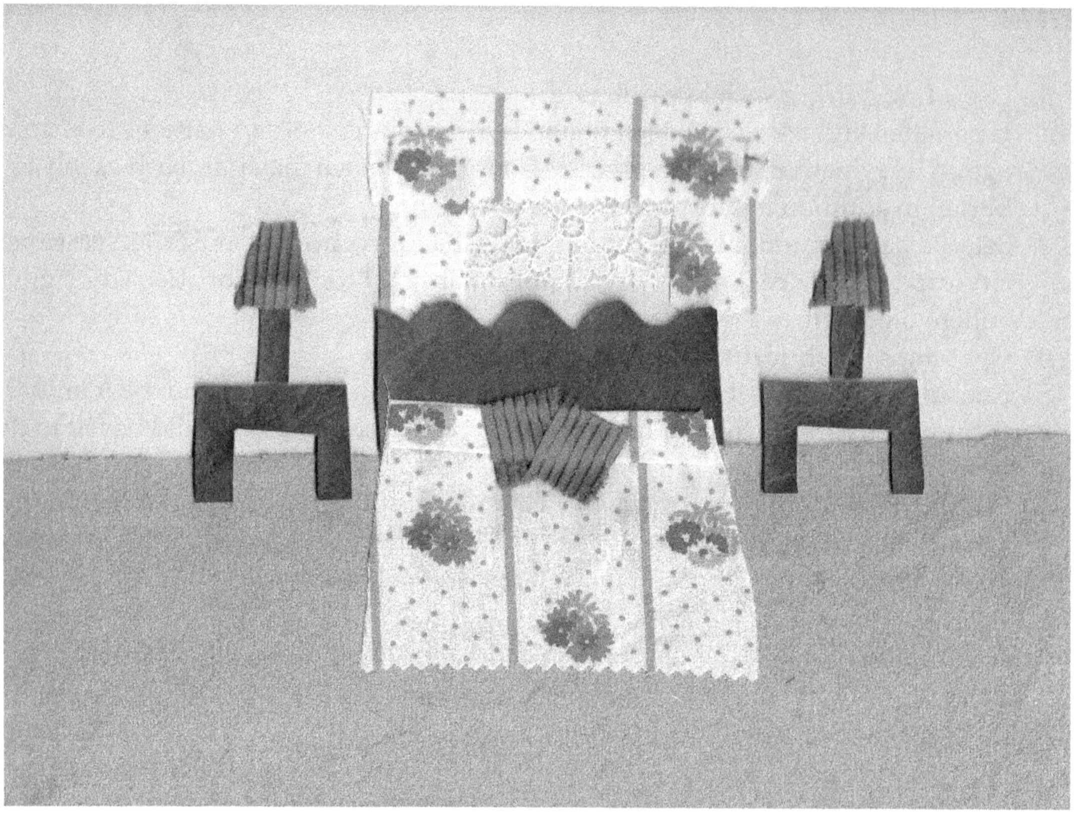

Figure 15.43 Fabric bed, night tables and lamps, student Norina Teitell

Figure 15.44 Fabric picture—Sunset and bird over mountain range by student William Dorsett

Figure 15.45 Fabric picture with drawing, softball player by student Susan McGuire

Figure 15.46 Fabric picture with buttons, cardboard and drawing, little girl in plaid jumper by student Donna Solimine

VI Puppets

Description: The puppets project, besides being a lot of fun, aims at developing imagination and increasing competence in handling materials. It is suited to both youth and adults. The puppets tend to be invested with distinctive personalities, their features suggested by the creator.

After the puppets are created, follow up with a group verbal interchange about the various personalities that have emerged. Ask questions such as: What is her name? How old is she? What does she do for a living? Where does she live. Married? Children . . .? Of course, the creator will be making these things up as she answers, but as the personalities emerge, a relationship can be established among the puppets and the start of an improvisational play.

Arrange the puppets into separate groups of five to six or so creators and fabricate a puppet play using the personalities to form a plot.

After the plot is established, practice the improvised parts and especially the voices which have to *project* their personalities.

Create a title for the play then set yourselves hidden behind a table with your arms raised to the surface and palm outstretched to hold your puppet aloft. Make sure to move the puppet physically when it speaks. Take turns, each group presenting a mini-show to others. A leader (or faculty) should introduce each play in turn and there should be much hoot and hollering, clapping and audience response.

Dramatic presentations can be stimulating in negative as well as positive ways and so groups engaged in the project should be fairly stable. Subdue the excitement if it creates excessive stimulation, which it may do among spirited youth. The project is not recommended in the psychiatric hospital or incarcerated setting.

Fabricating puppets can be a rewarding experience for the frail elderly. Although presenters must do much of the work, participants can make all the decisions to do with features and clothing. In this way, the puppet may stimulate memories of a well-loved friend, spouse or parent, and memories of other places and times. The rapport generated while creating the puppet aids intergroup socialization. Participants may talk and touch one another through the puppets where they might not do so independently.

Process:

1 Use a discarded toilet paper roll as the core of the puppet head. Coat this with white glue and put fiber fill around the roll as stuffing. (Cotton can be substituted.)
2 Place a length of discarded nylon stocking over the stuffing. A range of tones should be available for representing skin color.
3 Tie the nylon on top of the roll; secure it *under* the roll at the bottom by staples (flat side facing the interior to avoid scratching your hand later when the puppet is held).
4 Push the stuffing forward against the nylon in various places to pinch and pull out the facial features: forehead, ears, brows, cheeks, nose, lips and chin.
5 Sew a few stitches in various places, if desired, to give expression to the face, for example, by pinching the areas around the nostrils and lips.

6 Create hair with yarn. Styles can include braids, bangs, ribbons and so on. A hat can be made with fabric or even cardboard.
7 Use fabric, buttons, wool or other trimming materials for facial features and accessories as desired. Sew these onto the nylon or try fastening with white glue.
8 Use a length of doubled-over material, sufficient to cover your hand and wrists, for a body. Cut a tiny slit at the fold, slip the material tightly over the paper roll and staple it on. Sew the sides leaving space for your fingers to emerge on each side as the puppet's arms.
9 Decorate the puppet's clothing if desired.
10 Consider adding artifacts such as glasses, cigarettes, pipes and so on, using wire or whatever works, stapling these on.
11 When the puppets are complete, hold a roundtable discussion for everyone to talk about their puppet.
12 From these descriptions plays may be devised, each containing an assortment of **characters**, a **plot**, a series of **actions,** a point of **conflict** and an eventual **resolution**.
13 Rehearse the shows in an improvisational manner. Use a draped table as the puppet stage, with participants kneeling behind, unseen. Each group presents its play in turn to the other groups which provide the audience.
14 Speak puppet **voices clearly and loudly** to be heard from beneath the table. Exaggerate puppet **actions** "on stage" to vividly demonstrate which puppet is talking.

Figure 15.47 Puppet—"Artist," by student Kristie Henry

Figure 15.48 Puppet—"Woman with Curly Hair," by student Christina Suter

Figure 15.49 Puppet—"Grandma," by student Melissa Denneau

Figure 15.49a Puppet—"Man about Town," by student Andrea Kunst

Figure 15.50 Children from the housing project cuddling their puppets

Figure 15.51 Student with children performing their puppet show to an audience of children at the Paterson Housing Project.

15 To extend the project, create scenery as a backdrop. Using mural paper, create two or three continuous scenes, each as wide as the allotted background for the table. Tape the scenes onto two long broom handles and roll them up. Set up screens or curtains to flank the "stage," behind which two people stand to roll and unroll the scenes as they appear in the play.

16 Add music and sound effects to the improvisational play, live or recorded, as desired.

VII Jewelry Projects

Description: Jewelry has materialistic value which appeals to participants; in addition, products can be given as gifts adding another potential reward to doing the project. The approach is different from other projects in the step-by-step procedures that are necessary. Jewelry-making is most suitable for capable adults and teenaged youth. But note that due to the complexity of materials, in most institutions it will not be permitted.

A Copper Enamel

Process: The project is offered for situations where more sophisticated projects are wanted and the safety factor of handling a small kiln can be accommodated. Further outside instruction is strongly recommended, as the process involves high heat.

1. Inform the group in advance that full attention is needed; that all tools must be returned in good order; that spills can happen because the process is delicate but that new tries are easily made. Limit the number of copper pieces to be enameled; one to three per person is suggested to keep the session under control.
2. Place the copper enamel kiln on a fireproof pad and plug it in; dispense tools and materials.
3. Allow individuals to select from an assortment of copper shapes. Use large shapes—generally circles, ovals or squares—for frail elderly who have physical limitations such as poor vision and trembling.
4. If the finished product is for hanging, a pendant or charm, use a hole punch (a simple metal instrument) before starting.
5. Prepare only one side of the shape to fire (to keep the process simple). The back (if it will be seen) can be painted with acrylics after firing.
6. Sand the copper shape thoroughly in a cross-hatched pattern with a small square of carborundum paper.
7. Wash the shape with detergent, rinse it thoroughly, dry with paper towel then handle it only by its edges.
8. Apply Agar gum solution with a brush to hold the glass powder then place the copper shape on a piece of cardboard with a tweezer so that it can be turned without handling.
9. While still wet with gum solution, dust a base coat of glass powder on the shape using a sifter.
10. Add other colors through the sifter or with a tweezer according to the developing design. Add glass threads or stones as desired using the tweezer.
11. When the design is completed, lift the piece carefully with the spatula and guide it onto a grate. (Place a tweezer in your other hand to help guide the piece off the spatula and onto the grate. Make sure the grate is a size to fit in the kiln.) When the grate is loaded with copper pieces, guide it into the kiln with a long spatula and long tweezers. Close the kiln cover to begin the firing.
12. Pieces can take 5 to 15 minutes to melt, depending on their size and substance and on the kiln temperature. When the pieces become granular, they are still not ready to be removed. A shiny glaze should appear, indicating that the glass has fully melted. Using the long spatula, remove the whole grate or individual pieces, as you can, and place on a fireproof pad near the kiln so that the pieces will cool slowly. Colors will change in the firing and cooling process.
13. When cool enough to handle, copper pin-backs can be glued to the copper using 5-minute epoxy resin.

Illustration: Figure 15.52 shows examples of copper enamel jewelry.

Figure 15.52 Five copper enamel jewelry shapes after the colored glass melted into the prepared designs, by student Penelope Jones.

B Found Object Jewelry

Description: The fun of this craft is finding small, durable, non-hazardous material to connect with other finds (even fragments of actual costume jewelry) to create an object of wearable jewelry. The process is by nature improvisational and therefore methods of preparing, connecting parts and finishing will depend on the materials used. The project is best suited to non-institutionalized adults who have the ability to find suitable objects at home.

Process:

1 **Factors** in **selection**
   a Small objects with interesting *attributes* of shape, form, color, texture, light reflection and compatibility with other selected objects.
   b The ability to *connect* forms: some interesting objects may be unfeasible to secure together.
   c The *wearability* of objects: some interesting and feasible objects may be too heavy, sharp, bizarre or uncomfortable to consider wearing.
2 **Factors** in **fabrication**

The following list is intended not only to provide technical suggestions but ideas for suitable objects for jewelry-making:

Methods of preparation

a Cutting, sawing
b Punching or drilling holes
c Pulling apart, extracting or peeling

Methods of connecting or adhering parts

a Soldering
b Stringing or beading
c Gluing
d Bending, looping and hooking
e Tying

Methods of finishing

a Washing
b Filing
c Sanding
d Waxing
e Polishing
f Painting

Illustration: Figure 15.53 shows examples of found object jewelry made from seeds, a carved and polished scrap of wood, and computer parts.

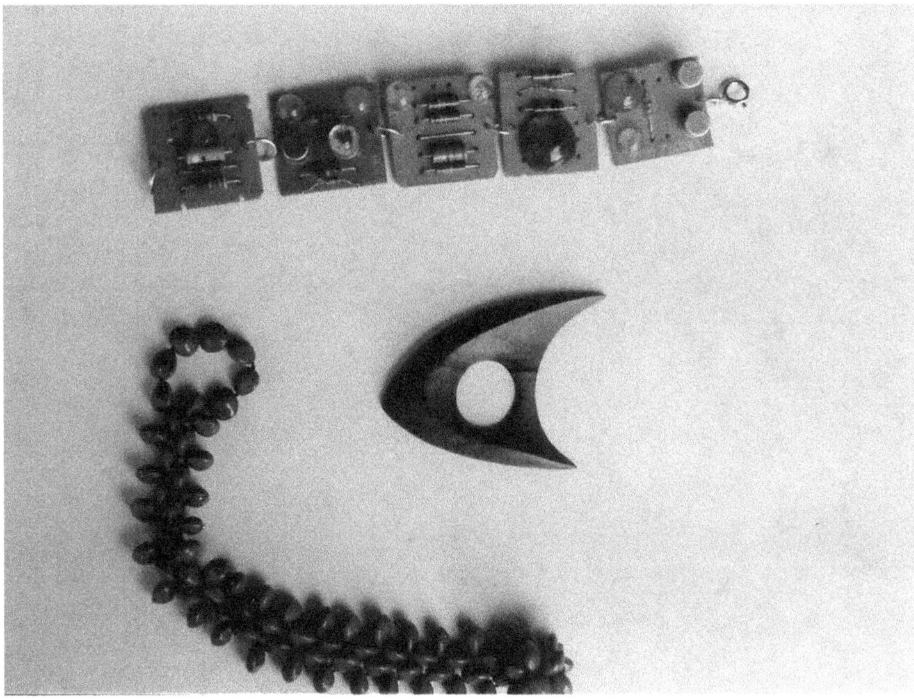

Figure 15.53 Found-object jewelry made from seeds, a carved and polished scrap of wood and computer parts

C Plaster Formed Jewelry

Description: This project can be prepared and completed at the site and requires little in the way of materials. See IV.D on creating sculpture in plaster for a description of the concept.

Process:

1. Consult Project III.D for step-by-step procedures on mixing plaster.
2. Pour plaster into 3-oz. paper cups; tip the cup to form a spout.
3. Guide the pour of plaster onto a flat sheet of wax paper into thick shapes or puddles. Shape with a wooden stick. The shapes should be small in order to serve as pins, earrings, charms or pendants, but full, not thin and fragile.
4. Make matched shapes for use as earrings.
5. When completely dry, loosen plaster forms gently from wax paper.
6. Fasten pinbacks with epoxy resin when the piece is completely dry, Alternatively, press a hole into the plaster while still damp to hang the shape from a leather cord or metal chain.

Illustration: Figure 15.54 shows examples of plaster formed jewelry shapes.

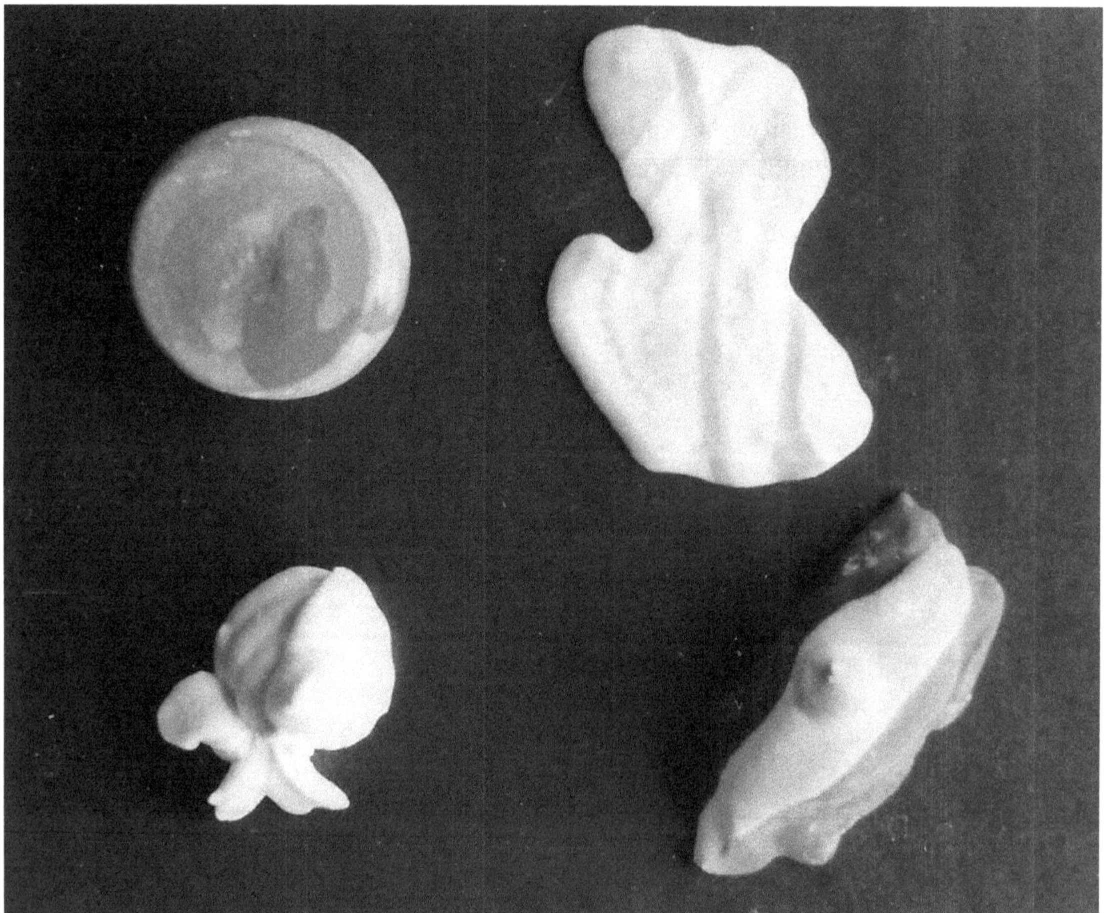

Figure 15.54 Four small, abstract shapes poured in plaster and later painted

VIII Innovations and Variations

Description: Listed below are variations on the projects using procedures already described but adding different materials and combinations. Try some, always considering the resources, needs and respective desires at the site.

Watercolor and ink compositions
Watercolor and ink with wet sponge applications
Tissue collage on objects such as a tissue box, or plastic jar
Cardboard games or toys
Movable cardboard toys with brass fasteners
Relief sculptures with string or cord glued on for texture and design
Xerox of gloves or other clothing or objects
Figure collages made from wallpaper
Figure or scene collages made from magazine pages
Oil paint drops on water pushed with a stick to create abstractions
Painting on alternate surfaces such as wood, plastic, metal etc.

Figure 15.55 Painted flowers on wood panel, student Alison Weber

Part Six

Enhancing, Expanding and Evaluating the Program

Figure 6.0 Student Carlos Salgado shows a group of children in the day-care center how to paint with watercolors

DOI: 10.4324/9781003592693-22

Chapter 16

Enhancing Interaction with Participants and Staff

Interactions among people will naturally be as individual as there are personalities and topics, but there are guidelines to follow when working in institutional settings.

Guidelines in Interacting with Participants

Avoid Emotional Involvement

Try to avoid causing a strain on the friendly relationships you establish with participants by becoming emotionally involved in their predicaments. You must also discourage emotional attachment to yourself. The keen interest taken in you—your home, work or school environment—may have you respond in ways appropriate elsewhere but not in the institutional setting and the limited context of the program.

The socialization that takes place during the sessions is best characterized as interest but not intimacy. Avoid granting special favors and handle requests for books, art materials and other program-related materials in a standardized manner. Some participants may mistake interest for intimacy by your actions and that may change the direction of their efforts. Moreover, an intimate relationship cannot lead to close friendship in the institutional setting and so will eventually lead to a sense of failure rather than success. This undermines the primary goal of the workshops. Should the tenor of socialization become sexual in tone, the participant and/or the presenter involved should not continue in the program.

Strike a Balance Between Art Activity and Social Interaction

The art activity should always accompany socialization. On some occasions the conversations may become so intense that the art activity is placed in the background. If this occurs and art activity is ignored, you become no more than a listener or conversationalist; you cease to be a provider of those special opportunities for personal creative growth that

DOI: 10.4324/9781003592693-23

constitute the program's objectives. Similarly, concentrating on your own art activity should not be so intense that it closes off others from interacting with you.

Avoid Judgmental Attitudes and Responses

Some participants may be used to eliciting negative or shocked responses to their behavior. Seeking that reaction may provide reinforcement for a negative self-image or have other psychological origins which are beyond the scope of the program. Your responses to such remarks can be significant, so aim to be nonjudgmental in both your attitude and words. This avoids giving the implied condemnation which may be expected or even solicited and free them to discover more positive aspects of their personalities.

A nonjudgmental attitude implies accepting people *in the present*, without forming judgments about their past behavior about which you can know little if anything. That domain of judgment requires its own distinctive processes in which you are not involved. Accepting this can help to reconcile conflicting concepts, such as the idea of giving pleasure to criminals who are incarcerated for punishment.

One way of responding when you are not sure what to say is simply to *repeat the last phrase of what has been said in a matter-of-fact tone*. This indicates that you have heard the comment and the speaker can then continue on as he or she wishes without having to weigh your remark. For example, Speaker: *I left home when I was sixteen*. You: *You left when you were sixteen*. Speaker: *Yes, I . . .*

Avoid Interpretation or Analysis of Artwork

While encouraging participants to talk about their artwork, you should avoid making your own interpretations or analyses which might be far removed from their intentions and at the same time possibly reinforce their notions of right and wrong. You provide encouragement but participants should feel they are working for themselves for goals which they establish, not to please others which they may be more used to doing. Since some lack confidence in their abilities, a *wrong* interpretation may be attributed to some failure or mistake. One of the underlying motivations in making art is the communication it affords. Misinterpreting those messages can further a sense of failure rather than create an exciting new avenue for communication.

Be Sensitive to the Direction of Personal Disclosure

Questions may arise about how to deal with personal disclosure and confidences that are shared. The informal, friendly atmosphere in the art workshops makes it not unlikely that personal confidences will comprise some of the topics of conversation. You should be receptive to this as to other concerns of the participant but at the same time try to maintain the kind of distance that would offer trust and the freedom to talk without negative consequences. You do not want the individual to become dependent on you as a confidant nor suffer the sense of loss—of privacy and your absence—when you leave the program, which protracted conversations of this nature might produce.

Self-Disclosure

You might also be cautious about self-disclosure. While a certain amount of self-disclosure is a natural part of most relationships of substance, in the institutional setting this may be misunderstood as a move toward intimacy. The participant might feel a responsibility to do something about the shared information, feel incompetent or helpless to manage it or worse, take some deleterious action. Either way, the situation can lead to a sense of failure, thus compromising a potentially successful relationship.

It is true that without a degree of trusting disclosure, communication may remain on a superficial level. But also true is that some institutionalized individuals, for complex reasons, are unable to develop trusting relationships. It is beyond the scope of this program to change that nor is it a goal to create trust relationships. What is important is that you do not add reasons for mistrust, something that may unwittingly be done if limitations in relationships are not observed. This is particularly salient with respect to emotional entanglements. Issues surrounding program duration and leave-taking with respect to this matter are addressed later in this section.

The Informal Interview

A procedure that can help to facilitate interaction without intimacy is the "informal interview." The answers not only help to achieve a successful program but provide you with cultural understanding you may not otherwise have access to. The interviews should take place during the first few sessions in a location somewhat apart from the working tables.

Insert 16.1 Suggested Format and Questions for Inmate Interviews

The purpose of the interview is stated in a tactful, nonthreatening way: "Some information is needed so that we can make the art program more personally meaningful for you." The questions are then asked in an informal, friendly manner, allowing sufficient time for response after each question.

1. What is your name?
2. What is your educational experience regarding school; for example, how long did you stay in school? What were your special interests in school? What subjects did you like best?
3. What are your educational experiences out of school; for example, what events were especially important? What people or situations provided learning or encouragement— family, others? Who had special importance for you in this regard?
4. What kind of work do you do or did you do in the past?
5. If you had the money, the time and the training, what kind of work would you do, that is, if nothing stood in your way?
6. How long do you expect to be detained in this facility and what is the nature of the charge—that is, if you care to discuss it?
7. What kind of art activity do you think you would be most interested in: drawing, painting, clay sculpture . . . ?

* Question No. 6 is, of course, sensitive and some institutions may prefer that this be eliminated.

It is conducted by one presenter while others continue to work with participants at the tables. The description and examples that follow center on the interview as conducted in the jail where it is a most valuable asset. Other sites can benefit from the interview format with questions prepared explicitly for the type of group addressed. A suggested format for inmate interviews appears in Insert 16.1.

Reasons for the Interview in the Jail Setting

The interviews serve a number of purposes: they allow the inmate to talk about him- or herself to an interested listener in a semi-formal manner. The concept of the interview is not invasive; the inmate is already used to the bureaucracy of providing information. It can, on the contrary, be expansive as the interviewer allows the inmate to think about important aspects of his or her life. The questions and answers may lead to other talk involving aspirations and goals.

No judgments should be made concerning the inmate's answers; the interview is a means to get to know the individual, not the record on file, meeting with him or her as a person, not a cellblock number. You may benefit equally from the interview as it may ease your fear of *dangerous* populations.

Recognizing the Limited Duration of the Program

One of the most basic program limitations is that of contact hours. Although the art workshop sessions may become high points for the participants and full of substance, they are of limited duration and only one facet of many in their lives. It is important, both for you as a presenter and for each person you work with, to understand from the outset that the sessions are scheduled for a certain time span and will terminate at the end of that time span.

That termination must be seen to be in the structure of the program and not with any individual relationship. Unless that understanding is verbalized and periodically repeated, albeit in a casual and friendly way, some participants might believe that *they did* something to cause the program's termination and an end to the relationship, as they may indeed believe they caused other relationships to end. The sense of rejection that may have accompanied past failed relationships would thus be repeated and much of the good you've done negated as a result. Mentioning the termination as something coming in the near future is a wise way to do it, saying, for example: "We have three sessions left, what project would you like to repeat?"

Accepting Program Termination

You must also clearly understand that you will be leaving your participants' lives at the end of the series, probably forever. You should not leave the impression that you will write or return from time to time to visit, something you might sincerely wish to do but for a number of reasons not care to do when the program is behind you.

Presenters may suffer an acute sense of guilt or loss upon termination of the program if the limitations of contact are not clearly perceived. In sum, the parting at the end of the series should not cancel nor reduce what has been gained if the concept of termination is felt throughout the workshop series. All involved must accept the fundamental limitation in the program's structure: its duration. Remaining in touch with fellow students who have shared your experiences is helpful if this can be accomplished.

Insert 16.2 Basic Guidelines for Presenters

In your work in institutions and agencies you will encounter a variety of people (clients, residents, patients) living in one or another kind of institutional setting. These clients and those associated with them (family, friends and social units) need help, and a portion of this will be provided by you. Here are suggestions to help you in establishing successful relationships:

1. For the most part, these individuals are living in institutions for a reason. The reason may not be clear to you at first, but it is a good idea to assume it exists. Staff personnel may help you to understand the causes of the clients' difficulties.
2. Listen to what individuals say. Try to understand their point of view. Sometimes it helps to say back to them the things they are telling you, particularly when they are having difficulty communicating.
3. Be straight about what you can and cannot do. Some of these individuals are indeed needy and you will want to give them what they need. But your time and energy are limited and both you and they should be clear about what these limitations are.
4. Confidentiality is important in all of these relationships. Be careful about what you repeat and to whom. There are rules for confidentiality, all of which you may not know, but assume that you may not identify any individual beyond the session and conversations should not be shared beyond your teammates and your assigned logs. If you have a question, consult the site representative.
5. Learn and observe the rules of the institution in which you work. Sometimes you will not see a reason for the rules. However, the staff you work with know their jobs better than you and have reasons for how they do things that you may not understand.
6. Your first source of help in the site is the staff member(s) on duty. You should feel free to ask for help when you need it.
7. Meeting your site responsibilities is extremely important. Individuals will count on you to a degree you may not at first realize. If you are unable to keep an appointment, be sure to let the institution know before the time you are expected. Keep necessary telephone numbers handy for this.

Conclusions

Acquiring understanding and skill in relationships may come easier to some presenters than to others but achieving success in those efforts is necessary for the program to succeed. You are not trained in counseling or therapy and this must be recognized throughout your interactions. Nevertheless, the service you do offer is valid: a caring person delivering creative artistic experiences in a friendly social atmosphere to people in need of the *freedom* inherent in artistic expression. You are a person comfortable with yourself or you would never have taken on this exposure to people ostensibly so different from yourself. And in the work of this program you are inviting others to be comfortable being themselves as well.

Insert 16.2 Basic Guidelines for Presenters (prepared by Dr. Paul Humphreys, psychologist) lists seven general points which should be observed in your relationships with people within an institutional setting.

Guidelines in Interacting with Staff

The logistics of your interaction with line staff is complicated by changing shifts, pressing duties and turnover of personnel. The suggestions that follow may not always be feasible for these reasons as well as the general complications within institutional life; however, where the suggestions can be used they will prove helpful.

Schedule Preliminary Discussions

The threat of disruption may concern staff more than actual disruption. The art program causes a change in routine; therefore, a preliminary discussion with staff about the program is a good idea.

- Use visual materials such as artwork to help explain the concept of the program.
- Give staff an opportunity to voice their concerns and then address and try to alleviate each in turn.
- Describe some of the potential benefits to clients which can occur when the program operates successfully and demonstrate how those developments might aid staff as well.

Recognize Staff Concerns

Listen carefully to staff advice. Although you may not always agree with the attitudes and actions of custodial staff, you must recognize your own position as transitory invitees to the institution. You are relating to residents and inmates in a limited way, while staff are with them on a regular basis and are involved in most aspects of their daily lives. It might also be said that as presenters, you have more to gain when the program goes well and therefore put efforts into seeing that it does, while staff has more to lose if the program presents problems and their efforts go into feelings of anxiety about that possibility.

Reduce Nonessential Demands

Try to reduce nonessential demands; for example, bring in support materials such as water cups, paper towels and newspaper, rather than asking staff to search for those things. Provide written lists of implements and materials to facilitate security checks. Help to assemble and return participants to their rooms or other events when permitted. In sum, look to alleviate the pressure of added materialistic and physical concerns when you can do so.

Recognize Staff Assistance

Recognize cooperation and enthusiasm among staff personnel when it occurs and encourage this, just as you do with the participants. When possible, praise incidents of special assistance to upper-level administrators.

Building good relationships with staff requires effort throughout the workshop series to keep the lines of communication open, so that staff and presenters may better perceive one another's mission and purpose.

Chapter 17

Expanding the Artistic and Social Experience

The Value of Displaying Artwork

The work of participants should be displayed only with their permission, but hanging artwork has several advantages described below. It might be done informally at the end of each artwork session as in the "critiques."

The "critique" is a discussion of artwork at the end of each workshop session, led by a presenter followed by the group's active participation. (See also "Critiques" in Chapter 9.) It is an important extension of every artwork session allowing the creator to claim the momentary spotlight. With limited space, artwork can be spread on the floor for these discussions or laid out on tables, but it is best taped with care onto the walls. The presenter describes the work on view: the scene, arrangement of colors, the mood conveyed, then asks the artist to suggest a title for the piece.

Participants creating more sophisticated works might benefit from constructive analysis of color, line, design, tone and other formal elements in the artistic process. Most "critiques," however, would consist of the artist being asked to comment on the intent of the work and what inspired it. After that, the presenter and others in the room would comment on the work. The discussion should be positive in tone, the essential purpose to enhance self-esteem.

Self-acknowledgment

Signing work and agreeing to have it displayed—two distinct steps—means that an individual acknowledges the achievement. That acknowledgment, particularly in cases where work was previously thrown away or left on work tables, indicates progress toward improved self-esteem.

Work displayed attractively is more impressive than when lying under the artist's gaze at the worktable. It is easier then to acknowledge that something significant was produced. As stated earlier describing barriers in making art, creative artwork is frequently felt to be childish or of little consequence because of its association with play; exhibitions, on the other hand, hold overtones of importance.

Moreover, with their work hanging with others, participants see it as part of a community of works, holding a purpose apart from themselves. The works become, in effect, an extension of themselves, a reaching out to others, as all exhibitions do.

DOI: 10.4324/9781003592693-24

When the work is placed on walls passed by daily during institutional routines, participants see their work side by side with that of others. This provides a sense of acceptance and belonging. When works are placed on walls in sleeping space, they are contributing to their own décor, a rare privilege in an institutional setting. Artwork is a personal statement, the artist alone selecting color, line, form and content. It is an unequivocal presence of individuality in a space where blandness and uniformity are generally standard.

Peer Acknowledgment

When work is displayed and discussed, an opportunity exists for peer acknowledgment of one another's efforts. Whether subject matter or technique is discussed, sharing ideas provides a sense of community. This kind of communication may not be the norm where non-communication, avoidance and even hostility may sometimes be more prevalent attitudes.

If work viewed by others is praised, an additional benefit accrues. Praise by peers may strongly influence one's own approval of the work and may have an effect for a limited time on self-esteem. Positive attention gives the work an importance which translates to the importance of the one who produced it.

The benefits of praise are not limited to the receiver but may also apply to the giver. The sense of sharing that one feels in giving something good to someone is positive in that it indicates the *capacity* to give. One must indeed own something in order to give. When the gift is well received, a certain power is transmitted. There is then a chance to return the gift of praise by acknowledging the other's work as well.

Staff Acknowledgment

The display of artwork offers an opportunity for staff to see the artists' productions and praise their efforts. Staff members must at times admonish the behavior, mess, problems and work their patients, residents and inmates cause. Any praise that staff members can legitimately offer to their charges is recognition of them as worthy individuals beyond their group identification and the duties that attend them.

It is also important to recognize that patients, residents and inmates are dependent on staff for the quality of their daily lives within the institution. Staff are involved with every phase of their activities—eating, working, recreation, smoking and sleeping—and granting rewards and punishments, approval and disapproval are regular commodities of exchange. Therefore, the positive attention that a staff member offers through praise of an art production can enhance the *immediate quality* of that person's institutional life. This is irrespective of any long-range influence on self-esteem.

Acknowledgment of Outsiders (Presenters)

Individuals may want to participate in the art activities to please the presenters. Although this is not an end itself, it may lift the lethargy that sometimes abounds in the institutional setting and serve as the initial motivation to *go for it*. Displaying artwork furthers an opportunity for presenters to praise work and add to that motivation, something they can do throughout the series. Such praise coming from people unconnected to the institution—people who represent the successful outside world—holds added significance.

Institutional Acknowledgment

When artwork is placed on the walls, a warmly humanistic environment is created. Simply stated, the presence of original art is beneficial to the institution's image as a place where individuality is encouraged. An institution may want to extend this image by mounting a formal exhibition of artwork at the end of the series with an opening reception for participants and their guests.

Photographs of artwork and sessions in progress might be taken throughout the course of the series and either displayed or placed in an album. When an institution acknowledges an individual's work by providing space to show it off, perhaps even adding the festivity of a reception, it is *listening* to what the individual has to say and making the effort to truly *look*.

Community Acknowledgment

The cultural backgrounds revealed in the artwork of inmates, the aged, psychiatric patients and youth can offer insights into personalities and predicaments. Artistic imagery as a medium of communication may present a bridge to generate such understanding. A carefully selected, well-mounted exhibition of individual personal expression gives the community an opportunity to see and respect these often rigidly classified groups as human beings and not merely "criminals" or "crazies," a perception that is an unfortunate result of the distance imposed by confinement. Moreover, by touching, however slightly, the thoughts, hopes, feelings, interests and problems of these individuals, one also comes to know something about the institutions in our society which confine or shelter them.

Optional Enterprises for Expanding the Experience

The program experience might be extended beyond the actual workshop sessions in a variety of enterprising ways should opportunities present themselves.

- Giving voluntary "homework" assignments
- Creating inter-site projects
- Designing culminating events

Implementing Voluntary Homework Assignments

You may get a feel as the series progresses that some participants would welcome having an "assignment" between sessions. Jail inmates and those in drug rehab programs, to improve their skills or merely to report industrious behavior to higher echelons, may want assignments and undertake these seriously. Home assignments may also give the art program more weight because of the studious implications of the word. Beyond all that, homework gives inmates purposeful activities to engage in during the week. Always be aware that any materials provided, even paper and pencils, must first be shown to officers in charge for approval.

Procedures and Suggested Topics

Consider first if you have time to add this to your other obligations. If so, plan an assignment related preferably to an art project of the sessions. Explain the assignment and the expected outcome. You might ask if spelling and grammatical corrections are desired. Follow through the following week by asking to see the completed assignment, then provide feedback, remembering that responsibility rests with both parties in a homework arrangement. Below are two suggested assignments which can relate to several different art projects:

1 Create a written, musical or dramatic work inspired by the art object made in the session. The work might be a poem, essay, song, short story, short play or letter to someone.
2 Suggest a theme for the work. The theme should be broadly based and ideally related to the interests of the group; for example, family life, future plans, successes, embarrassments, viewpoints on contemporary problems. Themes can be solicited from the group.

Inter-site Projects

As you come to know your constituents through the weekly art workshops and hear about what others are doing, you may have your own idea for a meaningful inter-site project. Be mindful that introducing anything new takes careful planning, and approval must first be secured by representatives of both sites involved. One such project is described here for the purpose of illustrating the concept.

Puppets (creative art project V.C) are made by nursing home residents for youth of the housing projects. The youth use the puppets to devise a puppet show. With presenters' help (quite a bit) they create a plot, rehearse the show and, kneeling behind a table, present it for the entertainment of the nursing home residents. The value of the project is equally for the residents and the youth by generating feelings of worth and usefulness. The elderly residents have the opportunity to meet the children to whom the puppets were gifted and learn something about them. The children learn from making the puppet show, the trip to another area, the exposure to what may be a new generational group of people for them, and in some instances a positive experience in race relationships. This inter-site project depends on logistical elements such as transportation.

Designing Culminating Events

An event or activity planned as a formal ending to the workshops can serve as an extension of the program experience and at the same time help to end the series in a positive way: (1) by participants acknowledging the termination of the series and (2) by participants receiving group recognition of their achievements. A few culminating events to consider are suggested below:

- A final exhibition.
- A group project such as a mural, wall hanging or puppet show.
- A party, including any or all of the following:

  - Refreshments (approved in advance by the facility)
  - A round table discussion evaluating the program and its significance for individuals.
  - A taping in which participants are separately interviewed by presenters about their reaction to the program.
  - A presentation of art-related gifts, such as a sketch pad and set of colored pencils, or box of crayons or felt markers.
  - A written certificate of participation.

The Written Certificate

A written certificate documenting participation in the program can be meaningful in almost all situations: the jail, rehab center, nursing home, mental health facility, domestic shelter and any youth facility. Presentation of the certificate can be accompanied by a ceremony of sorts to add to the spirit of accomplishment. Presenters would determine what amount of effort and time constitutes adequate participation. A sample certificate of participation is offered as Insert 17.1. The script here should be something like Old English Text to give it *class*.

Insert 17.1 Certificate of Participation

Certificate of Participation

________________ date

This is to acknowledge that ____________________ participant

participated in an art workshop series conducted by

____ presenter(s) (sponsoring agency if applicable)

from ________________ to _________________

beginning dates ending date

_____ sessions, each lasting ________ hours at

_____________________________________.

Site, City and State

The content of the program consisted of art projects in drawing, painting and sculpture. This certificate signifies that the participant named completed the program and actively participated in it.

____

Institutional Representative Program Sponsor

Foil Seal

(if desired)

Chapter 18

Evaluating Program Effectiveness

The Structure of an Evaluation Design

Evaluation of the Art and Social Interaction program is desirable for both presenters and institutions. Results can help to determine the strengths and weaknesses of the program. Positive feedback will encourage continued institutional support.

Limitations in the Evaluation Process

A controlled process of evaluation of the program intended to prove its impact on the well-being of participants and the acquired skills and learning gained by presenters is not within the scope of the program or this text. Although a controlled study on the value of the combined art and socialization experiences would be worthwhile and should be considered for future research, the prevalence of so many variables makes such evaluation difficult. Some such variables include age, ethnicity, family and economic background, talent and intellect, reasons for involvement and extent of commitment. In addition, there are variables connected with the diversity of populations in the very different institutions served by the program. Other confounding issues of a more transitory nature are the amounts and kinds of medication in use, the quality of staff intervention, family involvement, physical and emotional stress, and the immediacy of the many acute and chronic problems that attend the various situations of confinement.

Evaluation in the Pilot Program and Validity for Other Programs

The pilot program was judged to be successful in meeting its goals as indicated by its three years of funding in its early years by the Department of Higher Education under Title 1. Evaluation each consecutive year was required for funding approval. Instruments designed to evaluate the effectiveness of the program in meeting its objectives are offered in Appendix 3. (The names and affiliations of evaluators appear in Appendix 2.)

The program functioned in a total of 20 disparate facilities over a 49-year period, with different student presenters and a wide variety of agency and institutional participants. Notwithstanding that diversity of place and person, it remained a single program with

DOI: 10.4324/9781003592693-25

unique components. One of the most significant of these components is that the presenters (students) were trained specifically in the projects and approach to be used. This points to a conclusion that the longevity of the program seems contained in the type of spontaneous creative artwork presented and that undergraduate college students were the presenting component.

Leadership of the program (the author) remained constant from the outset until her retirement in 2014 after it was agreed a new faculty would be hired for the course continuance. The extent of program details required (albeit now contained in this book for future leaders), would confound evaluation of the program were past results claimed to be conclusive.

That the program continues at this writing in the institution in which it began, under different faculty leadership, speaks well for the prognosis of its longevity. This also demonstrates that the program can change and prosper with the priorities different faculty bring to it through their disciplines and personal preferences.

The necessity for evaluation of the pilot program, albeit informal in nature, resulted in guidelines being designed for observing the sessions—its presenters, participants and content—and instruments for determining that effectiveness. This was done through the collaboration of the author and members of the evaluation team. These guidelines and instruments can be adapted to similar settings elsewhere to help determine the strengths and weaknesses of the program, adjusted for a single facility or for multiple sites with diverse populations and situations.

Evaluation Components

Those who evaluated the pilot program were disparate in outlook, given that social work and psychology professionals, line staff, students and institutional participants afford a range of viewpoints. Nonetheless, each evaluation followed the same structural format with components that likely would remain similar in future situations:

1. A credentialed evaluator agreeable to observe and report on the institutional site.
2. Selected evaluation instrument(s) and a consistency of goals.
3. A completed observation report, document or commentary constituting the evaluative content of the program's efficacy.

Evaluation Processes

The evaluation procedures that were implemented in the pilot program had a number of objectives:

- To identify *criteria* for evaluating program success and weakness.
- To identify *observations* that would reveal program success and weakness.
- To standardize evaluation *procedures* by professional outside observers.
- To initiate evaluation methods by inside professional and lay observers, namely therapists, social workers, line staff and presenters.

- To initiate methods for self-evaluation of presenters and participants in personal or behavioral change.
- To produce viable designs for questionnaires, information sheets, guidelines and other instruments useful in the workshop sessions.

Evaluating Benefits to Presenters

The overall value of the program for presenters has been described previously. In this section, for the purpose of establishing reference points to which evaluation could be directed, five principal areas are identified in which learning experiences for presenters might occur.

- **The sociological and cultural value** of the experience: exposure to non-mainstream populations and facilities and related social problems.
- **The scholarly and issues-oriented value** of the experience: relevancy to academic work and/or research; the immediacy of current events in the news involving participant groups.
- **The artistic value** of the experience: motivation emanating from the process and product of work in various media.
- **The career value** of the experience: direction toward graduate education or employment.
- **The personal value** of the experience: values, skills, leadership, sense of responsibility, self-awareness.

Evaluating Benefits to Participants and Institutions

The list that follows identifies principal areas in which positive experiences might occur. Those can be viewed as criteria or reference points to which evaluation can be directed in assessing outcomes:

- **The value of the artistic experience:** the quality of participation; the extent of progress in various media; satisfaction in self-expression.
- **The quality of interaction:** with presenters; with other participants; with staff.

- **Fulfillment of needs:** beneficial behavioral changes; motivation for other activities.
- **Institutional involvement:** the willingness and reliability of support provided to the program; interest in continuing the program; quality of staff interaction during the sessions.

Verbal Evaluation Processes: Tapes

The Value of Taped Discussions

Questionnaires and other instruments can be distributed to all parties involved in the program and asked to be returned in timely manner. This would include presenters, participants, site personnel and evaluators. However, the depth of the responses may need enrichment in substantive content. Institutions might respond favorably but uncritically and some may not respond at all, whether due to lack of organization, sophistication, interest, responsibility or resources.

Logs kept by presenters may be observant, insightful and probing and provide excellent resources for evaluation. Or they may be cursory and haphazard and add little substantial observations or reflections. The fact that logs are graded and responded to by faculty incentivizes astute and comprehensive input. Participants may be eager to respond and do so with thoughtfulness about what worked for them or did not. But others may not be able to respond in depth due to hesitancy in writing, medication, fatigue or other impediments.

What may prove effective for obtaining more substantive responses to enrich the evaluation process are taped discussions conducted by presenters with participants and with staff.

Taping Participants, Line Staff and Evaluators

Taped "logs" made soon after the sessions by presenters often elicit observations that might not have been made when following the written log format or later, in the questionnaires completed by others. Discussions can begin with presenters asking simple questions concerning a participant's likes and dislikes in the course of the series. After an initial fascination with the tape machine, participants will tend to put the mechanism in the background and begin to talk about the program in more detail than they would on paper.

Guards or custodians are excellent resources for anecdotal observations. Seeing the group before, during and after the workshops, they are in a position to consider:

1. If participants look forward to the sessions.
2. If participants talk after the sessions about what they did and speak about what they created, and how they regarded the presenters.
3. To what extent participants value the program relative to other programs offered in the facility.

Discussions between outside evaluators and participants can be taped in a similar manner with special questions prepared by evaluators that address the distinctive nature of each group.

Additional Considerations in an Evaluation Process

Various other points pertaining to an evaluation process are worth noting:

- The "Code of Ethics for Protection of Human Subjects" should be studied by all observers and evaluators.
- If extended evaluation is possible, controls should be set up whereby the impact of the art activity alone and the impact of social interaction alone could be isolated and assessed.
- A uniform approach in evaluating the disparate sites of the program should be established to minimize conflicting reports and increase the reliability of results.
- The diversity of outside evaluators' credentials is an asset in the composition of an evaluation team to include, ideally, professionals from the areas of sociology, psychology, education and art.
- The total subject area and constituency covered by the art and social interaction program are probably too vast for comprehensive study but in-depth analysis of the program's effect on any single group could be significant in guiding similar endeavors.
- In-depth measurement of the learning experience for the presenters is a productive area for future research in light of higher education's role in furthering student career training and exposure to cultural diversity.
- A summary of the recommendations of an evaluation team after all individual reports are made would be advantageous for a comprehensive assessment and recommendations.

The art and social interaction program had an opportunity to do just this when a grant was awarded to the college for three consecutive years. The evaluation by the grant's evaluation team of professors is included in Chapter 20.

Chapter 19

Student Reflections on Learning, Experience and Career Goals

What I Learned

I learned that the interactions you have with people on a daily basis are probably the most important things in life. To be able to communicate and build something, anything with another person is something that is truly meaningful. **Meghan B.**

After having our last session this past Friday, I can honestly say visiting CarePlus twice a week has been one of the most rewarding experiences of my life. As a psychology major I got to witness disorders I had only read about in textbooks. **Caroline S.**

I learned a lot about myself from this course. That I need to take time to look around before life passes me by. I need to appreciate the people in my life and to tell them how much I am grateful for them. I need to think about how lucky I am to have all the things that I do and not dwell on what I don't have. I have freedom, a lot more than the girls at Holley. I have loving and supportive family, friends and a boyfriend who all treat me respectfully and who encourage me and I don't know what I would do without them, or how I would have turned out if I didn't have them. **Heather M.**

I'm so happy I took this class . . . I learned that I liked dealing with people face-to-face even though I always pictured myself really shy, especially in front of people that were older than me. I learned how to speak comfortably in front of a group of people, present my ideas in an organized fashion and become confident in myself and what I was doing. **Lisa F.**

I can sincerely say that taking this course was one of the best decisions I have made, because it not only taught me more about others, but it taught me more about myself as well. I absolutely enjoyed every minute of it. Between the Paterson Charter School and the children at Strengthen Our Sisters, I have learned so much. They were at times unruly but have taught me a lot. Children open up our eyes to things that we otherwise wouldn't see. They teach us to be curious, to examine everything closely and to ask questions. **Emily F.**

DOI: 10.4324/9781003592693-26

Overall, I believe that this was one of the best opportunities that I have ever come across, because I think that it made me into a better overall person and made me appreciate things a lot more than I used to. I often would take things, such as a good home and my friends and family for granted, but just being around the children from SOS and hearing about some of their stories made me appreciate what I have. **Alyssa D.**

Leaving this class, I think of art in a whole different light. Art is not just coloring, gluing, or painting. It is creating, communicating, imagining, reflecting, expressing, and so much more. Furthermore, as we have learned from being in this class, it is a splendid outlet and resource. **Alexa L.**

My art sessions at Father English have taught me valuable lessons. This experience proved the importance of preparation and classroom management. **Michele M.**

I have always known that I wanted to major in social work and work with abused children, but working with the children at my site confirmed this even more. **Cynthia F.**

Overall, I learned a lot about how nursing homes run from going to the Veterans hospital and also visiting Care One for my two additional sessions. It gave insight into how the elderly are being treated and how they live their daily lives. **Courtney S.**

I immediately learned that I was not there to teach the students, but more to guide them to reach into their emotions, to provide mediums for them to create with, all within an environment they could feel safe in. **Dean J.**

This program made me use what I've learned in this class when I'm out each day; it made me less judgmental. For example, when I see people in the news going to jail for drugs or choosing the wrong path, you have to see past that, more broadly. Maybe this person never had someone to guide them in their childhood, or struggling every day to change, but grew up around violence and that's the only thing they know. **Courtney V.**

I began to understand what it is like to live within the walls of a psychiatric center. I let myself see through the eyes of my participants and this allowed me to relate to them, something I would have never had a chance to experience if I had not taken Art and Interaction. **Samantha B.**

First and foremost, I learned to be myself and not let what others think affect my artistic ability or me. Each day I looked forward to creating something new and even going out of my element to do so. I admit some projects were harder than others but the more imagination the better, and that is something I have also learned. Along with learning a lot in the classroom, I was able to make friends with classmates through the sites we selected. I was able to think out of the box and make friends I'd never think I would be friends with before. **Liz P.**

I have learned that doing artwork can relax the mind and stimulate the brain at the same time. I also learned how to mold myself to adapt to a surrounding that is unfamiliar, such as the environment at CarePlus, to succeed. **Anthony N.**

This experience has taught me more about myself and has been more than just a learning experience in art. It has taught me about life in general. Life is short, and it's not always fair. We don't pick the hand we are dealt, so being sympathetic to others is extremely important. I did not realize how much influence we had on one another. **Caroline S.**

I have written down so many notes about this semester and am actually almost in tears as I type this. I have learned so much about not only art and the incredible role it can play in the lives of so many different people, but I have also learned about people and their thirst for originality and their deep need of interaction and self-worth. I have always known this to be true. There are jails, psychiatric hospitals, battered women's shelters and senior centers. However, most folks who know of these places did not have any interaction [with them]. I now have a more personal connection with the institutions that house some of these folks, and a better knowledge and understanding of these people as well as the individuals that maintain them. **Kathy C.**

Between spending my Monday and Thursday mornings with such a great class and getting to spend my Wednesday mornings with the women of the Bergen County drug and alcohol rehabilitation program I could not have asked for a more inspirational experience. I have gained a better understanding of those in total institutions. I now understand the feeling of no independence and no self-expression. **Rachael O.**

Through this interaction process, I've learned so much. First and foremost, I learned the importance of social relationships and how showing a bit of care and compassion can impact one's life in a significant way. **Alexandra B.**

I've not only had a once in a lifetime experience, but also an enlightenment about society as a whole. I worked with the elderly through multiple art projects. Writing logs has helped me to keep track of the progress I am making. It helps me realize which projects were useful and which were not that successful. It also let me keep track of which residents were attending and who was absent. Logs also help me to summarize the events that happened during the session and look for ways to improve myself or improve my methods and approaches. The logs were a good source of reflection and are good records of the projects we did and the events that happened at the session. The logs helped me become more organized and responsible. **Kaitlyn C.**

I know all the good things inside of me were lurking there somewhere, waiting to be revealed. Thanks to [this] class I have found an outlet for all my people skills that had never really been given a chance to blossom. I totally stepped outside my box in this class, and I'll never forget it. I feel like this experience also better prepared me for graduation. In all the years at Ramapo I have never had such a successful and enjoying experience. **Melissa B.**

What I Felt

This whole experience made me a better person on the inside. I was never good at doing art work, but I found myself in a position to teach someone different projects of art that could help him or her cope with their problems. **Matt S.**

I knew after reading the course description that it would be an experience like none I have ever had before. I was eager to get started at the sites from the moment I registered. However, words can't even begin to express all that I got out of the experience. It was so much more than I could have anticipated and I will take this experience with me forever. **Heather M.**

Because of all of the great people that I have met in and outside the class, I feel extremely proud and privileged to have sat in this course. **Cynthia F.**

Being in this class made my confidence boost because this class surrounds you with positive energy. **Courtney V.**

It has made me a better person overall and changed the way that I think. The diversity of the girls was something that I thought might create a barrier between us, however it made no difference in the connection that I made with any of them. It reinforced my belief that appearance truly is only skin deep and that you can never judge a person by this. I felt as though I did not only help the girls, but they helped me too. They showed me who I am and how sometimes you need to just let go to have fun. They restored my interest in art that I rarely do anymore despite my knack for it. They truly have improved my life and I cannot thank them enough for it. **Jeff B.**

The older male kids at future scholars really look up to me and want to be like me. They always ask where I get my clothing and watch from, they ask if they can play basketball with me, and so forth. That makes me feel good that somebody believes that I am a successful person and they want to be like me. **Andre K.**

In this art class, we actually got to apply what we learned in class to the outside world. I have never had a class that had a requirement to teach other people what we have learned. **Anthony N.**

Waking up every Tuesday morning knowing that I was making a difference in someone's life not only helped mold me into a better person but also allowed me to be more accepting of people for their differences, especially those suffering from issues as serious as schizophrenia or bipolar disorder. **Marissa R.**

It was weird saying goodbye, it has been a part of my life for the past three months. I didn't think of it as a chore anymore, but instead doing my part to help the community. The patients there had become my friends. I genuinely care about all of them and knowing that they'll forget about me tomorrow saddens me greatly. They have been a big part of my life. They have given me a totally new outlook on mental health. Though I had always been interested in psychology and good at learning it, this was my first one on one experience with it. **Caroline S.**

I have always thought that childhood was the most precious thing that anyone could go through, and visiting these sites instilled this feeling inside of me. Having a very short childhood, it was nice to act like a child and play with the kids every time I went. I showed up early and stayed late just so that I could gain bits and pieces of what I had missed. These children have honestly changed my life. **Emily F.**

Aside from the great experience I've gathered from the children, I enjoyed every single class because every day was a different and unique day with a project or assignment waiting for us to create. I must admit that I never thought I would enjoy creating art, especially since I am really bad. However, 1 managed to create some great designs, drawing, and paintings which was so much fun to do . . . I am not an art major or of any sort, but a chemistry major. There was no purpose for me to take this class, but I just heard so many good things about it, and that I am guaranteed to get such a great experience for it. Although I did hear that it was going to be a lot of work, I was also told it would be worth it. **Mohammad B.**

It has been an unforgettable 10 weeks that will remain with me for the rest of my life. **Kati L.**

The inevitability of aging and dying is something I've faced this semester a few times. I've come to understand that the connections we make with people are what really matters most. I'm not generally very materialistic but I've noticed that I hold on to my grandmother a little tighter when I see her and ask her more about what things were like for her before I was born. I also spend more time at the kids table at family parties. **Melissa B.**

First Impressions: Sites, Staff, Residents

I can still recall the uneasiness and the tension going in on the first day; I truly wasn't sure if this experience was going to be what I had hoped for. I was unsure that I would get along with the girls or be able to gain the respect of the staff. Even after the first 3 meetings I was unsure if I was going to walk away from this with actual feelings for any of the people that I had met. Now, at the end of the road, all of these questions have been answered, all of my wondering has been put to rest, and everything has turned out better than I could've hoped for. **Jeff B.**

The interaction I had with the aids also showed me how committed they were not only to their jobs, but the kids as well. I understand that at times they had to be strict and demanding towards misbehaving kids but in the end I saw how much the kids appreciated them. I see them conversing and laughing with each other about artwork. When the kids need something, the aids are quick to offer assistance or provide the materials being sought. When the children are behaving, they praise them and reward their positive attitudes. **Rhine S.**

I was scared the first day I went to the shelter. I was driving with one other guy I barely knew, to a place where we were not allowed to have the address, to do an art project with children we did not know. I immediately learned that I was not there to teach the students, but more to guide them to reach into their emotions, to provide mediums for them to create with, all within an environment they could feel safe in. **Dean J.**

I'll never forget walking into the facility for orientation. I was so scared of the patients there. I felt like they would infect me if I got too close. Though this is a shallow outlook, I have been pretty sheltered my whole life. I haven't been exposed to any mental disorders other than depression in myself. Now, I can honestly say walking into Care Plus did not faze me at all the last session we had. **Caroline S.**

When experiencing the different sites, it was different to see how each was run by their respective site representative. It was also interesting to see where each of the different facilities held their art lessons and what supplies they had on hand. You could tell which facilities were more organized. For example, when I visited the Veteran's home it was very organized; the people that were expected to take the class were punctual and excited for their art lesson. However, S.O.S. was a different story. The children were never ready, and the tables were hardly ever clean. They had no supplies we could ever borrow, and the site representative only showed up a handful of times. Hence, we usually were working independently as our own group. **Lori B.**

Insights and Observations

The idea behind arts and interaction may be to help others express themselves through improving their self-esteem, however, I think it also helped me as a presenter to improve my own self expressions. **Brooke L.**

Once people of all types—either poor, with disabilities, or incarcerated—know that they are somebody to someone, they feel good and become more confident in their artwork and within themselves. **Courtney V.**

I could tell by spending these weeks with the children that most of them don't get the attention that a three and four year old needs from their parents because they become attached and never want to leave once the session is over. Hearing how some of them didn't have dinner the night before or breakfast that morning makes me think how fortunate I am to have a family that can provide for me. **Courtney V.**

Listening to their stories of rape, drug use, depression, and delusions, has opened my eyes to a whole new world. These mentally ill individuals are no different than anyone else. Affected by chemical imbalances, or past events in their life, these patients would give anything to feel "normal" once again. Seeing them struggle with the reality that is their sickness can be difficult. **Caroline S.**

Within these long weeks I had the chance to interact with every single child and learn about their lives. I can see how things at their homes can influence their personalities at school. I've noticed that some of the kids that played violently with their peers are the ones without a father. Jake for instance only lives with his mother and happens to be one of the meanest kids I've ever met and I then learned that his mother plays a bad role in his life. I saw Jake's mother a few times as she came to pick him up, and she always had a cigarette either in her hand or buckled up behind her ear. However, the good news is that I have seen great progress with him as he interacts outside with the kids, and he started to participate more within the critiques towards the last few sessions. **Mohammad B.**

I have been brainwashed to believe that Paterson is a horrible, low-income town filled with crooks and drug addicts. Although for some parts this may be partially true at times, this experience let me see Paterson in a new light. The children were no different than any other children. They were full of enthusiasm, openly shared anecdotes, and had an attention span of five minutes. They are typical elementary school children. Whether they are aware of their situation or not, they showed the same innocence and carefree concern as most children their age. Although we've discussed resilience in class, this real life example puts the concept into context. **Michele M.**

Creativity leads to confidence. Supplying children with the chance to create opens many doors and outcomes. Interaction is effortless over an art project. It is a great way to communicate, collaborate, and improve teamwork. Art helps us find common ground and understand each other. Sometimes, art helps us understand ourselves. **Amanda F.**

[At the Children's Psychiatric Center] Keith told us that when the girls hit eighteen and they are still there, they try to place them in the apartments if they don't have a family. It is very hard to survive in the real world at the age of eighteen without a support system. These girls are a lot stronger than people give them credit for. Many people want to forget everything they have ever known because of things they have gone through. Cordelia wants to bleach her skin, live a different life and change her name to Bella. I think she wants to do this so no one can identify her with the things that happened in her past. **Adam R.**

We work with one another, and in some ways depend on one another, as all people do in life. When a person's success and happiness is in some way dependent on your involvement in their life, you make a connection with them that I think is really what this program is all about. I think all my classmates have gained inspiration and a greater sense of self from working with all the people that we have met on this journey. I know that I am a better person, not only because of what I've done for them, but also because of what they have done for me. I've recently been put in the middle of a rather unpredictable situation in which I am left feeling helpless and without control. The children and veterans [I've worked with in this program] live their lives feeling that way daily. The thought of them brings me the inspiration and patience I need. **Melissa Barone**

Comments from Participants and their Relationships with Students

I will never forget when one of the residents communicated the death of her son and husband in her wet on wet watercolour and shared it with us. At that moment, everyone offered her support and sympathy. Some of them even related with her and shared their own stories. Moments such as these displayed trust and comfortableness. I never imagined that these art sessions could cause residents to be more like a family and less like just strangers forced to live amongst one another. **Alexa L.**

Both the staff and the patients at the Nathan Kline Institute of the Rockland Psychiatric Hospital have told me that my art sessions with them were the highlight of their week. They look forward to sessions and came out as happier people. The patients began quiet, withdrawn, and some even angry. **Kati L.**

When I would walk into the classrooms these children would have a smile from ear to ear, even before we would get into explaining the day's project. The energy in the room went from very little to sky-high. This is one of the best feelings because I didn't even have to do anything for these children to appreciate my appearance. **Courtney V.**

As the kids from each unit filtered in, I did notice that Eliza was not here. I had promised Eliza I would finish my acrylic painting and give it to her since she gave me hers. I painted her a rainbow of yellow bouts of energy with pink clouds and a flying kitten under it. (Holley Child Care) **Sarah M.**

Lara told me I was like a sister to her and I almost cried. I have a sister and she is my best friend in the world. The hugs that I got the last day of Holley and the looks that I saw on the girls' faces made me want to . . . say to them every day, "I love you, you're beautiful, everything is going to be ok, sweethearts, it's not over yet." **Heather M.**

Each time we see them, we are welcomed with hugs and warm greetings from the children. One child even introduced us to her parents. "Mommy these are my art teachers." She was so happy to be in the program and to be a student with the chance to interact with us. Living in an institution or living under any circumstances is tough and I am grateful the Ramapo Arts and Interaction program allowed me to step into those lives even if it was only for a brief 10-week period. **Rhine S.**

The regulars knew our names and would even introduce us to any of the newcomers. **Kristen R.**

Another major aspect besides the actual artwork was interacting with the girls during the sessions. Because we were close in age to most of the girls who were mid to late teenagers, we had conversations about tv shows, sports, celebrities, the Twilight series, and asked them about things in their daily lives. **Laura G.**

Bailey refused to participate in the art program because he said that he hated art. However, in the last two weeks he pulled a complete 180 and began greeting us at the door when we pulled up and allowed us to enter his world. He also showed us a side of himself that we had never seen; Bailey embraced us when the session was over, whereas he previously ignored our presence to begin with. Moments like that, when Bailey invited us into his world, are what makes this program so worthwhile, not only for the participants but for the students. **Kristen L.**

Denmark once stated, "I was upset and everything was wrong, so I'm glad you came and I can have my 'happy hour' of painting." For many, our sessions were a much needed break. I feel that although we conducted our sessions in a strict, institutionalized setting, I brought about an air of freedom and easiness. This is important for keeping the patients spirits up and reminding them that there is life and freedom outside of the institution's walls. My classmates and I represented that life and freedom. **Carl P.**

From our Orientation to our Final Session we tried to communicate and give the patients positive attention that they needed. The very first session a woman by the name Naomi sat next to me. From that moment on every time I saw her she sat next to me and talked with me. She complimented me on my clothes and jewelry and I did the same to her. I tried to make her feel good about herself because you could tell she was lacking some self-esteem. Charlene shared with us her situation and why Naomi was a patient at Rockland. She would hear voices that sexually pleased her and these voices were so powerful that she would listen to them and hurt her beautiful daughter. She was battling with schizophrenia and she needed to choose whether the voices were more important to her than her little girl. I tried to show kindness and attention to Naomi because she took such a liking to me. I hope I made a difference in her life. Even if it was only for two hours a week. **Kristen C.**

Student Teams: Problems and Solutions

I feel working with your [team] partners at the sites, you really learn about them as well. Since the facilities were not so well off, there were often times where one would leave the facility very upset. Possibly an incident would happen, or just an event would make you upset. However, you have your partners there to talk about the situation that's bothering you and get their insight to help you process the day's events. **Lori B.**

At the onset of this fieldwork, I had extremely difficult times with my group. We butt heads about our difference in opinions, lack of communication and misunderstandings. Now, I am walking away from this class with two new friends. The three of us plan to get a cup of coffee after we hand in our portfolios. I did not foresee that happening and I am so glad we were able to work through our anxieties to come to an understanding of each other. **Sarah M.**

This class was particularly special for several different reasons. Being in this class gave me the opportunity to interact with my peers. This opportunity is not usually given in class because the focus is usually set on the professor, where this class had a little bit of both. **Amanda F.**

Working at the Domestic Abuse Shelter

There are many things that can be said about my experience at Strengthen Our Sister's Shelter this past semester. There were times it was overwhelming, chaotic, and frustrating. There were times it was rewarding, fulfilling and gratifying. Overall, I must say that the experience of performing art projects with the children touched on an assortment of emotions that I never thought I could feel around complete strangers from very different backgrounds. **Mike T.**

Working with the participants at Strengthen Our Sisters was both physically difficult and emotionally daunting. At times I felt myself feeling emotionally unavailable, physically exhausted, frustrated, appreciated, unappreciated, loved, and hated. The participants were unique in their own personalities and the extenuating circumstances that led to their arrival at Strengthen Our Sisters. **Kristen L.**

With a smaller group and a slightly older population, we were able to connect more with the children. I learned that Monica and Lazar are artistic and thoughtful people. Each week their mother stayed in the room with us and we learned that she was studying for a nursing test. We knew when she took her test and when she found out she passed she told us in excitement and we were so happy for her accomplishment. Spending time with us became a routine for her and we liked that. **Jackie K.**

At Strengthen Our Sisters, there were always hiccups and malfunctions. Entering a site with no structure, it was hard to conduct sessions at first, but Paul, Mariya and I soon learned how these kids worked and what we needed to do in order to keep them engaged. **Emily F.**

The only problem I can see with going to Strengthen our Sisters is how the children will deal with the fact that we are not coming back. **Dean J.**

The lessons I have learned from volunteering at S.O.S will be applied to my daily life. When I decide to start a family and raise my children in the future I will incorporate some of the methods of discipline and teaching I have learned when dealing with the children at the shelter. Even though at times it was stressful, I am proud to say that my time and energy spent at Strengthen Our Sisters Shelter was a wonderful learning experience. As a graduating senior, I know that this class will be one of the few courses that will bring back fond memories of my educational career at Ramapo College. **Mike T.**

Working with the Elderly

I completed the fieldwork requirement for this course at Care One at Wellington. I specifically chose this site to suit my interest and minor in gerontology. Every Wednesday afternoon for ten weeks, I went to this site with my classmates Lauren and Brittany, who are also gerontology minors. As part of satisfying the forty-hour minimum of fieldwork for the minor, we would hold the art sessions and then stay for an additional two and half hours just interacting with the residents. However, I must say that my favorite part was always the sessions. To me, the sessions provided the most optimal learning and life experience. **Alexa L.**

When I first went into the center . . . I was worried I would be feeling depressed about seeing them unable to remember things anymore such as their families or hobbies, but it ended up making me appreciate things more. It made me appreciate that I still have my memory and also appreciate my grandmother. She probably has such a hard time dealing with her husband's disease and . . . how difficult it must be for her every day, knowing that one day he will not remember her. **Courtney B.**

I am now conscious of what projects are better suited for older adults, based on the level of sophistication and complexity they exert. This way participating elders will not feel that they are being infantilized, a major issue that unfortunately continues to go on in nursing homes across the world. Additionally, I have learned that there are projects that do not just benefit elders mentally in terms of stimulation, emotional expression, and socialization, but also physically. Some projects, such as making figures out of clay, offer great exercise for fingers and hands. This helps to alleviate pain that many older people experience due to the deterioration of joints that often accompanies old age. Also, these sessions can help the countless older people who suffer from depression as a result of the many changes elders face in late life. These fluctuations include the death of loved ones, the loss of roles and functionality, medical problems, and so on. Such changes can be easily expressed through art. This expression is essential, as keeping things bottled up only fuels depression. I myself can recall many residents leaving the sessions in elevated moods. **Alexa L.**

It must also be hard for [the frail elderly] because they need to rely so much on other people. But through art we can help them become more capable and independent . . . It's hard to come up with ideas that are suitable for the sites because there are always safety measures that need to be taken. I believe the acrylic jewelry and watercolor works great with the elderly. It's harder for them to draw than paint. The poem and picture connections worked well with them and helped challenge their creative brains to delve deeper. I'm glad that I've learned all of these projects and now have examples to keep on file for the future. **Kaitlyn C.**

When we first began the sessions, the residents were polite, but that was about it. Only small talk ensued. However, as the sessions progressed, we really began forming bonds with the residents. We began to see their personalities. It was no longer just "thank you's" or "can you pass me the glue stick?" Conversations fostered by the projects caused them to open up to us and we felt our trust being earned as each session passed. By our last session, we could talk to the residents freely without having to depend on a project. **Alexa L.**

Working with the Mentally Ill

Being given the opportunity to work with the patients at The Nathan Kline Institute was an amazing first-hand experience. Because I am a senior graduating with a psychology degree,

I was thankful to become more familiar working with the mentally ill before going out into the field. After our group sessions were over, I am glad to say that this is the right field that I want to get into and that this was one of the most incredible experiences I've ever had. **Meliss K.**

I thought about how easily I could get any kind of food I wanted and how I took it for granted. It is hard to not have control over such a simple thing as feeding yourself. Humans have a natural relationship with the food they eat, and for my group, not being able to make decisions about their food was at the top of the list of the worst parts of the psychiatric center. **Samantha B.**

The session opened my eyes to the internal battle of schizophrenia. It seemed incredibly difficult and sometimes losing the battle to ignore the voices. Demarc and Naom often wore headphones to drown out the voices in their heads. **Samantha B.**

Going to CarePlus showed me how people who are mentally ill actually are, rather than just learning about them in class. I was able to have hands-on experience in the field that I wish to go into for my future occupation. **Anthony N.**

Erica, the site director, is a young and independent female. She takes care of business and doesn't let anyone push her around. She is tough when she needs to be but is always there for the patients. They all look up to her, and the fact that she was doing projects with us by the end of this process means a lot to me. I know she finally gained trust in us to run the session without feeling like she had to baby-sit us. **Caroline S.**

Both the staff and the patients at the Nathan Kline Institute of the Rockland Psychiatric Hospital have told me that my art sessions with them were the highlight of their week. They look forward to sessions and came out as happier people. The patients began quiet, withdrawn, and some even angry. One girl, Susanna, changed my perspective on mental hospital patients. Susanna is 19, just as old as I am. The difference is I am healthy, and lucky enough to have been born into a family that was able to provide me not only with material things, a college education, and money, but love, compassion, and support. Susanna's family did not provide her with all those things. It has been an unforgettable 10 weeks that will remain with me for the rest of my life. **Kati L.**

The people at CarePlus may have been a large group to work with, but it was more than worth it. The variety of personalities that we worked with made it all worthwhile. It saddens me to know that many people stay away from the mentally ill. Through working with these people, I have come to realize that I like them more than I like most other people. It was one of the most rewarding experiences I have ever encountered. Katie and I are keeping in contact with Adele because we are hoping to volunteer at the site in the fall. She said there was a very small possibility that we could get paid internships. **Jennifer B.**

Over time, you develop a bond with these people because they trust you and rely on you to be there each week. Also, by building trust and relationships with the patients, they would openly talk to us and we were able to eliminate our stereotype about the mentally ill. **Melissa K.**

Working with Abuse, Neglect and Youth at Disadvantage

I probably learned more about the girls from their artwork than talking to them. Their unrelenting need for more of everything, materials, paper, lemonade, ice cream and so on. They have an unquenchable thirst to get more out of life. **Heather M.**

How can a child educate a college student? These children all taught me things that an individual will not be able to learn in a classroom, such as patience, empathy, and a sense of compassion and understanding. **Cynthia F.**

The poverty-stricken and violent environment that exists inside Paterson is very eye opening to someone like me, who lives in a relatively safe and well-off environment like Wyckoff. The effects of the environment are clearly present within Eastside High School, as the kids are familiarized with violent games and weapons and are noticeably more aggressive amongst themselves than kids in other areas in New Jersey. In addition, the kids are always starved for materials and attention throughout the sessions—things they may not receive because they live in low-income housing with not many possessions of their own. This is a sad yet true fact that shapes their behavior patterns and attitudes towards each other. **Frank T.**

I understand that I do not know everything that happens in their personal lives . . . but it was clear that their personal issues affected their moods during the sessions. **Kristen R.**

Interacting with the children [at Friendship Corner] was unforgettable simply because their lifestyles are so different from mine. Quite a few of the children have divorced parents and many siblings; some don't even live with them. In a household where there is no paternal figure, sons as young as 7 years of age have stepped in to take the role of the dominant male in the house. Other kids haven't been exposed to people of other races, ethnicities, and cultures—they kept asking me what country I was from, and one girl even asked me why another girl's eyes were blue and her hair blond. **Rhine S.**

By the end of the semester, I no longer called them the kids in Paterson, they were my kids at Father English. During our 10 weeks at our site, I had gotten to know so many of the children, some more than others. I learned much about their personalities and how each one worked best and who liked what kind of art projects the most. It became important to me to make them happy and feel good about themselves and leaving them had gotten to me much more than I thought it would have. When I told the kids it was my last day, they all rushed up to hug me and bombarded me all at once and said thank you. It was one of the most rewarding moments I have had in my life thus far. **Amanda A.**

I sat with Azumii and watched her make something for her father. I asked her if she saw her father a lot and she told me that she goes to visit him every weekend. I told her that I used to visit my father every other weekend and we talked about that for a few more minutes.

After a few minutes, Jeremiah came over to sit with me. We talked a little, but he's very quiet. He was working on his paper doll, and I was making one too. I finished mine, and so did he, and then we started the interaction. His interaction with my puppet was kind of violent. He was making it jump on mine, and mine was trying to give his hugs and high fives. I told him to be nice to my puppet because he was hurting its feelings. It worked and he started to be nicer. **Courtney B.**

Rose had told me some things about her week at school as we shared our mutual anticipation for the arrival of summer vacation. I told the kids some things about my major and what I'd be doing after graduation. It was sweet to see how amazed they were that I was finally going to be finished with school. I remember what it was like at their age, and the way it felt like I'd be going to school forever. When I'm with the kids I remember what it was like thinking that at the end of college I would be on my way to becoming successful, that I would have everything I needed, and that I would understand and be happy with my life and the way I saw the world. At that age anything and everything was possible and all I had to worry about was the trivial problems tomorrow might bring. I miss those days, and coming to Holley just drives those thoughts home more and more. **Melissa B.**

The Course in Relation to the College Experience

This semester, my art and interaction class gave me one of the greater college experiences that I have encountered in my four years attending college. **Matt S.**

Being a part of Arts and Interaction was one of the best opportunities I have had in my college career thus far. Not only did I learn new art techniques, I worked with different mediums of art that I never have before. **Brooke L.**

I learned more about myself and other people through this class than any other course I've ever taken in my life. I became aware of other people, their desires, what they believe, how they act, and what motivates them. **Lisa F.**

I can honestly say now that this has been one of the most rewarding experiences that I have yet to gain from a course at Ramapo College. I have had many wonderful experiences here as a newer student; however, none have compared to the feeling I now am embodied with as this semester ends. **Marissa R.**

Many times, in college mostly I believe, we are stuck in a class for 15 weeks at a time, the class is quiet, we listen to the teacher lecture, we sit for the entire class time, and then we all get up and leave. That structure in a classroom gives no opportunity to really meet people, talk with them and get to know them, or form any kind of relationship with them, big or small. So all in all, I would have to say the thing that impacted me the most in Art and Interaction was most definitely the interaction part. I never once felt awkward in the classroom, from speaking to asking a question to just having a conversation with a classmate or professor. I knew our entire class was on the same page almost always, and the people I got the chance to meet even became friendly with me outside of class time. **Amanda A.**

As a freshman student transferring from Montclair State University to Ramapo College, I had no idea what I was getting into when I signed up for Art and Interaction. But what was a seemingly typical Arts and Humanities course quickly became a life changing experience. I gained a window into other people's way of life. Thrust into a complicated emotional situation with many children in a battered women's shelter, I was able to grasp a small view into the reality that the children of the shelter grew up with. **Dean J.**

The Art Projects

The first project . . . in the class was perfect. It got us to loosen up, relax and just draw. I had a very good first impression that day. We had to free-draw and let the pencil take us. I loved all the projects we did in class. They were so fun and reminded me of my childhood. All I did was arts and crafts when I was younger, so it allowed me to be a kid again for a little bit. It was the highlight of my week. A class I actually wanted to attend and do work in. It makes me think this must have been what the people at my site felt like. It was the one thing that got them looking forward to the next week. It was something they would be able to do and enjoy. **Lisa F.**

My personal favorite project was when we made the movable figures using construction paper, colored pencils, markers and the fasteners. I feel as though this project helped me to be the most creative because I was going through a lot at the time. I really blocked everything that I was going through out of my mind and focused only on that project. I believe I made a basketball player that was supposed to be me. That was my favorite project in class. **Andre K.**

The activities I have done this semester have helped to open my creative side In being spontaneous in my art work, rather than planning and mapping out every piece. It is a new way to look at the process of creating art. **Sarah M.**

Let me remind you that I am not an art major or of any sort, but a chemistry major . . . I am always stressed in general, but ever since I've started to construct art projects in this class, it has helped me relieve a lot of the stress. I truly think art is a very healthy hobby for an individual. So, whenever I feel stressed or overwhelmed, I just start drawing, painting, free drawing, and just letting my imagination go wild. **Mohammad B.**

I really enjoyed going to class, anticipating what new and exciting project I was going to create that day. I especially enjoyed this class because each project that we did gave me a sense of accomplishment. One thing that sticks out in my mind that I learned from this class is that I can pull a lot more creativity out than I thought. Usually when I ran out of ideas I would take a break, because I assumed that I had nothing left to think of. But this class forced me to pull creativity out when I did not think that I had any ideas left. I think that this is a crucial detail that I needed to learn for life because there are always going to be times where I have to push myself to the extreme and work when I feel like there is nothing left. It was nice to be able to learn this lesson quickly and easily. I hope that I can remember the feeling and remember to keep pushing. **Amanda F.**

Many of the girls just drew simple drawings that did not reflect much inner pain or depression, but the process is when their personalities and struggles came out. For example, Cordelia who often struggled to own up to her own identity would often either throw out her artwork, or try to take someone else's as her own, and often wanted to be referred to as Bella instead of her real name which she did not like. Other patients such as Heather drew very detailed elaborate pictures and artwork with an image such as a crying eye, flames, or images of herself crying and running away. For girls like Heather I feel the artwork did a tremendous amount for expressing feelings and using the creativity of the artwork both as a comfort and a therapy. **Laura G.**

Art is a wonderful [communication] project because participants and session conductors are enjoying the activity while conversing. Students revealed a lot to me about their lives during the processes of creating their art works. It was very interesting because I would simply sit next to a child while he or she talks about their family or tells me a story about something that happened to them. I am happy listening to them and in return they enjoy the company. Some children get so attached that they get upset when I would leave their sides to check up on another student. **Rhine S.**

Every week we struggled a little bit planning the projects. A lot of the projects we did in the classroom used prohibited materials that we couldn't bring into the jail. So a lot of the projects we had to manipulate and change to match the requirements of the jail. We started to get used to the men there and figured out which projects they enjoyed more. We catered to them and gave them projects to look forward to and talk about every week. Their favorite thing to work with was paint. They also liked to draw a lot. **Lisa F.**

I feel that I was successful in that I was able to inspire a great number of kids and provide them with some pretty neat drawing skills. For example, when we did a comic for our art session I had provided lots of examples of eyes, facial expressions, hair styles, etc. that the kids could use in their comic. In a later session when we did people cut-outs from construction paper, the kids remembered some of the details I drew on the chalkboard and incorporated them into their cut-outs. This shows that they are becoming more confident in their own abilities because they are able to take my art and reconstruct it on their own terms. **Frank T.**

Some of the art sessions that went exceptionally well at S.O.S. were art sessions such as: sculpturing, cartoons, paper dolls, and free draw. With the paper dolls the children were able to create their friends from school. Some created their favorite television show characters, and some created their families. **Lori B.**

Creativity leads to confidence. Supplying children with the chance to create opens many doors and outcomes. Interaction is effortless over an art project. It is a great way to communicate, collaborate, and improve teamwork. Art helps us find common ground and understand each other. Sometimes, art helps us understand ourselves. **Michele M.**

For our last project, we thought a great idea would be a large mural. Since there were so many individuals and the paper was so long, Luca proposed they make a giant caterpillar. In doing so, each inmate would trace a paper plate to create one circle of the caterpillar. Ultimately, all the circles would connect together to form the shape. In each individual's circle, they were to draw something representative of themselves. He then insisted that we, the students, would be in charge of the head. Everyone thought this idea was wonderful. We made the head with big eyes and a silly face and labeled the top of it "DRC." That session was my favorite yet. We sat around the table just drawing as a group discussing movies, school, rappers, television shows and more. **Alexandra B.**

Today's project was to make a unified mural that everyone can draw together [to] make one big scene that exemplifies everyone's feelings about the program and the future. We all drew a big, unified caterpillar. The reason we drew a caterpillar is the metaphor that one day it will be a butterfly. **Daniel C.**

Through the art, the women were able to express emotions regarding their arrest. During the comic strips project, almost every woman presented her arrest. **Kristen D.**

The Course Related to Choosing a Major or Future Career

Overall, this program working at Rockland Psychiatric Center has been a great help to me. Not only was the experience great because mental health is my major and I've learned new things and how to deal with certain situations that could only be taught in real life experience, but this was great because I am a graduating senior and as you can imagine, I am looking for a full time job now in my field. One main thing employers are looking for is experience and lots of it. All my interviewers have been so impressed with the fact that I had experience in a Psychiatric Hospital. Many of them are so interested, and they ask me to tell them my whole experience, asking me many questions. This will help me for many years to come. I hope it will help me secure a full time job. This was one of the best experiences I have had in my life. **Jalissa A.**

I am so blessed to have found my way into this class and to have chosen this site. I have wanted to work with kids in the institutional setting ever since I was a freshman in high school. This is truly the foundation for my career in which I will be doing very meaningful work. **Sarah M.**

Overall, I feel that this program was an exceptional opportunity as a student, a future educator and aspiring art therapist. In the past, I have worked with special education students and therefore began to understand some of the difficulties these individuals face. Now, I have some experience with individuals that come from very different situations and have gained insight to other factors affecting their social, behavioral, and cognitive practices. **Kristin L.**

Not only was it a great experience, but it was very helpful in me figuring myself out and what I want to do with my life in the future. I definitely would love to work with seniors . . . Hopefully one day I will be able to get my degree in art therapy and have a full time job working with senior citizens. It would be such a rewarding job and I can't think of anything that I would rather do with my life. **Courtney B.**

This program has given me the opportunity to look into the type of occupation that I [want]. After receiving my bachelor's as an art teacher, I would like to continue in school and learn of art therapy as a profession. I have always used my art as a therapy to help me cope with the chaos that I had to deal with in my life . . . I found myself creating my own world of safety where I was in control of my life, and it helped me realize that I am the only one who can control my life. I want to bring art and this experience to children who have had to deal with what I have and much more. **Sarah M.**

I can honestly say that working with the mentally ill at NKI was one of the best experiences I have had at Ramapo as an undergrad. Not only is it an experience that I can put on a resume for future employers, but it was also practice journaling and interacting with people. **Melissa K.**

This experience gave me the insight and hands on knowledge that will aid me in both my courses in school, and my future career as well. It has reinforced my decision to become a psychologist and made me even more eager to begin my career. **Brielle M.**

Overall, this has been a life changing experience for me. It has made me realize that without a doubt, Art therapy really is what I want to do with my life. **Jeff B.**

All of the projects done in the class reflected everyone's own personality, making nobody's artwork the same. This art class rekindled and has opened my mind to the world of art once again. I now have an idea of applying both this art class and my major for a future occupation—art therapy. **Anthony N.**

I have always been interested in Art Therapy as a career, but I was mostly interested in working with war veterans. I hadn't considered working with any other populations until I took this class. I am now interested in becoming a certified Alcohol and Substance Abuse counselor, and I am looking into masters' programs for Forensic Mental Health Counseling. I'm interested in continuing work similar to what I did in this class, and I'm grateful that I had the opportunity. **Alyssa M.**

I thought this would be a great class for me because I was trying to figure out what I wanted to major in. I've always liked art, so it would touch on that. During high school I took psychology and loved it, so I would also get a taste of that. I was really excited to start the course and when I did, it only made me happier. **Lisa F.**

Like any college student, I always question my future. I was not positive if becoming a substance abuse counselor was the right path for me, however after taking this course and spending time at the jail, I feel positive and anxious for the future. I now realize that Certified Alcohol and Drug Counselors are one of our world's many underrated heroes. They save the lives of these struggling addicts on a day-to-day basis. Yes, it is a difficult job, maybe one of the most difficult out there, but I am ready to be one of these heroes in the near future. **Brittney M.**

Chapter 20

Site Endorsements, Grants Team Report and Ex-student Survey

Excerpts of Letters from Institutions

(Note, the original name of the program was Art on the Outside)

Care Facilities for the Frail Elderly

Bergen County Senior Day Care Center, County of Bergen Department of Health Services, Paramus NJ—May 11, 2011

By way of background, The Bergen County Senior Care Center is an adult day care center that provides care for frail elderly clients with Alzheimer's Disease or other dementias. As part of the Bergen County Department of Health Services, the Senior Care Center provides loving, quality care to enhance the quality of life for both clients and caregivers.

The Art and Interaction Program is a wonderful program that brings in a fresh energy and enthusiasm that engages the clients and staff in the activities brought by the students. There is a relaxed, fun atmosphere in the room when the workshops are being conducted. The clients are very receptive to the students and enjoy the art projects [though with] short term memory impairment, it is not likely that they remember the different projects week-to-week.

I observe a definite brightening of demeanor and the clients'affect when the students are present and a fuller engagement in the process of the art project. The clients seem more engaged and talkative when the students are present and after the program.

Staff looks forward to the students' participation and enjoys seeing what project they will be doing with the clients. The Senior Care Center staff work alongside the students to assist the clients in the art projects. I find the interest and enthusiasm generated

DOI: 10.4324/9781003592693-27

by the students to be wonderful and the inter-generational aspect works wonders to engage elderly clients. The clients enjoy the art projects but it has been a challenge finding activities that they can do successfully as their skills are limited. I believe that over the course of the ten weeks that less reluctance was observed in the clients to participate in the art projects.

Nancy P. Warren, LCSW, Supervisor Adult Day Care

New Jersey Department of Military and Veterans Affairs New Jersey Veterans Memorial Home, Paramus, NJ—June 16, 2004

After working with two groups of students during the spring semester, I can honestly say that the college/community outreach program is one that has had a very positive impact on both the students and the residents. In a Long Term Care Facility working primarily with the Alzheimer population, the students adapted well to the residents behaviors and individual needs. The residents on the unit enjoyed working with the students and looked forward to the program. The residents recognized the students when they came down to the unit each week, which for this population was an improvement in their cognition.

I believe that the program had a positive impact on our residents and the students. The Alzheimer population was the perfect setting for this program and the residents responded positively to the projects that the students were engaging them in. There was also, as I stated earlier, an improvement in cognition. In the future, this population will be the one that the students will be working with due to the increase in the cognitive level of functioning following the program and the psychosocial skills used during the program.

Giudia V. Kirsch, CTRS, Supervisor of Recreation

Hillcrest Residence, Wyckoff NJ—June 7, 2001

Our Art and Interaction program was a great experience for the residents here at Hillcrest Residence. We did start with a larger group than we ended with, but those who participated throughout the entire 10 weeks not only enjoyed the art, but also the interaction with the students. The residents who dropped out expressed that they just did not feel artistic. I believe some of the projects intimidated them a bit. The program was unlike the usual arts and crafts where the focus is the end product and they were given everything they needed such as a kit with a concrete product at the end. They were now needing to use their own ideas and creativity more than they were used to. The program did enable one of our residents, who resides here with her mother, the opportunity to become a little more independent; by working on an individual project and through encouragement and support of the students to trust her choices. (This was an area that we were simultaneously trying to foster as well).

As the Activities Assistant, I never considered myself artistic but was amazed at what I was able to create with the help and guidance of the students. I really liked their free use of the paints, fabrics and pictures cut from magazines to create some unique artwork.

We were grateful to have both students and found both of them and their program quite pleasant to have. We enjoyed the whole Art and Interaction program and hope that we can be a part of it again in the spring, when the sessions start up again.

Jocelyn Paolucci, Activities Assistant

The Ridgewood Home, Ridgewood NJ 07450—June 5, 1978

Art on the Outside is a wonderful, innovative, and valuable therapeutic art program. The atmosphere in the Nursing Home is transformed while this program is in process. The Dining Room (where it is held) becomes a very positive, social environment. The participants and students can be seen smiling, laughing, talking, involved in art work and discussion, and even sometimes singing. The atmosphere is very warm and friendly. The students are responsible for creating this type of environment. They are very dedicated, interested, creative and motivated, and these traits influence our residents.

The residents receive a great deal of benefit from the program. Besides merely being an activity to fill free time and a means to release creative energy, it serves a variety of therapeutic goals. The therapeutic goals include socialization, increased positive attitudes, increased expressions of self-confidence, increased attention span, increased desire for learning and increased courage to attempt to try new things.

The participants seem more willing to get involved in other areas of the Recreation Program offered at the home. The residents always looked forward to the art sessions and would talk about what they had done in the days that followed. The projects were either taken by the artist or participant or they were kept by the Recreation Dept. and used in displays around the home. We have had a few residents who would not get involved in any areas of recreation, but with help from "Art on the Outside," these residents became active.

This program has great carry-over value, and with the program stopping for the summer, our home, our residents and our Recreation Program will feel the loss. We do hope the program will begin again in September and we will be lucky enough to have "Art on the Outside" Program here at Ridgewood.

Hillcrest Residence—January 6, 1997

During this past fall semester, I was fortunate to have four Art and Interaction students work at Hillcrest Residence. Myral Nefkizian, Sarah Abdillan, Irene Lewis and Christine DeRosa all participated in the program. All four students came to Hillcrest on a weekly basis. They were always well prepared, friendly, and patient with the residents.

Each week, the residents looked forward to the students' visit. Each project was explained carefully, and the residents were guided through the session. As the semester progressed, so did the leadership of each student. They became increasingly self-confident, which was evident in their work.

It was such a pleasure to have this group of students. I look forward to the next semester.

Suzanne Paulillo, CTRS. Activity Coordinator

Christian Health Care Center, Wyckoff—undated

I would like to thank the Art Therapy department and the three student interns for the opportunity to have them in our program this semester. The Ramapo students showed examples of each art project before each session began. The residents appreciated seeing the projects beforehand, so they could see a final result. The presentation of each week's project was clear and precise.

All the residents who participated in the Art and Interaction program had completed projects at Hillcrest. The residents looked forward to see what projects were being made each week. It was helpful that a background in art was not necessary in doing any of the art projects with the Ramapo students.

The students, Lindsey Stark, Christina LaMarca and Joe Niclas had their equipment and projects prepared each week. It was during each session that the residents and students would converse quietly, getting to know one another. The residents would talk of their backgrounds and in return learn about the students, their studies and their aspirations.

The residents were receptive to trying whatever the students presented. A favorite was the tissue paper project, where different colors and shaped tissue paper was applied to create a vibrant collage. Another favorite was the movable project where paper was cut, shaped and connected with fasteners to make a manipulative, changeable art project. Most of the projects were kept by the residents, given away or displayed in their own rooms.

A highlight of the ten week session was the final day; the day of the Art Show. We had requested that the residents save all the projects that they could. And then, we advertised the "Resident Art Show" throughout the building, telling everyone, even those who weren't involved in the ten week sessions with the art students, that they would be invited to a special event. There was a large diversity of styles and mediums presented at the show. The residents enjoyed the interaction with the Ramapo students.

Patti Lombardi, Activities Coordinator

Care One at Wellington, A Care One Senior Care Center—undated

It was a pleasure working with the three students, Brittany Faber, Alexa Levan and Lauren Wolf this past semester. They were always prepared, came on time and were very knowledgeable about what they were doing.

The Art and Interaction program proved to be both a very good intergenerational and art program for our residents. Our residents enjoyed socializing with the students, and creating art.

While the workshops are being conducted, the room is filled with good conversation and laughter between the students and our residents, as well as concentration on creating art by our residents.

Residents enjoyed having the workshop weekly as a part of their weekly scheduled routine, something they looked forward to. Our residents were able to speak and socialize with non-staff members and non-family members which proved to be very beneficial for our residents.

Discussion was common at the end of each session between staff and students. They were able to openly discuss what they felt went well during the program, and what they felt maybe could be adapted for next time. The students also voiced their brewing emotional connection with our residents.

The program, as a whole, met our objectives for an intergenerational art program for our residents. I spoke to our residents during our monthly Activity Planning program and they are looking forward to next semester's Art and Interaction Program.

Nadine Blowe, ADC

Care Facilities for Mental Illness

Rockland Psychiatric Center, Orangeburg NY 10962—May 30, 2013

Ms. Christina Hill brought her enthusiasm and creativity to each session that she conducted on the Deaf Unit. She had many patients interested in her art sessions, however, for the purpose of the 10 sessions, she worked specifically with 1–2 patients both of whom were Deaf. Her basic Sign Language skills assisted her in communicating with both patients.

Christina tailored her art work with the patients based on their preferences and focused on enabling one particular patient to become less withdrawn and more involved and focused. This enabled this patient to reduce her impulsive attention seeking tendencies. She would look forward to Christina's Art sessions weekly.

Lastly Christina initiated art projects that were enjoyable, appropriate, creative and fun to do. This greatly assisted in awakening these two patient's creative expressions.

The Art program at Ramapo College exceeded my expectations in terms of the dedication and professionalism your student displayed. I appreciate the opportunity to provide this experience to Ms. Hill as well as to Ramapo College for providing such a dedicated and professional student.

Olga Gonzalez, RN, MA Treatment Team Leader

Rockland Psychiatric Center, Orangeburg NY 10962—November 14, 2005

I'm thanking you and your wonderful art students for coming to our facility to share the Art and Interaction Program with our patients over the last two spring semesters. The student's presence and socialization with patients made a positive impact on them, while receiving clinical treatment for mental illness. Your program helped to enhance ours . . . Thank you so much.

Your students were no less than respectful, energetic and willing to teach. This program enabled our patients to express their feelings in art form, which is a task in itself, as most of our patients have difficulty verbally expressing their feelings. With weekly tasks presented by the students in a non-threatening manner, the majority of patients who attended the groups felt comfortable and eager to engage in projects. And that was important. I hope as you continue the Art and Interaction Program that you'll feel welcomed to call upon RPC/NKI-CREF to participate. Participating in this program has been equally rewarding for me as well.

Vera Hill, Rehabilitation Assistant 2

Rockland Psychiatric Center—May 12, 2004

The CREF Unit recently had the pleasure of having Sandy, Grace, Ivy, Emily, Chrissy, Karen and Kiera, students of the Ramapo College Art and Interaction Course. They were here from February 25 to May 5, 2004.

During this period, students introduced a variety of art projects to patients with focus on social interaction. Participation in groups with peers and students, completion of art projects, and then discussing the end product were the goals of these groups. Mediums such as watercolor painting, cartoon drawing, acrylic tile painting, tissue paper art with glue, group drawing of favorite food while sitting around a long table covered with paper and drawing to words/poetry are examples of works created.

In the end, the patients enjoyed displaying their artwork for all of RPC and NKI to see.

I too learned from them. Observing how comfortable they were teaching and interacting with patients said a lot about their character and their understanding of people suffering with mental illness. They have patience, they genuinely care and they've brought inspiration and . . . art to patients. It was a wonderful and rewarding experience. We look forward to the next group of students!

Vera Hill, Rehabilitation Assistant 2

Rockland Psych. Center/NKI-CREF Bldg. 35, Orangeburg, NY 10962—April 24, 2004

The majority of patients on the unit are inner city young adult males. It was good for them to interact with females in the same age group, because they were able to socialize on a positive superficial general level without feeling intimidated. Socialization and interpersonal relationship skills are treatment objectives that as a clinical institution, we focus on. Having the students here helped to promote healthy interactions with members from the community at large. They had an opportunity to practice interactive social skills.

The patients waited in sheer anticipation for the "female college students who taught art class". The students did not expect perfection when they engaged patients in specific tasks, yet the message they conveyed was to do the best one can and appreciate the efforts that went into the work then talk about it. And that's what they did.

The patients had a favorite student they preferred to sit with and chat while engaging in art tasks. It appeared to be the "in group" when the patients sat together with familiar students weekly. Though, there was an episode when a patient acted out and became disruptive and the group ended before completion. After the group, as in all sessions, the writer provided a debriefing session to lend insight into the behavior, a brief history and problems of specific patients. This enabled the students to have further understanding about people suffering with mental illness and why they act a certain way in groups.

The students' presence and interactions with patients were very much appreciated, because the students were the only visitors the patients had for months (or years), while hospitalized. The patients would say things like, "you remind me of . . . " or "you look just like . . . " or "are you coming back next week?" The students'arrival was anticipated weekly.

Another reason the program was needed here, art is a very good motivator and it sparked interest. A few patients did not participate in the scheduled groups on a regular basis. However, when the students came, these patients showed interest in art and participated in the sessions. Their performance in Art and Interaction would be the extent of socialization and participation until the following week. They demonstrated the ability to find interest in something that they felt comfortable doing, then later talking about the effort put into the work to completion. Thank you for choosing us to be a part of your program.

Vera Hill, Rehabilitation Assistant 2

Care Plus NJ Inc. Paramus, NJ—June 21, 2004

As the Coordinator for the Extended Care Program at Care Plus, NJ, I was pleased that our agency could participate in the Art and Interaction Program. Both the staff and clients at our facility found the program to be enriching and highly motivating. The students always presented themselves in a professional, yet friendly and open manner, and our clients looked forward to the weekly sessions.

As a group, our clients reported finding the sessions with the students to be fun and interesting. Those who were somewhat resistant at the beginning of the program, found that they enjoyed the one-to-one interaction with the students. Clients looked forward to seeing the students and discovering new and unusual ways to express their feelings through art. Observation of the group showed an increased ability to focus and concentrate on a project, and to complete a task. Social interaction was also increased, and clients looked forward to sharing their work with each other as well as with the students.

Specifically, several clients showed significant progress when interacting with the students. One young woman stated that she had no art talent but began to draw independently after working several weeks with the students. She continues to ask questions about various artists, and often shows staff pictures she has found of interesting artwork. Another client, who spends much of his time struggling with psychiatric symptoms, has begun to make collages. Usually nonverbal, he is able to explain his work and is developing some pride in his artwork. Another young man still remembers his "Picasso Pizza" and often asks if the "students" will be returning.

The overall program proved to be a great success. The variety of projects and art materials was especially helpful for our clients. Many got their first chance to work with plaster, and with watercolors. The projects were easily explained, fairly simple and yet interesting enough to hold the attention of our clients.

The quality of the program was a direct result of the students and their enthusiasm. Sandi Moreland, Jennifer Brother and Katie Regemie did an outstanding job of connecting with our difficult population. They each showed patience and compassion for the clients, and a willingness to not only teach, but to learn. It is my hope that each student took away from this experience as much as they brought to it.

Adelle Collin-Lloyd, Extended Care Coordinator, Partial Hospital Program Care Plus NJ

Youth Facilities for Mental Health Issues

Rockland Children's Psychiatric Center, Orangeburg NY 10962—May 15, 2011

Dr. Peck, so far the experience has been positive for our patients. I feel that your students have benefitted from it as well. Generally the overall atmosphere has been inviting and fun. The kids see this as an outlet for them from the normal daily routine. Often it is hard to stop them from their art projects when the time period is up.

As with anything that is new some of the kids were a bit reserved. Yet as the weeks went on and the comfort level improved so did the kids' interactions. One child entered this program very soon after the passing of her mother. As you could imagine she was very solemn and quiet. Your students handled the situation with great care and respect. The child seemed to appreciate that and as she continued to attend she became very open and comfortable in the activities.

The program has worked well and has met the needs of our kids. Thank you for setting this activity up with us. I look forward to having these activities continue in the future. Thank you for providing the opportunity.

Keith Walters LCAT-ATR

Rockland Children's Psychiatric Center, Orangeburg NY—December 29, 2010

This is the second time I've had the chance to work with your students. This session went over very well. It was nice to have met you this time around. Hopefully this activity will continue.

Kelly and Cassandra did a great job in presenting activities to engage our girls. Since the acuity level here varied throughout the weeks the atmosphere too varied. Yet all things considered it was a fun place to be for the 10 weeks. Our girls really looked forward to the activities.

As I mentioned above, our girls really enjoyed the various activities. One important thing occurred. Our girls did not feel as if they had to get the activity done right. Oftentimes they are afraid of messing up. That did not happen with these activities.

Each week all of our girls became more comfortable around Kelly and Cassandra. Some opened up socially during these activities. I'm not sure of any long term gains from being in these activities. Since the activities were always presented in a positive fashion I'm sure there were no negative effects for our girls.

In our facility we are limited to what kind of art activities the kids can participate in. Luckily Kelly and Cassandra were able to adapt not only to that but also the varying degrees of participation of our girls. Each week there was a different grouping of girls. Having these activities in the fall did present a small problem at the end. Some of our kids deal with separation issues. Since Kelly and Cassandra engaged so well with our girls there may have been some issues about the activities ending. One of our girls who regularly attended chose not to attend the last session, but did stop in to say goodbye.

On our end the kids were more acute in symptoms than the ones in the previous program. Kelly and Cassandra provided an outlet or an escape for our girls to put their problems aside for an hour a week. In that respect, the objective was met.

I look forward to having these activities continue in the future. Thank you for providing the opportunity.

Keith Walters LCAT-ATR

Rockland Children's Psychiatric Center, Orangeburg NY—December 29, 2010

I must reiterate the comments of Mr. Walters. Kelly and Cassandra were dynamic students and were able to adapt to our children's needs. Both of them will make fantastic Art Therapy teachers if that is the route they choose to pursue.

Lisa Shumate, Volunteer Services/Community Liaison

Rockland Children's Psychiatric Center—undated

My impression of this program was that it was organized and seemed to give students an introduction to a mentally ill population as well as art therapy.

The workshops gave the group of girls new people to talk with and extra programming from the activity department. The girls looked forward to the workshop each week and often talked of the students during the week.

The young girls involved in the group were usually receptive and could easily be redirected if acting out occurred. Unfortunately, there was a considerable amount of turnover in the group. Not one patient participant's length of stay was as long as the students' workshop program. The students' experience was not contingent on this factor, but I am certain that seeing a patient for the entire time would have been interesting. There was one young person that did seem to find some self-esteem through drawing. In the beginning she insisted she could not draw or paint, and through constant reinforcement and encouragement she ended up in the group without complaints of her own work. Before she left she also decided to join a group that is painting a mural on the girls' unit.

All of the students appeared to grow in being more comfortable with the patients. Their main learning experience seemed to be this point. They were trying very hard to relate to the young people. As a whole and at different times each of the four students tried different personal and interpersonal skills in relating to the patients.

The patients acted out at times, but this is part of their pathology. It did seem that they were more easily redirected in this group than other groups . . . The interaction between student and patient was a process that began in wonderment and ended in trust on both parties.

Theodora Barry

Youth Consultation Service (YCS)

Youth Consultation Service (YCS), Holley Center, Hackensack NJ 07601—December 13, 2012

Overall, the Arts and Interaction program was a highly valued resource for our program by both our staff and clients. Each week, upon your students' arrival, our residents were excited and ready to engage in the activities.

Our residents were able to verbalize favorite activities such as working with [clay] and paints and each week they would ask "when the next art group was." Over the 10 weeks, I was able to observe the positive relationships Tania and Christopher formed with our residents. As many of our residents do not have consistent, if any, family contact, these consistent weekly workshops were a source of joy for the children who participated.

Both Tania and Christopher demonstrated insight with some of the behaviors of the clients. They did not hesitate to ask questions or voice concerns if they observed some behaviors that were not typically seen. This information was essential to our therapeutic work, as I was able to relay information and concerns to the residents' primary clinicians.

During and after each workshop, I was able to observe an increase in the participants' moods and their willingness to cooperate with their peers. Many strengthened positive friendships with the other children who participated in the activity. Positive socialization skills were observed by myself and the staff helping out with the workshops.

YCS Holley Center views the Arts and Interaction program as beneficial to our clients' treatment and socialization. We would welcome future collaboration with your program.

Christine Bowman, LSW, YCS Holley Center/Sawtelle Hall Clinician

Youth Consultation Service, YCS Muller I-Newark, Newark NJ, 07104—December 9, 2011

I want to first take the time and tell you how great the program was. My girls appeared to love your students coming each week and really looked forward to their visit. My clients were sad to see the girls go. My supervisors are very pleased with all three of the girls and their ability to engage, encourage and interact with the girls. Which I know from experience can be difficult. The girls in the program are difficult clients at times. Alisa, Melissa and Jennifer were always timely and well prepared for their sessions. The girls were also dedicated, and very personable.

We all wish the program was longer than the 10 weeks and hope we have students next year willing to take the long trip to Newark from Ramapo.

Nicole Freedman, LSW, YCS Muller Hall Clinician
Cheryl Woolford YCS Muller Hall Ass Site Administrator

Youth Consultation Service (YCS), Muller South Hackensack NJ 07601—July 7, 2006

Our residents in both Holley and Muller IRTS thoroughly enjoyed the Art and Interaction program sponsored by Ramapo College's School of Contemporary Arts. The weekly sessions provided all the involved residents with something to look forward to, thus boasting their morale.

The art projects were challenging and helped our residents tap into their creativity. When our residents became frustrated they were able to turn to the students for support and help. It was evident that both the students and our residents enjoyed interacting with each other (sometimes more than the art project).

We look forward to hosting students for years to come. Many thanks.

Amanda Wagner, Muller IRTS Case Manager

Youth Consultation Service (YCS), Hackensack NJ 07601—July 1, 2004

After speaking with the administrators at the Holley Child Care and Development Center, there is nothing but praise for your program. The children at the Holley Center loved the experience. They enjoyed working with the students and loved the art projects.

Individual behaviors were relatively calm and relaxed while the students from Ramapo College were there. The staff also found it to be a learning experience. . . . about art in general and the uses of different mediums. The program runs smoothly and is very effective. The students were always prompt and respected the atmosphere they were working in. Thank you for thinking of YCS as part of your program.

Jean Marie Bellotti, Development Associate, YCS Foundation

Youth Consultation Service (YCS) Kilbarchan Residential Services—May 30, 2003

On behalf of the YCS Kilbarchan staff and the residents in our care, I thank you for the group of six art students you referred to us this spring semester. The students engaged our residents in various art activities such as making collages, drawing pictures, making clay figurines and other drawings.

It is YCS' mission to advocate for, educate, shelter and care for children in need and their families so that each can further develop the skills, self-worth and hope necessary for success within their communities. Because of the traumatic histories many of our youth have experienced, they often have difficulty expressing their thoughts and feelings in a productive manner. Since art is an excellent forum for self-expression, the residents had ample opportunity to express their thoughts and feelings in a creative format. In addition, the residents could socialize with each other while in the group strengthening their social and communication skills. All of the participants gained in this experience and looked forward to the weekly projects.

We too look forward to having another Art group next spring if it is deemed appropriate by your institution. It seems to be a terrific vehicle for learning for both the residents and your students. I welcome any suggestions you may have and anticipate that we will both gain from this wonderful opportunity.

Barbara Bishop Wells, LCSW, Kilbarchan Administrator

Families in Shelters for Domestic Abuse

Strengthen Our Sisters, Inc. Breaking the Cycle of Domestic Violence, Hewitt, New Jersey—September 17, 2012

We can't thank you enough for offering the Art Interaction Program to the children of Strengthen Our Sisters. The children truly enjoyed working with Amy, Megan and Russ. All three students demonstrated genuine concern, compassion and kindness and made the children feel special and created a safe and trusting environment in which the children no matter their past or present experience were able to explore, engage and transform.

As you know the children who reside at Strengthen Our Sisters often find non-verbal expression the only outlet to their intense feelings of fear, isolation, sadness, anger and loss. The Art Interaction Program and the students who facilitated the various art projects offered so much to the children that each week the children looked forward to working on projects with such anticipation and happiness.

Amy, Megan and Russ were very active and hands-on with the children and played a role in helping our children in promoting self-awareness, improved self-esteem, having stronger peer interaction, increased group and individual decision making and encouraged self-exploration that will aid in leading our children to a stronger future.

Again, thank you for hosting this very special program and we look forward to working with you on future projects.

Annemarie Tait, Wanaque Director

Strengthen Our Sisters, Inc. Breaking the Cycle of Domestic Violence, Hewitt, New Jersey—May 11, 2010

I see this program as an excellent opportunity for our children at the shelter to interact and develop a rapport with college students and, in particular, positive male role models. The atmosphere when sessions were in progress were active, positive and engaging; the children responded positively immediately to Michael, Dean and Lori, had fun during the art sessions and enjoyed the time. Some of the children expressed disappointment to find out they were not coming back.

The art projects were simple, age appropriate and allowed the children to use their imagination. They behaved and stayed focused very well during the sessions. There was one evening that there were too many young children in the room, but after that we moved the younger ones to another room so the older children could have more ability to focus on the project. Another time the children were preoccupied with playing outdoors and being flexible to the situations and children's temperaments is a good learning opportunity for Michael, Dean and Lori.

Engaging in these art classes . . . definitely increases self-confidence and ability to work with a group. Thank you to Michael, Dean and Lori, and others who came from Ramapo. We really enjoyed meeting you and having you at SOS. It is a challenging environment and you did a great job!

Sandra Ramos, Professor Ramapo College, Founder and Executive Director Strengthen Our Sisters

Strengthen Our Sisters, Inc. Breaking the Cycle of Domestic Violence, Hewitt, New Jersey—April 25, 2008

Strengthen our Sisters' overall impression of the Arts and Interaction program was that it is an excellent source of healing for children who reside at the shelter and several non-residential who participated. It has great potential for developing their bond with their mothers. Before the class took place the children were not focused on anything particular and sometimes were acting out. As the classes began the children became attentive and got very involved in participating in the art projects. They are now very eager to express their thoughts and feelings.

The children eagerly looked forward to the Art and Interaction Program each week. Their personalities have been more upbeat and vivacious since they have attended this program. It is incredibly heartwarming to see the youngsters actively drawing and creating artwork after school. It is also comforting to see them sharing with their mothers. Many of the women at the shelter are working towards independence and self-reliance. The Art and Interaction Program gave them a better forum for communications with their children.

Since the mothers and children at Strengthen our Sisters have been seriously abused mentally and physically many of them have withdrawn into a shell. This program gave them the opportunity to express themselves in a non-violent way. This modality is very consistent with our goals of breaking the cycle of violence. Change can only be successful if we work with the children, who are our future.

The children are very proud of their artwork and were happy that we had it displayed throughout the house. They are very starved for attention and [need] to do more things so they can receive recognition and feel important. As you may know many suffer from low self-esteem. Strengthen Our Sisters works diligently to support our people in breaking negative patterns.

We have had several children participate from the outside, particularly the children of Allison and Kim who unfortunately do not reside at the shelter at this time. These activities make them even more fervent in their desire to be reunited with their mothers.

I would like to thank you for the opportunity to participate in this fine enrichment program. On behalf of Ellen Kenny, Bexaida Barragan, and the residents and clients of Strengthen Our Sisters. I truly thank you. This year's Ramapo students had been an extremely enthusiastic, talented and capable group. In a mutual struggle for a just society I remain,

Sandra Ramos, Professor Ramapo College, Founder and Executive Director Strengthen Our Sisters

SOS [Strengthen our Sisters]—August 15, 2005

I was impressed by the communicative skills of students Kenia Liriano, Herminia Cedano and Jennifer Huebner. Shortly they became very good friends with the children. That created a very emotional and open relationship between them. It gave the children freedom of self-expression, which had a big impact on high quality of presentation. Everyone was very involved during the presentation and everybody worked as a team. It was a very big achievement for the students. In the beginning of the first few sessions, when the kids were done with their art, they would prefer to run outside and play. Then they learned to respect each other and stay as long as it was necessary to give their opinion about their friends' artwork. They also learned to concentrate and to do their own projects instead of taking other ideas from different kids. Participants were respectful to the projects because the workshop atmosphere was friendly.

Students were asking children questions about their families, loved ones, and kids were sharing with students their concerns and working simultaneously . . . There were a lot of conversations and discussions about the projects during the work. Then each child had to give a description and explanation about why he/she did what it did. The children were very happy to help the students to help set up for new sessions and to clean the room afterwards. Few children were resisting to do some of the projects complaining that they can't do it. Students handled the situation very professionally and got them involved with the group very easily.

By the end of the ten week sessions, the kids started to talk more about future orientated goals such as their future profession, or how they are planning to spend their weekend. The Program definitely helped children find ways of self-expression through art, which created self-image. They had opportunities to freely use any type of art medium without any limitation of shape or color and without control. That is very important for children's development. It stimulates fantasy and develops observational skills. Children become more supportive of each other.

I believe that having some music and some dance movements will make it more productive during the sessions. It will help move locked energy and release the stress.

Students had to use the refrigerator as a spot for the exhibition which worked very well. I liked that the students didn't complain about the difficulties that they had to face, but instead they found a solution. The staff at SOS was happy about how kids were excited and involved with the sessions. Everyone noticed how friendly they became with each other during the short period.

It is very important to continue this program at SOS . . . considering the fact that children at SOS come from dysfunctional families and they always need some help.

Karine Arshakyan, Child Physiologist and Art Therapist

Strengthen Our Sisters, Inc. Breaking the Cycle of Domestic Violence, Hewitt, New Jersey

On behalf of the mothers and children at Strengthen Our Sisters, I want to thank you for allowing your students to interact and teach the women and children of Strengthen Our Sisters.

Your students were wonderful and served a much needed task at the shelter. As you know our children have been through a lot of pain and turmoil. Being able to express themselves through art is very instrumental to their healing process. I would like to mention the following students who participated in the program, Melissa Johnson, Lisa Gangala, Jessie Cullari and Krista Satrot. In particular I would like to thank Sarah Siering who really found her way into the hearts of the children by sketching their portraits. This not only pleased them but totally raised their self-esteem and level of importance.

Thank you, thank you, thank you, we look forward to seeing you in the spring.

Sandra Ramos, Founder/Executive Director
Ellen Kenny, Director of Shelter Operations

Programs for Underprivileged Youth

Father English Community Center—A Division of Catholic Family and Community Services—June 4, 2013

It was a wonderful experience having the students, Michelle Megna, Tara Wagner and Brittney Meyer working with the children at our afterschool program. They were very professional, on time and prepared when it came to working with the children.

The children at Father English Community Center learned so much about artwork. They were introduced to a variety of activities including water coloring, pastels and working with clay. The children were given the opportunity to be creative on a weekly basis. It was not only a great learning experience for the children but they also enjoyed the activities.

I hope that we can continue working together in the future. Father English's motto is to make a difference which is exactly what the students at Ramapo College did this semester! Thanks again.

Jimmy Castro, LSW, Social Worker

Greater Faith Preparatory School, Paterson, NJ—November 15, 2010

Our overall impression of the art program was great. The teachers came prepared with all materials needed for the activities. The students were extremely receptive and engaged in every project presented. As always, during Art a child's harmonious flow is inevitable. The program certainly fits the academic objectives of our school. I look forward to increased motivation and self-confidence as their engagement in art increases.

Thank you for your service.

Krystal Lassiter, Executive Director

Friendship Corner, A Catholic Charities Agency of the Diocese of Paterson—undated

I am writing this after having successfully participated in and completed the Art and Interaction program. The program was a huge success on all fronts.

Through the Art and Interaction program, many of my students were introduced to art techniques that they may never have been exposed to otherwise. More importantly, they were taught that art is far more than applying paint to paper, but that art is a universal language that can allow children to be free and express themselves however they wish.

Our Mission as an After School Program is to provide underprivileged students, who are the overwhelming majority in my program, with the most comprehensive and inspirational program available. Too often, the impact that art has on the developing minds of the youth is minimized or totally neglected. However, it is my conviction that academics alone do not develop children to the peak of their intellectual or social potential. To that end, I have always eagerly anticipated the time of year that brings Art and Interaction into our midst.

The Ramapo students, who worked with the children in my program, were excellent at teaching specific art techniques, as well as relating to the kids. I was particularly amazed by how strongly the kids bonded with the students over such a short period of time. The kids here continue to ask about the students from Ramapo who came to work with them. They cannot wait until the program begins again next year. The time cannot arrive soon enough.

F. Kai Pettaway, Director Friendship Corner After School

Friendship Corner, Catholic Family and Community Services—July 30, 2004

I would like to take this opportunity to thank you and your students for providing such an exhilarating art program to our 4 year old children in classroom O on Tuesday mornings for the past few months. Ms. Kari and Ms Adela informed me that the children enjoyed all the projects that were made during the program and the wonderful quality time spent with the art students The children asked for Lisa Pisani and Kaitlin Rinaldi when they were not at the Center. The children could not stop talking about the positive experiences they shared with them. The children particularly enjoyed working with the different paints.

It is very important that this program continue for the benefit of both the children in our Paterson community and the students at your college. Your program has allowed the children of our community to work with people who show true concern and commitment to children in low socio-economic areas. This program is very therapeutic for the children and has helped with some behavior modification. We hope this program will continue and if so we look forward to working with your program in September.

Wanda M. Alicea, Director

Paterson New Jersey YMCA,—December 14, 2005

Just wanted to reach out to you in reference to the Art and Interaction program. Your program was unique and enhanced programs I coordinated in the past and I would love for the children I serve now through the Paterson YMCA to have the experience.

Ronald Cope, New Jersey After 3 Program Director

DHE Grant's Team Evaluation

A grant was awarded to Art On The Outside (the original name of the program), at Ramapo College Of New Jersey by the New Jersey Department of Higher Education under Title 1, Higher Education Act, Trenton, New Jersey November 2, 1977. The grant continued for three consecutive years.

Letter from the Department:

The Department would like to remind you of the successful nature of this project and the fact that it is continuing to operate at your institution. The project, as determined by the evaluation, is meeting a community need, and through the eyes of private individuals and representatives of public and private agencies, is fostering a positive image of your institution in the community.

Finally, the Department is continuing the grant with the understanding that your institution will make every effort to institutionalize the project by incorporating it into your regular structure. We will continue to support your project through the Department's various offices as much as possible and look forward to another good year of service to the community.

Robert C. Holmes, State Administrator, Title I, HEA

Excerpts of the Evaluation Team

Evaluation Team authorized by the Title 1 Grant: Roger Johnson PhD, Paul Elovitz PhD, Paul Humphries PhD, Spencer Jameson.

TO: Judith Peck
FROM: Paul Humphreys and Roger Johnson
RE: Final Evaluation for Art on the Outside
DATE: September 30, 1978
Methodology.

Art on the Outside is an educational program rich in evaluative measures. The progress on the Program was closely monitored from its inception and, as a result more information on the structures, directions, and outcomes of the program is available than is usual in educational research.

Evaluative measures are considered under the following headings:

1. Site visits. Visits to Program sites by staff and evaluators constitute the single most important source of information about the Program. Each site was visited three or four times a semester by Program staff. Each evaluator visited each site on the average of twice a semester. During two years of the program's life especially trained students also made site visits with an evaluative function.

   On-site evaluation consisted of scheduled observation of entire Program sessions, in vivo conferences with clients, and conferences with site based personnel. This meant it was possible to maintain close contact with the Program's operations with reference to activities, ongoing evaluation of site personnel, and client outcomes.
2. Paper and pencil measures. Many instruments were designed, administered, and analyzed during the course of the four years the Program was in operation. These measures were an important source of information about the Program functioning. In particular, many conclusions about program outcomes were based on information obtained in this manner.
3. Symposia. Each semester a symposium was held at Ramapo College attended by responsible site personnel, Program staff, the evaluators, and Art on the Outside students. The symposia were the occasion of important information exchange between site and College. They provided an opportunity for site personnel and College staff to exchange information in a structure conducive to free airing of opinions and to exploring and reconciling differences.
4. Student follow up study and client case histories. Dr. Roger Johnson designed and executed a special study in order to determine the long term effect of Program participation on Art on the Outside students. Analysis and conclusions from this special study is offered elsewhere in this report.

5. Staff meetings. Numerous meetings between evaluators and Program staff were scheduled during the four years of the Program's operation.
6. Student consultation and evaluation. Both the Program evaluators and the director enjoyed continuous contact with Art on the Outside students during the life of the Program. While this contact functioned in part to provide consultation to students it was also an important source of information to staff and evaluators about the ongoing operation of the Program.
7. Student logs. Each student in the Art on the Outside Program reported their experience of the sessions on a regular basis by means of an ongoing journal or log. These were read by the Program direction and by the evaluators. As well as being a valuable educational experience for students they were a rich source of information about the Program. The logs constitute a permanent record of the Program's outcomes and a vivid and entertaining account of the Program's many successes and occasional fa ilures.

Client Outcomes.

The most important outcomes of the Art on the Outside Program were those which directly affected client welfare. Client response to the Program was highly positive. The Program was well received by clients in all sites; indeed, clients looked forward to Program sessions and in some cases made special efforts to participate. In one site, client attendance was appreciably higher on the occasion of Program sessions. There were no instances of negative evaluation of the sessions by clients.

Certain client outcomes were short term; for example, patients' mood, which was often perceptibly improved during the session, might be evaluated only temporarily. Other outcomes were of greater duration. Client outcomes of the Art on the Outside Program are considered under the following headings:

1. Improved sociability. Clients in some sites tended to be solitary and antisocial. This was particularly true in the mental hospital and nursing home where patients, from one and another cause, were for the most part apathetic and listless. Clients were noticeably more social during sessions and, as they became more familiar with students and with one another, they became increasingly lively and interested in the projects and the people with which they were associated. Differences at a site between the beginning and end of a semester were noticeable in this respect.
2. Improved orientation to environment. With improved sociability patients often improved in their orientation to the people and events in their environment. Patients might become interested in the students and closely follow events in their lives at work or at College. As students were also interested in the world outside the institution these interests might be shared by clients. Clients in nursing homes and prisons were more likely to discuss life outside the institution with students than with one another.
3. Personal relationships. In many cases clients and students formed close personal ties. Certainly both clients and students experienced rewarding personal contact and will remember this experience in days to come. In a similar manner ties between institutionalized clients were observed to be strengthened as a direct result of Program participation. As institutionalized clients tend to be

deficient in areas of interpersonal competence, and, in some cases, may be institutionalized in part because of these deficiencies, improvement in these areas may well be one of the most important benefits to clients of participation in the Art on the Outside Program.

Survey of Ex-art on the Outside Students

In the spring of 1978, a one page questionnaire was sent to every student who took Art on the Outside during the last three years. (A copy of the questionnaire is attached.) The purpose of the questionnaire was to gain some perspective on what students remember about the program and what lasting benefits if any they cite.

Respondents. Sixty-seven former students returned the questionnaire. About three-quarters signed their name (listed as optional to provide some anonymity), and 88% of the respondents were female. The largest proportion of students came from various majors in the School of Contemporary Arts. This was followed by psychology and education and a scattering of other majors. About 15% of those responding have transferred to another college since taking Art on the Outside.

Results

1. Looking back on Art on the Outside, how would you rate it in comparison with other courses and experiences in the college?
   74% extremely valuable
   22% above average
   - 3% average
   0% below average
   1% poor
2. Has Art on the Outside led to any changes in your life?
   58% Yes, it resulted in definite changes
   33% It resulted in minor changes
   9% It caused no changes
3. Please indicate what changes (the numbers below indicate the number of respondents who checked each choice)
   31 people:
   10 people:
   7 people:
   16 people:
   38 people:
   10 people:
   16 people:
   It helped me formulate career goals.
   It made me change my previous career goals.

It helped me get a job.
It helped me decide on a major in college.
It made what I learned in other courses more meaningful.
It had little effect on my education.
It had little effect on my career plans.

4. Rate each of the following according to importance

	VERY IMPORTANT	MODERATELY IMPORTANT	NOT VERY IMPORTANT
A. learning the art projects	39%	43%	18%
B. writing logs	54	36	10
C. seeing the various sites	77	20	3
D. getting to know clients	86	12	2
E. developing friendships with other students in class	42	43	15
F. satisfaction of helping others	89	11	0
G. improving my self-esteem and confidence	80	17	3
H. learning to work with others	81	19	1
I. becoming aware of social problems	85	12	3
J. learning responsibility and self-discipline	70	21	9

5. Do you really feel that you helped at least some of the clients?
   52% Yes, I helped some in an important way.
   44% I helped some in a small way.
   0% I don't think I had any effect on them.
   5% I am not sure whether or not I had any effect.
6. Did any of the clients have a lasting effect on you?
   76% Definitely yes.
   20% Only a slight effect.
   5% No lasting effect on me.
7. List by name any clients you can remember.
   57% named some of their clients (one student listed 19 names) 16% said they could not, or that they remembered only faces 27% did not answer
8. If you had it to do over, would you take this course again?
   71% Definitely yes.
   18% Probably yes.
   5%. Probably not.
   6% Definitely not

Interpretation. These data speak for themselves, however some **conclusions** can be drawn. Three-quarters of the students who responded consider Art on the Outside an extremely valuable experience compared to other college experiences. Over 90% stated that it led to some kind of change in their life. Although only a few were able to get jobs because of it, many felt it helped formulate career goals and helped make other courses more meaningful.

All of the items in question 4 (what did they get out of Art on the Outside) were rated as very important by many of the ex-students. The only two items which seemed less important dealt with learning the art projects and developing friendships with other students in the class. It might be noted that the vast majority of students are art majors, yet what seemed important was not the art but helping others, learning about social problems, improving self-esteem, and so on. It would seem that students in many majors other than art would benefit considerably from this course.

Only slightly more than half felt that they helped the clients in some important way, yet no one believed that they had no effect at all. Three-quarters felt that the clients definitely had a lasting effect on them. The relative permanence of the relationship is indicated by the fact that most students remembered at least some of their clients vividly and could recall many by name.

Overall, most students had a very positive and significant experience with the program. Almost 90% indicated they would take the course again. It is possible that those who do not remember the program so positively did not answer the questionnaire, however it is clear from those who did answer that many students were strongly and positively influenced. Many students have changed their career and life goals as a result of the course. A few even mentioned that after seeing the conditions of the institutionalized they decided not to pursue a career in this direction. But the vast majority of those who cited career influences decided to enter the general area of social services.

Many respondents went on at length with regard to their feelings about the program. Below are some quotations:

> "I feel that your Art on the Outside has influenced my life more than I would have thought while I was taking the course. Thank you for that experience. I learned quite a bit about life, people, and myself."
>
> "On the whole, Art on the Outside was the most fulfilling course I have taken. If there is anything I can do to help encourage more curses of this nature I will be glad to help."
>
> "Art on the Outside has made me much more aware in the different ways and conditions which people live. To me, there can be no better course than one which exposes you to as many people, outlooks, and ways of life as this one has. My town is a small, upper middle class community which has few of the less fortunate ways of living. By visiting a prison, a mental institution, and a welfare division I have become more aware of what life really is."
>
> "When I arrived at Rockland Psychiatric Ward I noticed that one of the clients named Franz was very withdrawn and would not speak to anyone. It took a lot of talking with no response and a lot of patience on my part, but by the end of the semester Franz was not only speaking to people but actively involved in the program and enthusiastic about it. Art on the Outside has proved to be beneficial to him and to me also. After we ended the program for that semester, I heard that Franz had left Rockland."

"I took Art on the Outside 2 years ago, and to this day it has had an effect on me. It was a very important class for intercommunications, writing skills, community work. It is one of the best programs I've had in college. I'm very glad to hear the course is still going, and I think it should keep on!"

"Art on the Outside opened up a world that I was never in touch with. The emotional stress of intercity life, the mental and physical handicaps of hospital patients, and the end of the road feelings of the aged. All of the above led me into a field of teaching which I hadn't thought of before your class. Since graduation, I have been involved with a class of emotionally disturbed children. Working with them gives me such satisfaction—a satisfaction which I often felt while enrolled in Art on the Outside."

"It was through my experience with Art on the Outside that I realized that I wanted to devote my efforts to working with people. I directed my goals accordingly. It was an awakening to so many dependent people, institutionalized or otherwise who need supplementary programs in their daily lives."

"Although Art on the Outside had no direct effect upon my career, it left me with many valuable and important experiences. I became aware of many different lifestyles in the world as I was about to enter into the social world outside the sheltered college atmosphere. There are faces and feelings of people that will remain with me all my life. I have some of my clients' works hanging in my home."

Roger N. Johnson, Ph.D. Professor of Psychology, School of Theoretical and Applied Science,
Ramapo College of New Jersey

Chapter 21

The Jail Experience

History of Art on the Outside Inside the Jail

One of the most memorable aspects of the Art and Social Interaction Program over the 50 years of its existence has been its work with incarcerated men and women. It seems right to give this topic a chapter of its own. The program concentrated these efforts in the jail system. This was due in part to the way in which it began. Judith was contacted by Keith Ali, an officer at the Essex County Jail, asking if she would consider a program of art there. How her name came up in this regard is not remembered. She surmises he must have seen a news article about some work she was doing in the community with students and art, possibly with youth in the Paterson housing projects. He explained that an art program was particularly valuable in the jail prison system where the situation was so in flux: inmates, many new to incarceration awaiting trial, some already sentenced and awaiting move to a Federal prison. Anxiety was high and the release that art might offer would be helpful. Judith appreciated his sensitivity—to both his people and to art and they met. Officer Keith Ali was a tough young Black police officer and she a mild-mannered Jewish mother, artist and professor but they shared a cause.

More aspects of the cause Keith envisioned emerged as the program got underway. The age similarity between the inmates and the college students made for immediate ease of relationships with their common interests of music, movies, popular artists and more. More profoundly, the gender difference had far reaching impact. In the beginning of the arrangement only men were given the opportunity to sign up, while more females than males signed up for the college course. The inmates had an opportunity to see females in a different light as conversations became culturally oriented towards educational and leisure interests rather than on the more ubiquitous pursuit of sexual conquest. Rules had to be strictly obeyed regarding any contact beyond the jail setting including notes, letters, anything beyond the workshops in present or future time.

The college students, male and female, became de facto mentors, as the studies they were engaged in became a source of interest to the inmates opening ideas toward new goals. And students learned as well: how one mistake could change the course of a life. It should be noted that conversations always accompanied the art activity, whatever the specific project of the session, a rule of the program's mission: art and interaction.

Later, when the female wards of the jail were included and again both male and female college students were the presenters, the mix of genres in this unusual setting of tension

DOI: 10.4324/9781003592693-28

had gifts of insights and understanding to bestow on both groups. But with all the good that could be seen in the effectiveness of both the art and the interaction, it was difficult to keep the program going each year. There were always more reasons not to have the program than have it. This is entirely understandable. It is easier, less risky, not really necessary and replete with potential problems. Faculty running the program have far less obstacles to encounter setting up other sites for student engagement. That it continues is an accomplishment. Wardens and top officials can be led to see its advantages, line staff grudgingly come around. That the program works and works well ends up always being a surprise.

Student Reflections on their Jail Experience

Delaney Hall, a male correctional facility in Newark, NJ, was my site choice. Along with two other girls from my class, Lauren and Madinah, I assisted in instructing inmates with art activities for 90 minutes each session, once a week.

The majority of these inmates suffer from addictive behavior, and the individual's own personality, the environment, and his own behavior cause many of these inmates to relapse into their drug history. This is evident by the number of inmates who are repeat offenders at the correctional facility. The presence of students to interact with as well as the ability to use and understand their own skills has been a wonderful way to interrupt what might be a negative reciprocal process for these men. Through their artwork, the inmates slowly learned that it is safe to open up, try new things like sketch a self-portrait, express a future goal and seek positive ways of conflict resolution. **Katherine M.**

Lisa made up this project where the men would have to create song lyrics or write the lyrics of their favorite song and draw about it. One table did a Beatles song. Another table did a Biggie song. Mike was singing, having a great time. **Samantha O.**

During this semester I was able to make new friends, create magical pieces of art and also help others who need a bit of art and interaction to get by day to day. The women at the jail helped me remember not to take my freedom for yes! granted because being between those four walls is nothing but hell. **Liz P.**

Mike began to speak. He said that he was speaking on behalf of all the inmates. He said that he was so thankful that we did this for them. That he had been in jail for the longest out of anybody and being able to look forward to Wednesdays was really nice. It offered him a chance to relax and forget about all the drama that was happening [even] if just for an hour. **Lisa F.**

This was our last week at the Hackensack County Jail. Lisa and I decided to do watercolors as our project, because that is what we did during our first session where it was a hit. The men were so excited to see us. They helped us set up by taping down the sheets of paper and filling cups with water for each table.

The theme was to paint something positive that represents you. William painted his family. Another inmate painted himself playing basketball, because that's when he's at his happiest. Jor painted himself hanging out with his friends. He was talking about his childhood, and how much he would love to reconnect with some of his old friends when he gets out. **Samantha O.**

Every week we struggled a little bit planning the projects. A lot of the projects we did in the classroom used prohibited materials that we couldn't bring into the jail. So, a lot of the projects we had to manipulate and change to match the requirements of the jail. **Lisa F.**

I never expected to be upset that the semester is ending, and my trips to the Hackensack Jail have come to an end. In the beginning, the men did not help us set up. They were pessimistic. Only a handful of the inmates attended our sessions. Fortunately, as time went on more and more inmates joined. We went from having 12 participants to 22. They started looking forward to our visits. They would help us set up and clean up. They looked forward to showing their artwork to one another. One inmate said that it was a great way to express themselves. It gave them a positive outlet that allowed them to forget that they were in jail. **Samantha O.**

While attending my regular site, Bergen County Jail, I got to spend my Wednesday mornings with numerous females suffering from alcohol and drug addiction. What I have seen on television is grime and instability. However, as I walked through the corridors of Bergen County Jail I could not feel safer. The inmates that walk through the corridors do not catcall, grope or harass us as we make our way to N3. There is never a problem when I am there, and I have never felt that my safety was at risk, not even when I was in a room unsupervised with eight women trying to beat their addiction. I have learned to look at these women as people, not inmates. Yes, they have an addiction they need to conquer, but that does not make them any less human. **Rachael O.**

These facilities have reinforced my appreciation for my mother's hard work to discipline me and make me the person I am today. I have learned that creativity and self- expression are not always welcomed, and that I am more blessed than I thought. I have always had a sense of individuality and creativity, and I have always known that I have had restrictions. But in some of these institutions, the jail especially, individuals have restrictions I could never imagine conforming to. **Rachael O.**

We would talk about simple topics in the beginning. We spoke of current events such as the Olympics or sports. Soon, however, we began to talk about more intimate topics such as their families. Bryant told me about his sisters and I told him about mine. This brought to my attention the fact that they had been taken away from their families. I saw what it was like to be locked up and missing your family. I saw what it was like to not be sure how long your stay is or when you can leave. **Samantha B.**

At first it was awkward and I was not sure what to talk about. Now, when we walk in [to the Bergen County Jail Female Wing] we are greeted with eager smiles and eager artists. We talk about anything. **Rachael O.**

Never in a million years did I think I would have so much in common with inmates. We liked the same movies, music, television shows and even sports teams. We always had something to talk about and there was never a dull moment. My favorite thing to talk about with the men was, shockingly, school. I loved when they asked me about school and loved even more when they would talk about wanting to go back to school. **Brittney M.**

I have learned more about human nature from watching these men, assisting them with projects and sharing in conversations than in any other experience I have had in my life. Butler, Levi, Cruz, Jesus, Juan, Shaheed, McHarris and the others, all had very different personalities but the efforts that each man put forth every week has changed my perspective on rehabilitation through the use of art and interaction. I feel that we did impact these men during this program in a very real way. **Katherine M.**

While working at Bergen County Jail, not only did I learn about incarceration, criminals and the jail system, but I also learned about substance abuse. **Kristen D.**

This was a very inspirational class and it made me feel so mature and special to not only myself and the people I was helping, but also the people I was telling about my experience. I earned so much respect and recognition from doing work at the jail. My family and friends were taken aback and proud of me for doing this. **Lisa F.**

An addiction to drugs can force people to do things they normally wouldn't do just to support their habit. I grew to genuinely care for these individuals and it ultimately opened my eyes to larger societal issues regarding substance abuse. This experience made me much more open-minded, compassionate and less judgmental. **Alexandra B.**

We went to the on-site Jail orientation and I think I was shaking the whole time. I had never been so nervous or uncomfortable for so long. The orientation took about four hours and didn't make me feel any more comfortable about the jail. I looked at Samantha, [my site partner] and said I couldn't do it. I wouldn't be able to handle it, especially if it was with the men. She looked at me and said, 'look you're totally safe here. All you have to do is relax and stay by me. We'll get through this together'. I reluctantly said ok and we began planning for the site. **Lisa F.**

Bergen County Jail was not scary at all. I was a little intimidated on the first day I went to orientation, but that was because of the appearance on the outside. The jail was a tall, brick building with several windows with bars on it, and it was surrounded with barbed wire. There was a lot of security. During our orientation in the jail, we were warned that there might be lockdowns during our visits. However, we were also advised that there are rarely any lockdowns and that we would be secure in the jail. **Jesenia C.**

The thought of spending my Tuesday mornings with criminals frightened me and made me feel uneasy about the whole experience. What if they killed someone? What if they were in a gang? What if they raped someone? These were all questions I kept asking myself and it was making me question whether or not this was the right choice for me. I felt more comfortable when I learned that the men I was going to be working with were in jail strictly for drug charges and substance abuse. **Brittney M.**

Dana, the supervisor of the Delaney Hall program, said that they were all members from infamous gangs, including the Bloods, the Krypts and the Latin Kings. During the first few sessions, everything felt awkward. We were not sure what to say to the residents and they were not sure what to say to us. **Kevin H.**

The doors soon became very symbolic to me [as] I realized that I had a chance to walk through the locked doors and experience what happens behind them. **Samantha B.**

I believe that nothing is a coincidence and that everything happens for a reason. I was meant to take this class and meet the wonderful women at the Bergen County Jail who are striving and working toward their goal of a lifetime of sobriety and the men and women at the Bergen Senior Day care who have given all their lives and now are in need of some comfort and support. **Kathy C.**

These men are fathers, sons, brothers and friends. Some came from nothing, and were from the wrong side of the tracks, yet some had lived in beautiful suburban towns, similar to my own, but got involved with the wrong people, or were at the wrong place at the wrong time. It was some of the men's first time being caught and they were terrified. Others, unfortunately, have been in this position time and time again. **Brittney M.**

The greatest thing I have learned is how to prevent personal bias and judgment from interfering in the healthcare profession. It is easy to enter a jail or drug rehab center with prior misconceptions. By simply conversing with the inmates, I learned not to judge. Inmates are humans too. **Kristen D.**

Delaney Hall has classes and programs that allow the residents to get their GEDs, take college courses and art classes. Some of the residents are even given jobs. Not all people who go to jail are bad people. It's just they made bad choices from living under difficult circumstances. Some of the residents have been through more than I can imagine. One resident I will always remember is named Macho. He told me that he grew up in a poor neighborhood with no friends and family. Consequently, he joined a gang. He said he didn't join for the drugs or the money but to have his own family. His gang was his family, his brothers. **Lauren T.**

During that hour every week, they said they were able to forget that they were in jail and have fun. They also mentioned that it gave them an idea of how to express themselves and that they felt they had the ability to do things without being judged, such as creating artwork. **Daniel C.**

Many of the inmates mentioned how the program was an "escape" for them. [One] mentioned that it was the little things, such as art, that allowed him to escape from the regimented jail life which ultimately kept him sane. **Alexandra B.**

The isolation from society seems to be one of the coldest feelings in the world. Bringing art into the jail system seemed to provide these women with a sense of joy. One inmate at the male's DRC shared that the art program "allowed [him] to smile for one hour a week instead of sitting there thinking how messed up [he was]." **Kristen D.**

Rashaan, one of the residents who was released during the course of the sessions, used watercolors to express his past, present and future. He painted a guitar to represent the "rock star lifestyle" he used to abide by. He painted a peace sign to symbolize the state of mind he was in at Delaney Hall. For his future, he painted a heart to show that he wants to find someone to settle down with. **Kevin H.**

Correctional Facilities' Letters of Evaluation

Delaney Hall, Newark, NJ, September 29, 2021

When I was contacted by Judith concerning an art program for the residents at Delaney Hall, I was absolutely thrilled to be a part of something that was healing to our population. Once the class started, more and more residents took an interest in the program. The art students were absolutely wonderful and you could see how excited they became week after week at the interest in the program. I saw residents who had barely interacted with staff begin to open up. The program was healing the residents in a way that traditional forms of therapy could and would not do alone. Being creative is an outlet that allows healing in people who are suffering from substance use disorders and co-occurring disorders. It was an emotional outlet that allowed their anger, sorrow and joy to transcend the traditional therapeutic relationship and in turn gave them a sense of healing. It also gave them something to reflect upon because their artwork became a piece of their psyche, or inner self. I would certainly welcome it again as a form of therapy.

Ellyn Gannon LPC, MA, NCC, ACS, CCS

*Delaney Hall—Fall, 2010

I believe this program is an asset to any facility that chooses to take part in it. It has, for the second time, in my facility, been a success in expanding the opinions, views and attitude of residents living in a correctional setting.

I brief both the residents and the students before they begin as to what is expected of both parties. I try to create a creative, casual and comfortable atmosphere. The workshops are held in my classroom. This is not the largest of rooms but allows for the residents and students to be at a closer proximity to one another so their conversations are more intimate and engaging as opposed to a larger space that can promote segregation. I closely monitor the conversations, body language and attitude of both parties to maintain appropriateness.

The residents are told from the beginning that this is a judgment free workshop, and their artistic ability is irrelevant. The apprehension usually lies in the residents ability or lack of ability to be an "artist." However, once someone who isn't artistically inclined participates and shares, it opens up the door for the apprehensive resident to participate. The range of work that has come out of this workshop is amazing. We have seen full scale portraits and sculptures . . . and stick figures. However, each of them has the same amount of meaning and depth and are equally as cathartic to the residents.

There is always a change in behavior when the relationship dynamic changes in the classroom. In a traditional setting these people would not generally encounter each other on this intimate level. So, initially there is a sense of intrigue in both parties. On the resident side of things, this intrigue can bring out a more outgoing side or cause them to become introverted. However, either tends to fade after a few encounters, and the conversation flows as well as the openness to participate in the projects.

The residents who participate in this program generally find themselves working harder in their classroom endeavors, getting written up less and being more respectful to staff and other residents.

The residents were more open to participating in other artistic and educational activities. I also saw some residents become more outgoing and confident in themselves and their voice.

Ms. Dana Manginelli, Teacher

*Delaney Hall—Spring, May 21, 2010

The residents were open to anything the students assigned them. Even if the medium was one they had never used before, the residents felt comfortable asking questions about how to use it or how to manipulate it.

There will always be a separation between residents because of their different affiliations. However, in this arena the communication was more open because in order to do these projects they had to make themselves vulnerable and open themselves up to the possibility of sharing feelings about their work with people that they wouldn't normally communicate with.

I would love to have this program present in my department all year round. It is most certainly conducive to the overall objective of Delaney Hall. The staff has 100% embraced this program, and we wish it could be more often!

Ms. Dana Manginelli, Teacher

*Delaney Hall—Undated

This has been the third semester that Dr. Peck's Art and Interaction class has come to Delaney Hall, and it was amazing. It is so thrilling to see the transformation that takes place between both students and residents during each meeting. Since this is the third time Ramapo has collaborated with Delaney Hall there is a buzz that surrounds the Art and Interaction class and residents are very eager to participate being they have seen some of the wonderful works of art that have come from it. The residents are eager and open minded to the assignments given by the students.

As I mentioned before, it is a privilege to watch the transformation in the students and the residents. Initially, residents and students are more reserved for different reasons.

Residents are sometimes worried about how they will be perceived as incarcerated individuals, and students are apprehensive about the behavior or "danger" of an incarcerated individual. As the sessions progress, it never fails that the relationship between the students and the residents is never what is expected and they both learn so much from one another.

This program coincides with the clinical mission statement at Delaney Hall. It is a major asset to the cultural, social and personal enrichment of the residents. I wish that this program could happen all year and look forward to the next group of students.

Ms. Dana Manginelli, Teacher

Office of the Bergen County Sheriff, Bergen County Justice Center, Hackensack NJ Michael Saudino SHERIFF—July 15, 2013

My overall impression of the Art and Interaction Program at the Bergen County Jail is a very positive one. The three students: Catherine Desmond, Brittney Mastroangelo and Jesenia Chamarro were at all times professional, worked well with both inmates and staff and maintained appropriate boundaries.

The atmosphere in the room was calm, and the main focus was on the art activity which was accompanied by the social interaction. The inmates were surprisingly receptive to the projects, which is unusual because they seldom like to try anything new. They made comments like "This looks like fun", and "I've never done this before".

There were several notable changes in behavior related to the program. Most notable was the change in the jail environment that was created by the presenters, which gave the inmates an opportunity to temporarily let go of their normal criminal environment and involve themselves in the more positive creative environment. These changes in the environment are consistent with the objectives of the DRC program which are to demonstrate that attitudes of learning and achievement exist in the jail environment along with those attitudes that promote crime, drugs and other deviant behavior, and, hopefully, inmates may take advantage of these positive attitudes and begin to change themselves.

The Art and Interaction program presented a very positive experience for the inmates at the Bergen County Jail, and for that we are grateful.

Sam Watson, LCSW

Office of the Bergen County Sheriff, Bergen County Justice Center, Hackensack NJ—May 12, 2011

We enjoyed having the students. They were all dedicated to the process and were respectful in following the rules of the institution. The inmates responded very positively to the program as well.

The sessions were conducted in a warm and supportive manner. The inmates felt that they were treated in a non-judgmental and supportive manner.

The inmates were very grateful for the opportunity to participate in activities outside that of their routines. It also gave them a chance to interact with new people who bring fresh perspectives.

I think the women were more open and relaxed. My sense is that there is a disarming quality to Art Interaction that allows them to lower their defenses.

I do sense that the unit, particularly directly after sessions, was more relaxed and that the women were more comfortable around each other

The clinical staff is grateful to be able to afford our treatment unit with a different experience. We were able to support the process. The security staff were appreciative that all institutional rules and regulations were adhered to. They offered their support by providing regular smooth access to the treatment unit and inmate participants.

Again, I think the program allows for a loosening of defensiveness which is paramount to any treatment/change process. I don't know that I could recommend any specific changes at this time.

This program is in line with the overall goals and objectives of the Behavioral Health Department in that it seeks to foster openness and insight in a safe and productive manner.

The women have continued to discuss art and have also continued to express themselves through this medium. Many times it is safer for them to self-express through this avenue than to risk a more vulnerable and direct approach.

Patrick Hughes, LCSW. Director of Behavioral Health Services

Office of the Bergen County Sheriff, Bergen County Justice Center Michael Saudino SHERIFF—undated

I would like to thank you, Danielle Tricoli and Mark Merone for the amazing art workshops conducted this semester in our women's unit. Each week both Danielle and Mark would bring in creative assignments in which the women were fully engaged. They were both professional and understanding of the unique population that we have here in our jail. They maintained good boundaries while offering emotional support for the clients. The women spoke about the experience with nothing but positivity in hopes to have the workshops again. After each session, the women were encouraged to talk about the art they created which often evoked emotional content and further expression of feelings regarding their struggles. I hope that next semester we can continue with this program as I feel it was therapeutic for our clientele.

Julie Dietch LCSW, Mental Health Clinician

Office of the Bergen County Sheriff, Bergen County Justice Center Leo P. McGuire SHERIFF—June 7, 2006

The Art and Interaction program was a wonderful addition to our Mental Health program. The sessions were well structured, goal orientated and purposeful. While the workshops were in progress, the atmosphere was relaxed and the inmates appeared to be engaged in the artwork.

The inmates were very receptive to the projects and were eager to complete the work. It provided them with a unique opportunity to express themselves. The groups presented the completed work to the inmates differently. Wednesday's group accumulated the inmates' artwork in individual portfolios. At the final session the work was displayed on the unit. The inmates were then given their completed artwork. Thursday's group gave the artwork to the inmates at the end of each session. The group leaders introduced the inmates to different mediums, and they were receptive to these new projects.

The presenters developed a good rapport with the inmates. The behavior changes that were observed as the group progressed were increased cohesiveness, and the development of more supportive relationships.

The program provided an opportunity for the inmates to express themselves in a creative way, and the workshops provided a sense of structure to the inmates' day. The participants were able to develop a sense of accomplishment from completing the tasks and were given positive reinforcement from both the other inmates and the presenters.

Due to the nature of this setting, it is essential that the students have a sense of strong boundaries, are dressed appropriately and are willing to take the suggestions of the supervising staff.

There were no physical limitations that interfered with the group. The participants set up the sessions in the dayroom. The officers only allowed the assigned participants to attend the group, and all televisions were turned off so the group would not be distracted.

Both staff and the inmates felt the program was effective and beneficial. We appreciate all the hard work and dedication from your students and would like the program to continue, if possible.

Julie Dietch, LSW

Office of the Bergen County Sheriff, Bergen County Justice Center Jay Alpert SHERIFF—June 15, 1998

As always, we were pleased to sponsor your students and find this program to be mutually beneficial. Thank you for sponsoring the program at the Jail.

In general, the program works well in a jail setting as it provides a necessary but non-threatening outlet for incarcerated women. Although it is difficult to measure the impact on the overall institution atmosphere, I can address the attitude of the participants and find it to be quite positive. The women look forward to this creative outlet, often using the projects to foster communication with loved ones, whether by personalizing their projects or creating greeting cards or simply providing a pretty picture to their children.

In particular, the students participating this semester worked extremely well both as a group and individually. They rotated the weekly responsibility for preparing for the project but worked in unison to assist the women in its completion. Each of the students was fully involved in the program delivery and interacted positively and willingly with the participants. Ms. McKim brought a mature and quiet effort to her interaction with participants. Ms. Poitier had a more youthful approach in her contact. Ms. Sheridan and Ms. Sloezen were both fully involved, mature in their approach and seemingly undaunted by the experience. All of the students made a remarkable creative effort and sought to engage the students to the fullest.

You know that we have been pleased with this program in years past. This remains the case.

Thank you once again for bringing this program to our institution and providing us with another quality team of students. Forward to the Spring '99 semester.

Jay Alpert, Acting Sheriff of Bergen County
Karen E. Amy, Program Coordinator

Delaney Hall Participant Evaluations—Spring 2013

The class has given me a chance to refine a way to express what I feel in an articulate way of colors, like fresh drinking water in the desert. My love for the art of music is an expression too. This art class has opened me up to a new world of art that I totally forgot about. I really enjoyed it. **Levi J.**

I believe I got somewhat a better understanding of myself, saying in so many words, although I'm not a great drawer I gave it my best effort and learned from the young ladies in the class not to put limits on myself. So in other words I really believe Jonica and Alyssa inspired me to continue in the class, which I learned a lot in and very much enjoyed the whole ten weeks. In addition, I wish them the very best in their careers. **Hakim B.**

I learned in this class that you don't necessarily have to be an artist to do art. In my personal opinion, everything is art . . . music, food, life and everything in between. I really enjoyed coming to this class and I would love to do something like this again, except on the free side. I appreciate the time you guys took out to come and do art with us, so THANK YOU and good luck on your life journey. **Harry-Shawn M.**

Since being here in this class I've been more aware of myself in my artwork. I also seem to express myself a little bit better. **Bernard B.**

I have learned to find peace in a lot of things, as in doing art relaxes the mind and opens doors to a peaceful life. Alyssa is very respectful and helps you open up to notice and understand things. Taking this course has opened up other doors of peace to myself. Jonica has been very open to helping others. **James R.**

I really enjoyed this art class Ms. M has me in. At first, I really was not interested in it, until I really sat down and gave it a chance, Alyssa and Jonica are really great with us. Those two have a lot of brilliant and creative ideas. In this art class I have gained a lot of self-control, respect and that there is more to art than a paintbrush and colors. It relieves a lot of stress, feelings and emotions. This class has kept me out of trouble too. I feel a lot of positive energy, which brightens up my day. If I'm still here I would love to do art class again in September just to see the marvelous projects that are planned. **Dashaun T.**

Messages from Inmates

Retained from two students' logs, are interviews the students conducted with inmates from Delany Hall which contain remarks reflecting their experience. It was at the end of their sessions where the students served a group of incarcerated men.

Included in the team's logs were letters inmates wrote delivered at the last sessions of the ten-week program, one by males who had participated in the series and the other by females.

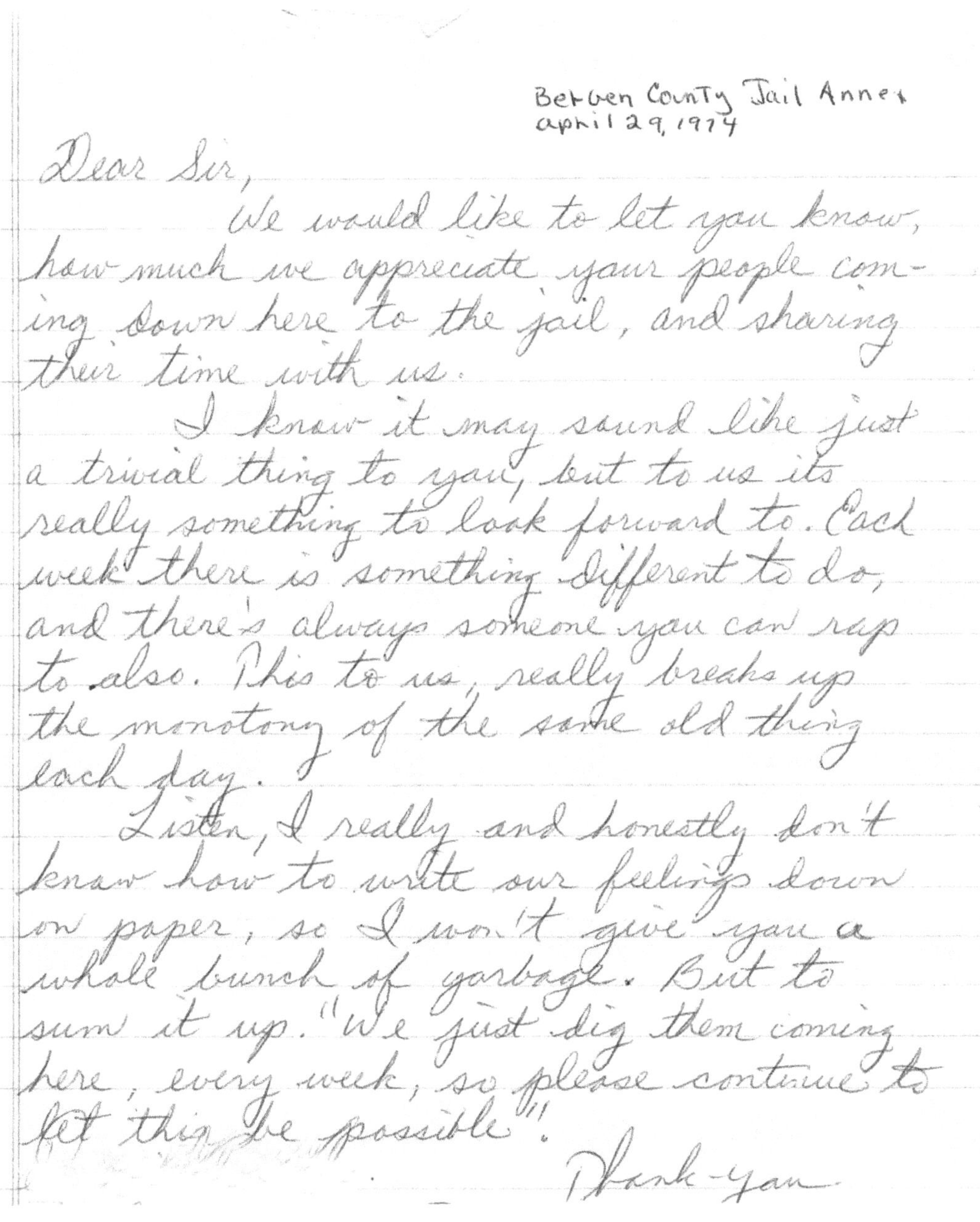

Bergen County Jail Annex
April 29, 1974

Dear Sir,

We would like to let you know, how much we appreciate your people coming down here to the jail, and sharing their time with us.

I know it may sound like just a trivial thing to you, but to us its really something to look forward to. Each week there is something different to do, and there's always someone you can rap to also. This to us, really breaks up the monotony of the same old thing each day.

Listen, I really and honestly don't know how to write our feelings down on paper, so I won't give you a whole bunch of garbage. But to sum it up. "We just dig them coming here, every week, so please continue to let this be possible"!

Thank-you

Figure 21.1 Letter from inmates at Bergen County Jail Annex, 18 signatures removed for privacy

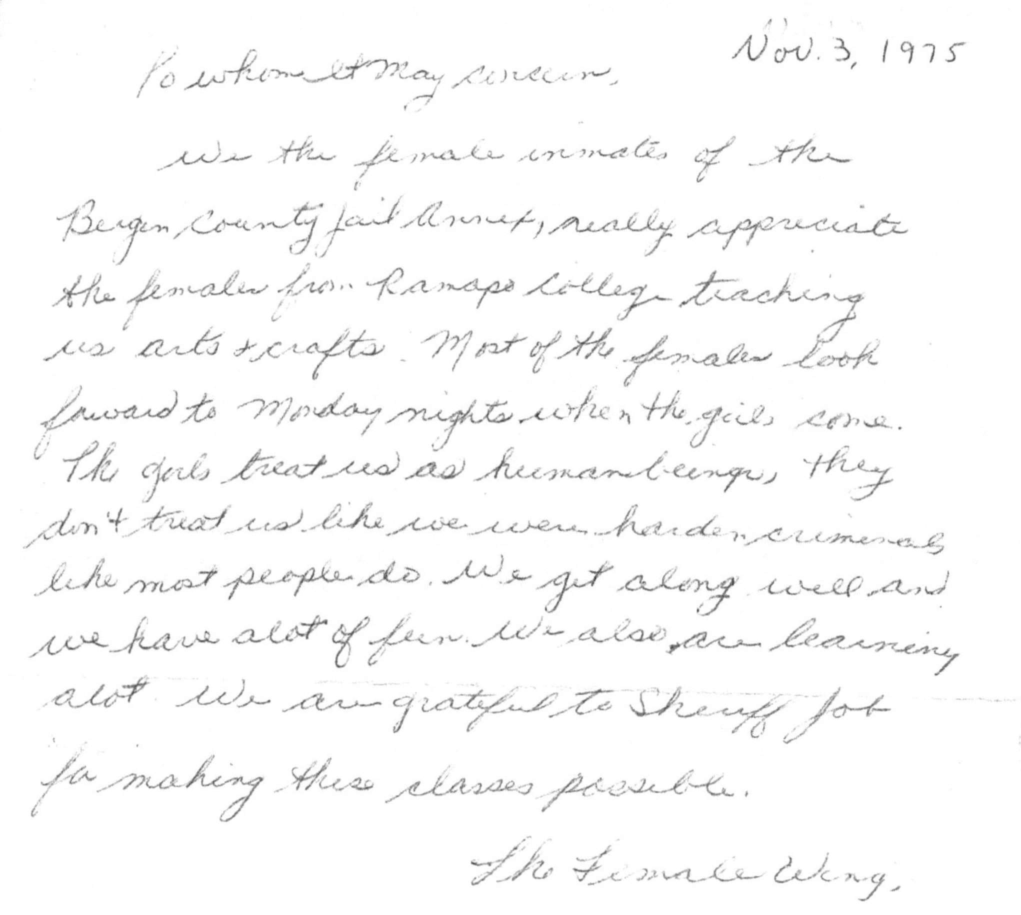

Nov. 3, 1975

To whom it May concern,

We the female inmates of the Bergen County Jail Annex, really appreciate the females from Ramapo College teaching us arts & crafts. Most of the females look foward to Monday nights when the girls come. The girls treat us as human beings, they don't treat us like we were harden criminals like most people do. We get along well and we have alot of fun. We also are learning alot. We are grateful to Sheriff Job for making these classes possible.

The Female Wing.

Figure 21.2 Letter from the female inmates at Bergen County Jail Annex, 10 signatures removed for privacy

Team Member's Final Evalution of the Jail Experience

Spencer Jameson, Assistant Professor of Curriculum and Teaching, Teachers College, Columbia University.

Art on the Outside Project at the Bergen County Jail (Annex)

Aspects of a Situation

Persons awaiting trial or serving short sentences have generally not been involved in programs of rehabilitation and it is conceivable that these are the people who could receive most benefit from such programs. There is need for a greater development of educational, training and rehabilitation programs within institutions of correction. The attempt to meet the need for rehabilitation was the justification of this project for developing a unique art experience for the men and women incarcerated at the Bergen County Jail. The young men and women who attended the program were often products of broken impoverished families, had unhappy school experiences which caused them to drop out, and were often burdened with the special problems of drug abuse and prostitution. Such aspects as these were but part of a total need structure to which Art on the Outside attempted to address itself.

Program Objectives

To develop and maintain a healthy self-concept and an appreciation of one's personal image and worth.

To provide art experiences that will enhance one's capacity to enjoy life, broaden one's appreciation of career possibilities and allow for the enjoyment of the leisure time that is a part of life.

To reinforce artistic skills as a tool of communication which facilitates social interaction.

It is against this backdrop of perspectives, that I intend to evaluate and report on Art on the Outside's attempts to reach its objectives.

Focal Points for Evaluation.

A. The Art Experience

The Art Experience had functional value for the pupils [participants] involved as these comments attest:

> "Most of the men and women had no initial confidence in their ability to produce anything worthwhile, nevertheless, by the end of our first session there were excellent abstract colored strip designs and drawings on the walls . . . "
>
> "This program has given me a chance to get back into art and drawing, something I missed a great deal . . . "
>
> "Some of the men did not realize they could make anything pleasing for themselves and were surprised and had pride in what they did . . ."
>
> "Most of the pieces were displayed in the cafeteria or the library. Other prisoners were proud enough to send things home with their families to display in their homes . . . "

The art experience also served as a vehicle for interaction between student teachers and the pupils [constituents].

> "Andy told me about his crime. He was going to the Berkeley School of music in Boston before he became involved with drugs. Later he rolled a man for $56.00. It was his first offense and he didn't meet bail, so he was spending time in the Annex until his trial comes up. We talked about music which is his major interest and how he wants to get back into this field when he is released . . . "
>
> "There was a black man 39 years old, who in 1954 went to Tennessee A&I college, after getting out of the army, having a family, not graduating from college got involved with heroin addiction. We spoke on social issues and his desire to go

back to college and get into social·services, helping people not to get involved in drugs as he did and to make a better life for people of all races . . . "

The impact of the program on the people involved was really positive. It enabled many of the men and women to get an immediate sense of success when they were able to complete a creative project in one session, a project they could display with pride. For some the act of involvement satisfied a strong need to do something with their hands to relieve the anxiety and boredom that was connected to being "1ocked up." Interaction with the students from Ramapo gave many men and women in the program an opportunity to relate to someone from their age group who in a sense was almost a role model, doing something that at one time they aspired to do or perhaps a role model doing something that they hoped to do in the future. I think the men and women in the program sensed that the students really cared for them and as a result they began to care, end result a warm relationship evolved that was clearly evident in all of my conversations with the parties involved.

In attempting to meet the needs of the men and women directly involved in the program I feel that Art on the Outside reached the objectives stated in the beginning of this report.

B. Student Teachers

Since the characteristics and effectiveness of those directly responsible for the instruction of the men and women represent critical variables to the learning process, they too must be regarded as essential focal points in the evaluation.

Conclusions of the students after the program were uniformly positive regarding the success of the projects and their personal gain.

> "The project was quite successful and all inmates enjoyed doing something with their hands, along with witty conversation . . . "
>
> "The men appreciated our program immensely—not only the art aspect, but we were also listeners to their stories, we laughed at their jokes . . . "
>
> "It's hard for me to sit down and try to recall all that went on in the eight weeks at the jail. It became a great part of my life. I enjoyed it. I honestly did not expect to enjoy it, but the fact that I enjoyed it, and that a lot of people who participated in the program enjoyed it really thrilled me . . . "

I think the students from Ramapo played an important role in helping the Project reach its objectives. There were some minor breakdowns that resulted in the men and women in the program being denied adequate time to gain the benefit of project instruction. Due to breakdown in transportation and poor communication between students involved, some of the students missed sessions or came late to sessions; this caused problems with the correction staff, and the people who suffered the most were the men and women who enjoyed and needed the program.

C. Program Administration

An excellent job was done by the Project Administration in the area of staff training when it involved the functional aspects of the Art Experience. Many of the students went through a testing period set up for them by some of the more manipulative prisoners. Failure to deal with this form of manipulation resulted in incidents that curtailed activity, thus depriving the project of much needed time.

Some of the students found it rather difficult to deal with the Custodial Mentality that pervades most jails. This inability to cope affected their performance level.

D. Prison Administration and Staff

The Sheriff of the prison appeared to be committed to the concept of rehabilitation. There is some doubt about the rest of the staff at the prison. It's important to point out that most of the people working in a prison environment are trained to be custodians, with a custodial mentality that is based on order and structure. Their views about people who commit crimes are different from people who come from an educational institution like Ramapo. Some of the Ramapo students failed to work within the structure of the prison and problems began to evolve which resulted in breakdowns in communication. These breakdowns caused the time allotment to be modified and the people to suffer were the men and women who participated in the program. Time and space were the major contributions made by the prison staff and administration in helping the project reach its stated objectives.

It is without equivocation that I recommend that the project Art on the Outside be continued at the Bergen County Jail. I feel that the project did reach the objectives stated in this report.

Part Seven

Beyond the Program

Figure 7.0 Inmate drawing a new picture in pencil

DOI: 10.4324/9781003592693-29

Chapter 22

Careers in Art Therapy and Social Work

Overview

This chapter might be helpful for students who want to obtain some insights about these potential careers by reading about the experience of other students who did go forward. You will read interviews from former students who became interested in pursuing careers in art therapy or social work by their personal experiences matching up with what these disciplines offer.

As an undergraduate, there are courses you would take to be eligible to apply for graduate school. Be sure to seek out that information in a timely way with your college advisor. Most likely, they will be courses that interest you anyway by their relationship to your field of interest. Later, there doubtless will be further graduate level coursework in a particular aspect of art therapy or social work that you have thoughts of pursuing.

Art Therapy

The American Art Therapy Association (AATA) can provide detailed information on how to become a licensed art therapist; this is the organization which administers the credentials for colleges to be certified in offering degrees, and information to students on what is needed for licensing as an art therapist. Here is a summary statement of purpose:

> Art therapists are clinicians with master's-level or higher degrees trained in art and therapy that serve communities in different settings. Guided by ethical standards and scope of practice, their education and supervised training prepares them for culturally proficient work with diverse populations.

DOI: 10.4324/9781003592693-30

Art therapists support their clients' mental, emotional, and physical well-being, including children experiencing behavioral challenges, such as Autism Spectrum Disorder; people and caregivers in medical crises; victims of violence or other trauma—from military service members to student survivors of mass shootings; older adults struggling with dementia or Alzheimer's Disease; or anyone that needs help coping with life's challenges.

info@arttherapy.org Tel.703-548-5860 P.O. Box 6240, Arlington, VA 22206 www.arttherapy.org.

Social Work

Students seeking a career in social work should begin by seeking advice from related faculty in the discipline, remembering that states have different requirements so it will save time to use information from the geographic location that interests you. Most social work positions require at least a bachelor's in social work degree (BSW) from an accredited school. The BSW allows you to pursue entry-level social work jobs in most states but not clinical roles. With a master's degree (MSW) you will develop clinical assessment skills and be able to specialize in a particular area.

Most states require applicants to pass the Association of Social Work Boards (ASWB) to become licensed. The National Association of Social Workers (NASW) provides professional resources, sets ethical standards and advocates for policies that benefit society. NASW also helps social workers stay updated on the latest research and best practices, ensuring they provide the best care to those in need. Joining NASW can offer valuable networking opportunities and professional development for students and experienced social workers alike.

membership@socialworkers.org Tel. 800-742-4089 National Association of Social Workers, 750 First Street, NE Suite 800 Washington, DC 20002. www.socialworkers.org/practice.

Out of School and Into the Swim

Four former students who took the plunge agreed to be interviewed about what their life was like as licensed professionals in the field. Their words offer insights to the practice: some of the choices they had to make, and some of the rewards; their difficulties and satisfactions with the career. The three interviews and the single essay tell a composite story about their professional lives.

Interview with Sara E. Siering LPAT, ATR-BC, BCBA, PMH-C

Interview with Kenia Liriano, LCSW

Interview with Megan Cormier ATR-BC, LPC (currently in inactive status, art teacher Pre K-5, Anne Arundel County Public Schools)

Essay by LeeAnn Cameron, MSW, LCSW

Interview with Art Therapist Sarah E. Siering, LPAT, ATR-BC, BCBA, PMH-C

Q. What path within education, therapy, counseling or social work did you pursue?
A. I am a Board Certified Registered Art Therapist (ATR-BC) and a Licensed Professional Art Therapist (LPAT). Board Certified Behavior Analyst, Certified in Perinatal Mental Health

Q. How did your interest in art therapy begin?
A. I was a high school student when I first learned that there was such a thing as art therapy. I remember the exact moment it happened, because from that moment on, I never seriously considered being anything else. I had always loved creating art and I had always believed in the importance of helping others, and once I learned that it was possible to help others through creativity, I knew it was what I was meant to do.

Q. How and why did you become interested in the career path within art therapy that you decided upon?
A. As an undergraduate, in the course Art and Interaction, I was placed at a residence for the elderly and at a shelter for women and children who had experienced domestic violence. One of the most memorable experiences in the class was my time in the domestic violence shelter. In this type of setting, the constellation of residents is constantly shifting, and it is natural to experience lulls in participation. I had a few sessions in which nobody seemed to want to engage with the art activities, and so I started drawing portraits of the children, who proudly showed them off to their mothers. The mothers immediately started requesting portraits of their own. They would sit as still as they could in that crowded kitchen, dignified and regal. I would sit with them in silence, taking in their faces, sketching as best I could with the materials I had. It was the first moment when I really understood the value of being seen. In fact, my experience with Art and Interaction had a direct influence on my future career, in that I developed a passion for helping survivors of domestic violence. I would go on to spend some of the early years of my career working with this population. I am very proud of the work I have done in this field.

Q. Did creating your own art or sharing the art processes with others have any effect on your choice of career or life style and purpose?
A. As an art major, I was already quite accustomed to creating and sharing my art with classmates. Of course, sharing one's art in a typical academic setting is for the purpose of improving one's technical skills. The artist receives feedback on her form, her perspective, her color choice, etc. and then modifies her art to make it a little bit closer to perfect. Art and Interaction was the first time that I recall sharing art with the purpose of connection rather than in the pursuit of perfection. This basic concept was built upon in my higher education and in my career as an art therapist.

Q. What was the general progression of your studies toward completion?
A. As an undergraduate, I took a combination of art courses and psychology courses. Although I chose to major in art with a minor in psychology, some art therapists choose to focus more heavily on the psychology coursework during their undergraduate studies. I then went on to graduate school, graduating with a Master of Arts in Art Therapy/Counseling. Upon the completion of 1,500 supervised clinical hours and the passing of the Art Therapy Credentials Board Examination, I became a Board Certified Registered Art Therapist (ATR-BC). Once New Jersey finalized art therapy licensure, I became a Licensed Professional Art Therapist (LPAT).

Q. How would you describe the nature of your practice?
A. In my 17 years as an art therapist, I have helped people in a wide variety of settings. I started my career at a counseling center in a rural community where we provided the only mental health services for miles around. I spent several years at a domestic violence treatment center creating art and cultivating a sense of safety with children who had experienced trauma. At a rehabilitation program for adults in recovery from substance abuse, art therapy groups were an opportunity to process the past and visualize a healthier future. For the past seven years, I have been providing individual and group art sessions to teens with autism living in a residential program. For these residents, art provides an opportunity for empowerment, autonomy, expression and self-regulation without the need for words. I also have a private practice, where both adults and children are welcome in the art therapy studio. Here I help people with trauma, ADHD, family conflicts, self-esteem issues, anxiety, depression and other mental health concerns explore their issues through creative expression. I have recently become certified in perinatal mental health, and the next step in my ever-evolving practice will be to support birthing parents with the specific mood disorders that can accompany pregnancy and the postpartum period of life: depression, anxiety, perinatal OCD and postpartum psychosis.

Q. Thank you for your generosity in taking the time to respond to these questions. Is there anything you might want to add?
A. Yes. I should mention that requirements to become licensed as an art therapist vary from state to state and the criteria evolve over time. Any students looking to pursue a career in art therapy should check the requirements in their state before pursuing higher education.

Interview with a Social Worker Kenia Liriano, LCSW

Vice President of Programs—Division of Prevention & Intervention, Health Equity & Domestic Violence & Trauma Services, Community Health Action of Staten Island

Q. You are a trained social worker. How would you describe the nature of your practice?
A. I have proudly worked in the human services field for the last 17 years of my career. I hold a Bachelor's degree in Contemporary Arts from Ramapo College of NJ and a Master's degree in Social Work from New York University.

Currently, I serve as Vice President of Programs within a community-based organization. I oversee initiatives in HIV and Viral hepatitis Prevention, Domestic Violence and Trauma Services, and I also provide oversight to a Health Equity portfolio of services focused on Hypertension Prevention. Our Hypertension Prevention main objective is to reduce the prevalence of high blood pressure through equitable access to education, screenings and health resources.

My practice centers on outreach and engagement, alongside clinical and non-clinical interventions aimed at addressing social determinants of health in vulnerable communities. The work is focused on critical factors that shape well-being, like behavioral and healthcare access, stable housing, food security, education and social supports in order to actively reduce health disparities and elevate the overall quality of life of our community members.

Q. Did your studies as an undergraduate influence your path towards a career and if so, in what way?
A. At Ramapo, while a student in the course Art and Interaction, I facilitated a series of workshops with a cohort of HIV-positive clients who were also facing comorbidities of severe mental health issues and substance use. This took place while I was working on one of our HIV case management programs at our community-based organization. The workshops were designed to provide creative outlets for participants, helping them explore their emotions, build coping skills and foster a sense of community. Through the art-making process, clients were able to express their experiences in a supportive environment, enhancing both their emotional and mental well-being as part of a holistic approach to HIV care.

One of the most successful aspects of the workshops was how the process of art making became not only a healing tool for our participants, but also a powerful means to confront the negative impact of stigma and discrimination associated with HIV/AIDS. The workshops created opportunities for community discussion, education and mutual support, fostering greater understanding among participants. The art created became both a personal and collective tool for healing, self-advocacy and empowerment, allowing individuals to express their experiences and challenge the stigma surrounding HIV/AIDS. Through this creative exploration, participants were not only able to process their own emotions, but also engage in dialogue that helped build solidarity, promote education, and increase awareness within the community.

Participants were able to externalize their feelings about stigma, challenge negative perceptions and reframe their identities in a more empowering way. The workshops provided a safe space for participants to reflect on their experiences and confront difficult emotions related to societal judgment, while fostering a sense of community and solidarity among those facing similar challenges. Participants were also able to use their artwork as a form of activism. It served to help amplify their voices demanding better access, better healthcare and social justice for those affected by the epidemic.

Q. How or why did you become interested in the career path within social work that you decided upon?
A. Artmaking offered me a unique way of shaping my critical skills, skills that are highly valuable in nonprofit work and leadership. From creativity and empathy to strategic thinking and collaboration, the lessons I have learned and mastered through art are transferable and applicable to every aspect of my personal and professional life. As a leader in the nonprofit sector, there is an expectation to adapt to the constant changes within the nonprofit landscape while fostering innovation. This involves staying responsive to evolving community needs, navigating shifting funding environments and embracing new approaches to

problem-solving. Creativity and Innovation in this context means not only finding creative solutions to challenges, but also continuously improving programs and services to maximize impact. Whether this involves engaging communities, developing new partnerships, or finding unique ways to deliver services, the solutions using the creative process allows me to think outside the box and approach problems with fresh perspectives while encouraging my team to do the same. I lead both clinical and non-clinical interventions. I focus on integrating art into the design of these interventions, using creative approaches to address social and emotional challenges. I am applying art-based methods to help in the healing of individuals and support community needs.

Q. What was the general progression of your studies toward completion?
A. During my undergraduate studies, while working as front-line staff at my non-profit agency, I was also enrolled in the Art and Interaction course, along with other art therapy-related classes. The Art and Interaction class allowed me to put art concepts into practice. It provided me with a valuable platform for integrating the theoretical art concepts I was learning with practical application, particularly in the context of healing and exploration. Through hands-on projects and interactive techniques, I gained insight into how art could serve as a powerful tool, helping individuals express emotions, process experiences and foster personal growth. Taking the class was pivotal in my professional development and it deepened my understanding of the powerful connection between creativity and healing.

During this time, I began to explore how to incorporate art into social justice issues, which led me to decide to pursue a master's in social work. I focused on integrating art into the design of interventions, using creative approaches to address social and emotional challenges.

Q. Did creating your own art or sharing the art processes with others have any effect on your choice of career or lifestyle and purpose?
A. I feel incredibly fortunate to have a foundation in the arts. Creating art has always been a powerful way for me to navigate life's challenges, deepening my sense of agency and building my confidence. Whether I am working on an art piece that explores personal emotions, societal issues or community experiences, this process has helped me develop a deeper understanding of others' feelings, needs and struggles.

In my work, art has been an invaluable tool that has helped me shape impactful interventions across our clinical and non-clinical programs. It has helped me hone my creativity and use it as a tool for navigating changing landscapes and challenges in innovative ways. My engagement in the Art and Interaction course exposed me to a diverse set of ideas, practices and philosophies that deepened my interest in art. This led me to explore careers that blend art making, creativity, social justice, health equity, social engagement and interdisciplinary collaboration. It has influenced my understanding of the possibilities within the broader field of art and social work. I now use my artmaking within my career striving toward innovative, community-focused social justice goals.

Q. Thank you for taking the time to respond to these questions. Is there anything you might want to add?
A. Yes, I'd like to say, this journey of my own has allowed me to merge my passion for creativity with my commitment to social justice, guiding the work I do in the social work field. How inspiring it is to be able to combine work and creativity with a fervent life passion.

Interview with Megan Cormier ATR-BC, LPC

(currently in inactive status, art teacher PreK-5, Anne Arundel County Public Schools)

Q. I understand you are or were working in the health care profession. How would you describe the nature of your work or practice?
A. I began my work in the healthcare system as a 2nd-year Art Therapy graduate student, completing my internship (three days a week) and getting immediately hired upon graduation. I worked as an art therapist at The Children's Hospital of Philadelphia for 15 years. I ran art therapy groups in playrooms and individual sessions with patients, siblings and/or caregivers at bedside or in various conference rooms throughout the hospital. I also held staff groups to help with vicarious trauma and burnout.

Q. What was the general progression of your studies toward completion?
A. I knew I needed a master's to get an entry level position in art therapy, but I was also interested in education and took every education class I could to complete my teacher certification. I finished my student teaching at Mahwah High School the semester after my May graduation. While at Ramapo, I got a taste of what art therapy work could look like with the Art and Interaction course. It is not clinical art therapy, but definitely an art as therapy practicum.

Q. As an undergraduate of Ramapo College of New Jersey you took the course Art and Interaction. In the approximate ten weeks during which you presented the art workshops, in what facility and with what clientele did you conduct your sessions?
A. I got to experience two very different programs: an Alzheimer's day program and an adolescent treatment/delinquent? program.

Q. Did your engagement in the Art and Interaction course procedures and requirements or your interactions in the facility have any influence on your choice of career and if so, in what way?
A. Absolutely. I got a better sense of what it might feel like working in a group setting. I experienced the vastly different approaches to art making, introducing a task, how to introduce/use the materials needed, depending in which site I was working. I realized something as simple as a dixie cup filled with painting water (to wash off brushes) could be mistaken for drinking water. (The participants didn't recall using it to clean their brush off just a minute earlier).

Q. Do you remember individual client(s) with whom you shared the art projects? Staff supervising the sessions? Characteristics, concepts, methods or approaches of the course?
A. There are certain participants that I still remember from the Alzheimer's day program that stay with me (and that was back in 1999!). Staff supervising the sessions? I do not recall this. I do remember writing up logs each visit we went and submitting to Dr. Peck. This was

valuable teaching and a great prep for graduate school in art therapy. There we had to do the same and use in supervision.

Q. Did creating your own art or sharing the art processes with others have any effect on your choice of career or life style and purpose?
A. Creating my own artwork while in the Art and Interaction Course was the beginning of how I began to process my own artwork and the experiences I was having. I became aware of the continuum of materials (structured vs unstructured) and what they elicit affectively. I love working with people and being able to offer materials to create and empower via art. I knew I wanted to be in the medical field somehow and found the purest happiness working as an art therapist in a pediatric medical hospital.

Q. Can you tell us anything more about your work as an art therapist?
A. Yes, I also had contract art therapy jobs. I worked in the Family Court of Philadelphia (PA) for approximately 16 years. I facilitated groups during court mandated supervised visitations. I ran art therapy groups in Camden, NJ for a program, *My Family Has Changed*, as well. This was for children who were experiencing parents' divorce, custody battles, etc., a grant-funded program that ran for several years. I facilitated closed art therapy groups for adolescents with epilepsy through the Epilepsy Foundation of Eastern Pennsylvania. These groups ran for approximately 5–6 weeks for two consecutive falls.

I was a guest speaker on pediatric medical art therapy at Temple University, University of the Arts, and Rowan University. I had been hired to teach an undergraduate art therapy course at Bryn Mawr College in 2017, just before I relocated to Maryland. I had to rescind and was able to suggest a colleague who accepted the position.

Q. You stated you are inactive at this time. Can you explain?
A. After moving to Maryland, I decided to put my art therapy career on the back burner and pick up the education track I once had. I began volunteering at the local elementary school and then became a substitute teacher. I applied for a part-time art position to see if this is what I wanted. Thankfully, I had reciprocity with my NJ certification, my Praxis raw scores were still valid and I am now a Maryland certified teacher in Art Pre K-12 (I do need to take a reading course before I get my certification renewed). One year later, I am a full-time art teacher.

Q. Thank you for answering these questions. Is there anything you would like to add?
A. I will say that education is a lot more work to bring home. There is more prep, more clean up, lesson plans, etc. It never seems to end. Art therapy, you leave work and unless you are in private practice, your documentation is done at work. I only brought back emotional baggage which I utilized in supervision and in my own artwork.

Essay by Leeann Cameron, MSW, LCSW

Certified in Clinical Social Work Supervision, Nonprofit Leadership, Victim Advocacy, Paralegalism and School Social Work

My Story as a Social Worker

One day you will tell your story of how you overcame what you went through, and it will be someone else's survival guide.

Dr. Brene Brown, Social Worker, Researcher, Professor, Author, TEDx Presenter, and Podcaster

Never underestimate the power of small meaningful gestures. I was at a trauma-informed education training for social workers a few years ago and one of the activities involved having attendees reflect back on their educational journey to the first memory of feeling safe in school. I remembered in early elementary school, there was a time in which I was not permitted to use erasers. The person I lived with would remind me on a regular basis that "children are meant to be seen and not heard" and that "erasers weren't allowed because you should get it right the first time."

Part of our daily homework at that time was to correct our prior work so that we could deepen our understanding of the concepts that were taught in class. One of my teachers would let me stay after school with her a couple of days a week to do this; I suspect because she saw me coming in without my homework and suspected I was embarrassed to explain in class why it wasn't done. That teacher, perhaps without knowing it, created a safe space for me to work after school.

Indeed, we are expected to learn from mistakes: erase and correct. This I did and improved my work as I never had been able to before. Sometimes I had to try multiple times, but I was progressing and felt safe to keep trying because I wasn't afraid of this teacher. I highlight this story to share that though it may sometimes seem like we are not doing much in therapy or inspiring huge change (especially in trauma survivors), change can be internal and not easily seen. This corrective experience is a memory I still hold on to.

No matter where we find ourselves, small thoughtful gestures are healing and can bring a glimmer of hope to a child who otherwise doesn't see much care in their daily life. While we can't erase the traumas of ourselves or others, we can do what it takes to create a safe space to empower ourselves and others to learn ways of healing, to move forward in a constructive manner and to build the life we want, however the direction adjusts through our journey.

Creating a sense of safety is an undervalued skill and intervention. My own protective factor was art; it would take me a few years to realize that art was my first safe and therapeutic encounter, as it provided a creative space to work through my lived experience. My approach to life had been to be as invisible and perfect as possible in search of safety. Art provided that hidden space.

Fast forward to high school. The words of my guidance counselor stung, "You very likely won't get into a college as competitive as Ramapo having under a 3.5 GPA." What was I doing wrong? In that moment, I perceived my guidance counselor as just another person who thought I wasn't good enough.

My initial motivation to attend college was that it was a means-to-an-end escape. But I needed better grades to get out of my household and into college. Following that meeting, I made honor role.

What my guidance counselor didn't know was what I was experiencing in my household. That I couldn't productively focus to do school work there: the continual inner distraction I experienced replaying the traumas throughout the day; my inability to sleep due to nightmares or to sleep at all through the fighting; being overtired and struggling to focus in class. The counselor knew that I would linger after school for "tutoring" but not that I needed that safe place to be, even for a little while after school.

During lunch, I either chose not to eat or to purchase the cheapest snack, so that I could save money to put towards going to college. Following my first year of undergrad, I changed my major from visual arts to psychology.

I loved my classes in undergrad, which were immensely helpful in learning the foundations of the discipline. My favorite class was, "Art as Therapy" where I learned about developmental stages of art in children and concrete art-based interventions, such as kinetic family drawings, animal genograms, sculpting conflict resolution activities, and other hands-on methods which were helpful in setting a spark for me to learn more ways to build engagement with clients.

I completed my undergraduate internship at a hospital in a psychoeducation program which connected patients with resources post-partum. It gave me the opportunity to learn about research processes and grant writing as well. But this initial internship was only for a couple of months in summer; I wanted something that would take me deeper and allow me to learn more.

I independently sought out an internship with an outpatient therapy center. I participated in that during my senior year of undergrad. There I had the opportunity to collaborate with therapists and outpatients of diverse abilities and mental health needs and could incorporate some of the creative arts activities I learned about in my "Art as Therapy" course.

I am proud to share that I am a first-generation college student and I graduated with a BA in Psychology from Ramapo College in 2010! A challenging aspect about my experience as an undergrad was finances: completing unpaid internships and sacrificing a social life for paid work. My incentive throughout was that financial stability meant independence and never having to go back. Still, I should better have utilized the advisors and supports that were available at my college, as this could have saved tuition money. Going for a social work major would also have provided a more realistic view of the field post-graduation.

I soon realized that in order to secure a position in the field, I would need a minimum of a master's degree and began looking into different majors at various institutions of higher education. I was drawn to the human rights and social justice foundation of social work; it was a flexible degree, and licensable.

I applied to Fordham University's master's in social work (MSW) program, was accepted, and in my studies made the Dean's List. My first year MSW internship was working with older adults in independent living and assisted living facilities where I had the opportunity to learn about the function of the Department of Health and to provide therapy and case management services.

My second year MSW internship was with a program that worked with families who were referred by Child Protective Services. In this program I worked with guardians who lost custody of their children due to abuse and/or neglect, and those guardians were working towards reunification with their children. In this role I provided therapeutic supervised visitations, facilitated groups, wrote court reports and provided case management services. I learned that my experience growing up, although isolating, was not unique. I also observed how differently the system treated people of diverse backgrounds. I am grateful to the inspiring mentor I worked with at my second year MSW internship who hired me and continues to support me.

I graduated with my master's degree in social work from Fordham in 2013 and subsequently went on to earn my license in Social Work (LSW) and then my clinical license in Social Work (LCSW)!

As I reflect on the progress of my education, I realize that my interest in entering the field was aroused by the adversities in my life and failure of systems that might help: medical, police, legal, school, family or even bystanders who did not intervene. I recognized that the only way to impact the system towards change was to become part of it, to tackle it from the inside out. This is what motivates me.

I am grateful for the opportunity to work with a domestic violence organization, specifically in an outpatient creative arts based program for adult and child survivors. I not only served in this role within my program, but increasingly was requested to support additional projects in other programs such as supporting clients going to the Prosecutor's office for trial prep; public speaking engagements at area high schools.

During this time, I also independently earned certifications from a paralegal program and victim advocacy program. This investment helped me expand my skillset to better support my clients. Considering my next steps, I applied for and obtained certifications in Executive Non-Profit Leadership and Clinical Social Work Supervision. There was a time when I considered applying to law school and I very well might have if it didn't involve taking out more student loans.

In my career, I have collaborated with my mentors in trainings; done fee-for-service work with a private practice; worked at a special needs camp; provided supplemental supervision for LSW's working towards clinical hours; and went back to Ramapo to speak with students in the "Community Mental Health" course to share about my career journey and opportunities post-graduation.

It took me a long time to realize that I had subconsciously learned to cope by throwing myself into school, subsequent certification programs, and work because that was easier to focus on, kept me busy, provided external reinforcement, a sense of accomplishment—and safety.

Slowing down is hard. Shifting gears to focus on my work/life balance is one of the most painful processes I am still negotiating, but at this stage of my career and life journey, I have to sacrifice my passion of working with survivors of domestic violence for a better work/life balance, a more realistic schedule, better financial compensation with improved benefits, the protection of a union and a pension: practical considerations in today's economy.

It really took me a while to not feel like a sellout, but I ultimately realized that self-neglect was a form of selling out myself. Shifting my mindset was necessary to work toward balance for all areas of my health. Social workers don't need to be martyrs; it's okay to choose ourselves too.

My first job in a public school was as a Mental Health Clinician, providing school-based counseling, in class lessons, trainings, program development and crisis intervention.

I currently work as a School Social Worker at a public school. The majority of my work includes collaborating with staff and families, evaluations, developing Individualized Education Plans (IEP's) and school-based counseling. Now in a public school, I may view my impact as advocating for an appropriate placement or therapies for a child, greater accessibility for learning, connecting families with resources and related advocacy.

What brings me joy in my daily work are those moments when a colleague shows that they value my input, when a parent expresses gratitude, or when a child shows growth. Acknowledgement is rare and progress can be inconsistent, but I strive to find glimmers in every day.

I have heard people say that they think social workers get "burnt out" because of the work. I would strongly disagree and push back on that and highlight that it is rather the unsustainable conditions of the work that push social workers out of the field. Some issues that *I* have seen in the field are ethical and legal conflicts, pressure to make decisions which might jeopardize my license, high case loads, no breaks, carry over work after hours, low financial return for the cost investment of education and certifications, lack of leadership, worker safety, politics and conflicting interests of stakeholders.

I have learned some harsh realities as well: the business of business is business and at the end of the day, every employer is a business. There is no ideal situation, job, pay, boss, client or workplace culture, just environments with different pros and cons. For me it is now about creating a path that can lead me closest to the life I want to create while making a positive impact.

I would encourage you who are entering or in the field to separate your value as a social worker from that which you have as a human being and to fill your cup with aspects outside of your work identity. I am still working on this. I have been fortunate enough to develop friendships and a professional network through the years. I encourage you to learn from those gems of people and nurture those relationships, for they will be a life raft of guidance during challenging work situations and a support when you are job searching.

I have a quote posted by my workspace to help ground me: "Grant me the strength to accept the things that I cannot change, the courage to change the things that I can, and the wisdom to know the difference." The quote is familiar from AA, NA or Al-Anon, but I find the reminder helpful in all aspects of my personal and professional life.

The core of social work is about social justice and the attempt to disrupt broken systems. The problem is, however, that we often can't do this without risking our job security. Therefore, we need to pick our battles and then carefully choose how to approach them. For me, learning that I have a voice and using it strategically for the justice I seek has been the equivalent of walking on a balance beam surrounded by hot coals.

One of the most valuable lessons I have learned is that social work isn't about a specific approach, intervention or methodology when working with people—especially trauma survivors. It is about connection, grieving, finding corrective experiences, healing attachment wounds, regulating the nervous system and empowering people to see possibilities within and beyond themselves. We as humans have a much greater capacity for resilience and growth than we realize; we just need a little help to see it.

Chapter 23

Music in the Prisons

Invited Essay by Andy Teirstein

Arts Professor, New York University Prison Education Program

Breaking Out in Song: Music in the Prison

There are very few times when a person is removed from common society and placed out of sight. It happens when someone is ill, or when someone dies. And we do it in our penal system, where an incarcerated individual is isolated. After several years of very little educational programming, an increasing number of prisons are once again facilitating education in partnership with universities, providing a sense of community that comes with classroom learning. Within this framework, the arts can play a meaningful role. When a teaching artist steps into a prison, the tools of self-expression are brought into the isolated space. The arts are about connection. They can create a bridge, a way for an individual to reach out to others. What is the effect of art in a prison? And what is the effect that prison work can have on the teaching artist?

Beyond the Campus

Artists are often drawn to borders. We're fascinated by the edges of society, and what some refer to as the "contact zone," the point at which different cultures meet. As a professor and a composer, I decided some years ago to reach beyond my campus classes and go behind the wall, into prisons. What follows are some general reflections on the experience of working in a men's correctional facility, and a few of the challenges and insights that one may encounter.

On the first day of a semester, after being processed through the gates and the metal detectors, hearing the loud buzz and the metal bolts snapping open, the teaching artist enters a room that may seem to be full of imposing men, convicted criminals, many having committed violent crimes. But by the second week, as discussion and group work evolves, there is a sense of community, essential to the classroom. Some of the men may have trepidation about taking classes, and many have significant fear of expressing themselves. On that first day, they are also checking the teacher out, wondering, *is this going to be okay?* Engaging with the arts may be a new experience for them, which can be challenging. The teacher

DOI: 10.4324/9781003592693-31

needs to find a welcoming path into creative work. Many participants are likely to find it difficult to sing, and especially to move their bodies with music in the group setting. Movement, as I will discuss, can be a transformative key. As they become more comfortable with the creative environment, they begin to explore the process of working with music and creating songs. The teaching artist quickly comes to understand that these are men who miss their parents, spouses, siblings and friends, and who are willingly engaging in education as a step in rebuilding their broken lives. They have requested to be permitted to take courses, and they value the class time.

Maximum Security

The United States doesn't have *one* criminal legal system; we have a myriad of federal, state, local and tribal systems—at a cost of at least $182 billion each year. You may have heard about Rikers Island in New York City. Suicide rates there continue to climb. The city recently agreed to pay more than 28 million dollars to Nicholas Feliciano's family. He tried to take his life in 2019, as the guards waited eight minutes to open the cell door, and he suffered severe brain damage as a result. Contrary to closing, Rikers has grown by 11% since 2022, and 87% of the incarcerated individuals there are awaiting pre-trial hearings. But what of all the institutions that are not on your radar, the ones you don't hear about? In my limited experience, much depends on the specific prison administration, the Deputy Superintendents and Correction Officers.

For several years I went into a maximum security prison. I was working with a theater director, on plays like *Twelve Angry Men* and *Julius Caeser*. I have no photos of my work in these places. Cell phones, electronic watches, recording equipment, or any computing devices, are not allowed in. You get your TB shots, clear the requirements, get fingerprinted and leave everything at the gate. You're told not to wear green; if there's a riot, they would need to be able to quickly pull you out. When we did *12 Angry Men*, we were granted permission to bring a pair of pants and a shirt for each actor. Imagine that you have been wearing green pajamas for 20, 30 years, and then, one day, you put on a pair of slacks and a white button shirt. A feeling of transformation descends on the room. The first time I saw this happen I was moved—to observe the men putting on their costumes, and see how lucky they felt, how honored and elevated, how their faces beamed. Sometimes we were permitted to present a performance to the other incarcerated individuals. For a couple of these, outsiders were allowed to attend, including incarcerated individuals' family members. At other times this was not permitted, depending on prison guidelines.

Movement and Rhythm

In order to reach the final performance, we did improvisation work, building the confidence to perform in a group. As I mentioned above, getting incarcerated individuals to move their bodies is a challenge. Movement is the key. We hold our histories, both cultural, familial, but also personal, in our bodies. At first, they feel like it's not cool to move. But with a little rhythm, it becomes inviting and enjoyable. We begin with simple movement and sound exercises, standing in a circle. An easy folk song can be used as call and response, repeating lines and then finding a clapped rhythm. Once they are comfortable with this chant, an improvisational layer can be added, and they begin creating word couplets in rhythm. It is good to have a similar format for each class meeting, beginning with the song circle, and then embarking on a series of exercises in basic musicianship, including elemental music reading skills, harmony and rhythmic training. The goal of the course is for each participant to create one complete song by the end of the semester.

Creative Process and Community Building

To create a song, one needs to write lyrics. The blues, as a musical genre, provides a historical root at the basis of many American song styles. Students begin with creating blues lyrics and move from there into rap, country, rock, Latin and other song styles. In creating lyrics, students learn to free associate in writing. They begin by responding to prompts. For instance, I may ask them to describe a significant person in their lives. They create word collections on these assigned themes, which are then written on the blackboard. The process of creating a song is personal. It entails introspection, reflection and emotional engagement. But once the student has expressed an emotional concept in word phrases, the class can help in the process of sorting and editing them into song lyrics. At times they work in small groups, learning to collaborate. The musical concept of ensemble is a model. In a musical ensemble, each member of the group plays a role in producing the song. Although they've been incarcerated together, it's a new experience to work together with movement, music and poetry. Over several weeks, if class is working well, they develop a degree of spontaneity, improvising words over a rhythm held by the group. These two tools, improvisation and collaboration, are the essential ingredients of developmental work in the performing arts, and they can also be personally and socially transformational. After the song is created, there is the act of singing it, which is a separate, sometimes larger challenge for incarcerated individuals. It requires enormous confidence to stand in front of a group and project clearly and expressively.

Telling One Another's Stories

I recall one student, we'll call him James, who pulled me aside as he entered the class and told me he didn't want to have to tell his own story. I assured him he would not be required to do anything he didn't want to do. At some point in the class, I had planned to have them write about a transformational moment in their lives, positive or negative. As they worked on this exercise, I considered the next step, where they would read their writing aloud, and I looked at James. I knew that this would be frightening for him, a moment of vulnerability in the group. So, I pivoted. Instead of asking them to read their own writings, I put them into pairs and had them spend some time learning their partner's story. They then developed a monologue, telling their partner's story in the first person, as if it were their own. When James's turn came, he was able to tell his partner's story as though he were the one who had experienced it. The class cheered him on. From James, I learned that a voice can be released through partnership, and that an individual can be empowered by another's story. This is one example of how the teaching artist can learn from working in a community setting.

Challenges

The carceral system is not built for classwork, and there are stumbling blocks. It may be rare to have all the group together for the allotted class time, as some will be called out for different duties at periodic intervals, called "movement." And there are other disruptions. At one facility, there was an incarcerated individual who seemed to be a promising actor—a poet and a good mover. We were doing an adaptation of *Moby Dick,* and he stopped showing up for the meetings. There had, apparently, been an altercation in a hallway during movement, and this person wound up in solitary confinement. That was before the HALT act was passed in 2021, Humane Alternatives to Long-Term Solitary Confinement. But even now, the Correctional Association of New York, an independent organization that monitors prison conditions, found numerous departures from basic adherence to HALT, in some cases resulting in individuals being placed in solitary confinement for up to six times longer than the law allows.

NYU Prison Education

In 2015, NYU started the Prison Education Program at Wallkill Correctional Facility, a medium-security prison in upstate New York. The NYU program does a superb, mindful and supportive orientation for the professors. The participants at PEP are not called inmates or prisoners. They're students. Most of the men in this facility come there from other prisons, toward the end of lengthy sentences, and do their last few years at Wallkill. In addition to a music class, NYU offers courses in Math, Environmental Science, Sociology, Public Health, Creative Writing, History and other topics. Through this program, they can get an Associate's Degree in Liberal Studies; they can also be part of NYU's Bridge Program, which, upon reentry, helps them make the difficult transition back into larger society. In some cases, they can begin studying at the Manhattan campus to receive a Bachelor's Degree.

Ensemble

The Arts can play a significant role in prison education. Artists are trained to observe, listen and to collaborate. When I go into the prison, I'm aware that I'm crossing a border. And I leave the prison each week humming the new song fragments that were created inside. In this passage, in both directions, there is the potential for new perspective. In the performing arts we learn the meaning of ensemble. We learn about the power of improvisation. We strive to be active culturally, not passive. Artists, like most other people, try to use what they've learned, the skills they've honed, to make a living, to get ahead, maybe even to compete for a leading role or a world premiere. But the training that we receive as artists can also be directly impactful on communities. And community work can be meaningful to our own lives in ways we might not anticipate. It's not easy work. These are unwieldy institutions, and there's scant money for it. But it is rewarding in the only way that is truly priceless: as lived experience.

Sources

Carlton, Genevieve. "Second Chance Programs Increase Access to Higher Education." https://www.bestcolleges.com/blog/second-chance-programs/. Last modified March 24, 2023.

Prison Policy Initiative. Accessed October 21, 2014. https://www.prisonpolicy.org/research/education/.

New York University Prison Education Program. Accessed October 21, 2024. https://prisoneducation.nyu.edu/.

Equal Justice Initiative. "Criminal Justice Reform." Accessed October 21, 2024. https://eji.org/criminal-justice-reform/.

Chapter 24

The Brain and Art in Collaboration

This chapter is addressed directly to you, the reader, head on, immersed as it is on that region of your body that holds all the remarkable endowments that can combine to produce a creative work. You are the organizer, college student, group participant or overseer engaged in the process of making art. When you create images in art which grow out of your sensitivities, emotions and experiences, you focus upon and organize those visual expressions. The result of this concentrated effort using the multiple resources of your personality produces something of importance. A receptive absorption of that effort by others who are open to it deepens their understanding of their own emotions and experiences. In this way, art becomes a link to meaningful communication. This two-way operation is replete with innumerable synaptic connections as the neurotransmitters of both artist and audience fire in the brains of each. All this worthy traffic is over and beyond the multiple other processes engaged in the actual act of making art.

For you the art maker, there is the exciting integration of energy, vision, intelligence, sensitivity and emotion, passing through specific processes and emerging into an eventual product. It is, in each instance, a journey of discovery about yourself and your perceptions of the world around you. More about that as we proceed through some of the surprising effects of art making on the brain and on general well- being.

The Hidden Power of Art Making

Much has been learned about the brain since researchers using positron emission tomography (PET) scans and other imagery techniques have been able to look inside the living brain. Far from a luxury, as art often figures to be—drapery for the essential room—the arts can be remarkably effective in changing lives, mentally and physically. Awakening the senses, reviving memories, soothing the caprices of the body and bringing meaning to experience, art making helps the person meet its brain with new self-confidence, ready to take on new challenges and endeavors, each one ever more enriching the brain's own power to grow itself.

DOI: 10.4324/9781003592693-32

Learning empowers the brain, has it growing ever more cells and synaptic connections. And self-confidence is a key factor in learning. No one can respect the validity of what is perceived without self-confidence. Seeing enlightens perception through self-confidence, through placing *value* on one's observations.

Making art—approaching a piece of paper, placing a production upon it that emanates from your mind and hand not ever there before and embellishing it with color, or squeezing a mound of clay into an original shape—what power. What control a young child feels, knowing and possessing something others don't. No wonder children instinctively love art and will draw on walls or in the sand if their environment affords no other way. While on the topic, if you the reader are a parent of a young child, you will find it productive to buy some white shelf paper to cover a table with to make a great white wave of drawable space.

It should be noted that children are motivated by their own markings on paper. As they make these markings, they are moved to produce others. It is scribbling now but will be pictures later and then words and reading and composing. But neurons are firing with every progression, so what children do at each stage helps the brain steer them to doing more. Could the same development occur without drawing or sculpting, simply with toys? Probably, but not so comprehensively, using so many brain resources at once: color decisions, manipulating textures, hand/eye observation and application, mind/body coordination, all compressed into short time spans with easy accessibility to continued experimentation.

Learning and the Arts

Your brain affords every opportunity for learning even before birth and throughout your life. Billions of neurons form in embryo and in infancy, linking up to create trillions of synaptic connections with use. Neurons that are not used or can't be are pruned away but some will last through old age. Children seem naturally inclined to creative pursuits in the early years as if programed to make use of their vast neural powers. Art making, like movement and play, is eagerly taken up, activities that create new neural pathways and connections, and with this, learning.

We all want our children to be good at learning, but childhood strengths are not patient reasoning, intellectual deduction and sequential logic, which is how we sometimes approach the task. The natural inclinations of youth can be summed up by three attributes. We know them well because they sometimes drive us crazy: vivid imagination, abundant physical energy and a burning need for self-expression.

How well the arts fit these talents. (Just about every mature artist we know has managed to keep those same childhood traits and use them.) **Imagination** in children's play enlivens the child's efforts to understand—what if, why, how, where?—helping to solve the mysteries of everyday life. Watching young children at play, pretending this or that action—boats at violent sea with couch bolsters, for one example—I see the neural activity, the brain power fired off for learning and understand why imagination figures so prominently in their play.

It is what they use to conjure the mysteries of the world to bring back to their lairs, transforming the unknowable around them into play and thereby under their control.

Their bodies are fitted to do this vanquishing of the unknown by the **physical energy** with which with young children are endowed, a fuel naturally loaded during their waking days to help them *go for it*. This purpose and energy combines with an urgency for **self-expression**, evident since birth with the evocation of their cries and smiles relayed to those who care for them: vital expressions depended upon for their survival.

So, encouraging kids to use in productive ways what they already have plenty of—imagination, physical energy and methods of self-expression—enhances that total sense of well-being because it is already something kids do well and they know it. When kids feel they are good at something, they feel pretty good about themselves. When things feel balanced from within without excessive anger or resentment or confusion, kids are free to reach outward to take things in. Their brains are receptive to learning. Building a foundation of self-worth is a bedrock against those debilitating situations sure to come. And making art has the attributes that help this along. It's a no-brainer.

It is not a stretch to observe that those three traits of childhood—imagination, physical energy, and the urgency for self-expression—means by which children incorporate in their lives their truths and solutions—are those of the practicing artist, all three needed to generate original productions.

For Whom the Brain Toils

It toils for you. All parts of you. As you and the participants in your group join you in art making, your mind is problem-solving (frontal lobe); your hands are working (cerebellum); your eyes are focusing (occipital lobe); your sense of touch is engaged (parietal lobe); your grasp of spatial relationships is sharpening (so called right brain); your emotions are engaged and you are admitting new knowledge and efforts into consciousness (so called left brain); you are bringing the memory of other experiences to the tasks (the limbic system); and all this while you are having fun and producing something tangible.

The brain controls and regulates all of our internal organs. What if we had to program our heart beats, push buttons to digest our food, pull strings to lift our arms and bend our joints? So involved with our functions we would be, we could do little else like hold a job, play, love, create. Well, the brain just as mysteriously performs other functions we do not consciously see but feel and intuit: our understanding, emotions, creativity, sensitivity.

Emotions and Sensitivities

It is wise not to underestimate the role of the brain in the domain of our emotions, as this plays a major role in using the information that is there; attention paid to our senses as well. The brain seeks information from the senses to determine what connections to keep and what to prune away. Emotional well-being is as important as intellectual growth, though the effort at enhancement of a child's emotional well-being can regrettably be overlooked given the plethora of routines that encompass *a day in the life*. The tasks at hand will take priority, emotions will feel overwhelming, mistakes and rebukes will occur, and consequent criticism or self-flagellating can be crushing.

Curiosity and its Rewards

There is an invigorating effect on the brain and increased feeling of general well-being involved in *viewing* art, as well as making it. The natural curiosity we were born with and exercised so extensively as children, our brains have fed on, regrowing itself with use as in everything. Curiosity figures in our eagerness to view and understand art (all arts—drama, literature, music, dance). Curiosity is an evolutionary need. Its impact on our lives is immeasurable: responsible for our lofty scientific advances, our attraction to any and all of the arts to ascertain knowledge, to discover meaning and find entertainment; our outreach to anything and anyone that catches our fancy. In doing all that, curiosity is responsible for our survival; we're programmed to want to get to the bottom of things, to fathom the meaning. Curiosity is what we're engaged in when we focus on some original idea that compels our understanding. Probably, this is why we love crime stories so much in books and on TV, probing the clues for who done it. Wherever it takes us, curiosity is a scout that bursts upon the world to find its riches; the arts are exceedingly good at taking us to those places of discovery. The area of the brain most responsible for that search for meaning is the hippocampus and satisfying that curiosity is dopamine, the brain's reward chemical, filling you with happiness. What a happy thing it is that the more curiosity we have which we move to satisfy, the more our brain cells multiply to keep up.

Brain Works

Maintaining levels of attention is a challenge for most of us in this chaotic world with so much going on in and around us personally and globally. We think we can cut through it and get everything done in the time we have by accomplishing several things at once. But multitasking, contrary to common thinking, is not easily done by humans. The brain cannot do it; instead it toggles quickly between tasks so it appears you are doing two things at once. I found this true eating my morning breakfast cereal. If I put on the TV and listened to the news as I ate, I was not tasting the burst of flavor from the blueberries in my dish. The moment I focused on the food, I actually *tasted* it. I had to choose which was most important for me at the time, I couldn't have both. Just one at a time. I tested myself to see if even thinking random thoughts was an intrusion on the sensations attending the food, and sadly it was. No tart blueberry taste burst upon my brain until I mentally fastened on the berries.

Young children start out wanting to see and experience everything, naturally eager to learn; that is the norm of human nature. Later, something thwarts that drive and many children find learning simply a task. Distracted, perhaps, by transient life of the moment, these children have not developed attention-based executive function skills and are unable to incorporate the necessary executive function of reflection. Children who lack executive function skills struggle not only in school but in life, say the authors of *Your Brain on Art* (Magsamen and Ross, 2023). The authors do not take a stance that this failure should be addressed in the schools and home but instead bring attention to the arts which can activate the neural connections related to executive function as well as other regions of the brain and strengthen them.

What *can* be addressed in school and home, in this author's view, is building on the self-assurance that making art provides: "Hey, I'm good at this!" And getting excited by the next new challenge, new ideas, new learning. Feeling good about past success at learning and looking forward to the next. The brain which strives to do what you want it to do picks up on that and helps speed, not slow the task of learning.

Happening mainly in the prefrontal cortex, the functions of working memory, cognition, and inhibitory control combine with other areas of the brain to promote the actions involved in learning. Effective learning involves recruiting multiple areas of the brain. But using these resources effectively requires an attitude of self-confidence conveying "Hey, I'm good at this! what's next?"

Inventiveness, Vision and Taking Risks

In making art, as in other endeavors involving a degree of challenge, taking risks goes with the territory. Art teachers who will be using this book to guide those in their charge know this full well. Some participants in the program will be familiar with taking risks, perhaps in more consequential ways, lured by the excitement in it. But those new to artistic excursions, as many will be who are participating in the program, might be encouraged from the start towards this attitude. All should begin this launch of bravado by abandoning cliche images such as hearts, mushrooms, balloon letters and so on.

Instead, search for images that have some relation to yourself: your interests, personality, experiences, recollections. Perhaps you already find these in nature—a fascination with spiders, a love of trees—or a particular sport; or in family; or in feelings that inspire or anger or threaten you; or experiences generated by memorable events, by travel, by life itself.

Artistic "accidents" can help make such meaningful content come to the fore. The methods described in the art and social interaction program with their emphasis on spontaneity, will cause you to produce "accidents," unique events which may alternately dismay and delight you. Let these events *lead you* at times, while at other times you may *lead them* to where you want to go—a puddle of paint pushed into forms. Sometimes it is the newness of the art methods and materials that motivates creativity, inspiring you to produce something fresh and original, a surprise to yourself.

Projects need not be contrived or "gimmicky" to be fresh and new. Instead, surprise might be the change of colors as paints mix, or the blend of wet-on-wet watercolors, or color transformations when wet tissues are overlaid upon each other, or the emergence of shapes that morph into images you recognize from your life. Guiding such elements of change is understandably exciting, for you are controlling and mastering events.

Ultimately, it is your personal vision from which you will produce original art. With thoughtfulness, inventiveness and the courage to be honest, you will find that vision. A fascinating accompaniment to this bravado of invention is the brain's approval: firing neurons and sending dopamine, the happy neurotransmitter, your way with each achievement.

An Attitude of Openness

Whether professional or lay artist, having an attitude of openness is a challenge; it's always easier to do things in the tried and true way. The irony is, the way may be tried, but it is not always true, for truth lies in continual discovery. A minimal study of the brain leaves the reader to conclude how maximal is the element of newness and discovery in its workings. So use your brain, which is there for you—only you—there to do what it "thinks" you want. Unlike everything else in the world and every other person in the world, that entity is *there for you alone with no other priority.*

Allow yourself to be open and honest as you explore art-making. Remain open, as you begin each project, to discovering what the medium itself can do; and be open, as well, to what may be lurking in your heart and mind and sensibilities, waiting to find expression. Openness to the challenging adventure of art might be one of your most difficult tasks in the beginning and you will recognize this if you find yourself reverting to the safe images you feel comfortable with.

Many of us do not honor our personal vision, accepting only the validation of "professionals" to determine beauty and meaning. Those external viewpoints should not be ignored but balanced by the validation of our own perceptions. How we see is intimately related to our personalities, insights, wisdom and wit; our sensitivities, tempo, and our concepts of self.

An attitude of openness is also necessary for those observing and perhaps evaluating what you produce. Viewers who see your work may be limited in their aesthetic awareness or their familiarity with the processes you've used. The viewer, as well as the artist, must try to be open to new ways of seeing. Rich rewards can follow in enhanced communication and understanding.

Spontaneity

The blank paper surface can feel almost threatening to adults new to visual arts creation in its invitation to failure. But art making designed to be more intuitive than reflective can often stop fear at the pass. For this reason projects in the manual are created to encourage spontaneity. An example of such a project is "free form drawing." The project emanates from a scribble. The scribble is a "warm-up" for free spontaneous imagery, much like scales are a warm up for piano playing. Though the word "scribble" tends to be associated with childish or inconsequential action, it is far from that when it leads, as it inevitably does, to the creative discoveries found in "free form drawing." In the free form project you *select* from the many lines and designs you produce rather than *decide* what to put down on the paper.

Other processes such as colored ink pictures and tissue collage are similarly designed as processes which may help you try new things with less fear of risk.

As your exploration with the projects moves on, you will recognize the importance of *process* over *end product* and understand that each move generates other moves and all experience counts. You don't "ruin" an art work; you *use* the effort, subsequently in a different version of that work, or in a more confident effort down the line.

Freedom and Confinement

Participants in the Art and Social Interaction Program are by the nature of their situations often confined in some way. An absence of control in some aspect of their life may affect their freedom of choice or mobility or actions: incarcerated individuals confined by their situation; mentally ill individuals confined by the inability of their mind to fully function; the frail elderly, confined by the physical capability of their bodies. Other freedoms exist such as the restrictions imposed by poverty and the inability to move to better conditions. In each of these situations art can help to alleviate the sting of confinement if not the actualities of situation, status, place and time. Making art embodies freedom.

Freedom to portray what you want in the way that you want, without risk.
Freedom that puts you in control.
Freedom in the artistic process: to choose color, line, design, texture and image.
Freedom to move forms through space.
Freedom to direct your inner emotions and perceptions of reality onto a medium of your choosing—paper, cardboard, clay—and manipulate it as you please.
Freedom to make artistic decisions, which may increase your ability to make personal decisions and thereby strengthen your competence and power.

Learning Throughout Life

An enormity of neural activity occurs in the first several months of life, billions of neurons reaching out to billions of other neurons to form trillions of connections, exuberant with electrical activity. These connections begin to decline, connections surviving or dying depending on mental stimulation or need to adapt to demands of the environment one is born into. A surge of neural activity, however, occurs again in adolescence. The onset of all this new chemical energy is beneficial for a host of reasons and needed with the onset of puberty but can have negative effects as well: rebellious behavior of teenagers towards their family for some, a reckless outreach for thrills and adventure for others for whom the mature understanding of consequences has not yet taken hold. Mistakes that ensue can cost one's freedom.

The burst of neural energy at this time, robust as it is, presents an opportunity to take advantage of the challenges embodied in the arts. All artistic disciplines whether visual art, music, dance, drama or writing, are repositories to which that new surge of chemical energy searching for neural pathways can be directed. Most contain opportunities for introspection; offer built in progressions for success; contain occasions for praise and commendation so needed at this time; and illuminate engaging glimpses towards prospects for the future. What should be recognized whatever endeavor is pursued within the fervency of this time—perhaps sports will fill the urgency or obsessive spurts of reading, eating, fantasy—is that it is a volatile time with energies to burn—or not.

Learning, we know, continues throughout life. Brain cells survive through the surges of separate stages of development. They are available if they are used. Such use means activating brain cells to make connections: thinking, inventing, perceiving, exploring, figuring out; in short, exercising the physical, emotional, perceptive and cognitive resources that our brains, devoted as they are to our personal survivals, provide.

One of the most productive ways to use the biological miracle of synoptic connections is to engage in hands-on creativity. This is because creativity makes use of just about all of our diverse capabilities, doing so in the rewarding service of producing something original. This book aims to have you and those diverse others you have come to know make all sorts of things that promise to be unique by introducing the art making experience. This will happen because of the unique perceptions, sensitivities and experiences every one of you bring to them.

Sources

Davis, Joel. *Mapping the Mind: The Secrets of the Human Brain and How it Works*. Secaucus, NJ: Carol Publishing Co., 1997.

Dowling, John. *Creating Mind*. New York and London: W.W. Norton, 1998.

Kotulak, Ronald. *Inside the Brain: Revolutionary Discoveries of How the Mind Works*. Kansas City, MO: Andrews McMeel Publishing Co., 1996.

Magsamen, Susan and Ross, Ivy. *Your Brain on Art: How the Arts Transform Us*. New York: Penguin Random House, 2023.

Nash, J. Madeleine. "Fertile Minds." *Time*, February 3, 1997.

Peck, Judith. *Art Activities for Mind and Imagination*. Mahwah, NJ: Imagination Arts, 2004.

Peck, Judith. *Smart Starts in the Arts*. Mahwah, NJ: Imagination Arts, 2003.

Ramsburg, Dawn. "Brain Development in Young Children." *Parent News*, April 1997.

Ratey, John J., M.D. *A User's Guide to the Brain*. New York: Pantheon, 2001.

Sylwester, Robert. "Art for the Brain's Sake." *Educational Leadership*, 56 (3): 31–35, November, 1998.

The Secret Life of the Brain, Thirteen/WNET New York, distributed by PBS Home Video. www.pbs.org, 2001.

Chapter 25

Artwork by Participants in the Institutions

It is deserving that the final chapter in this book be devoted to a sampling of art created by the individuals in the sites while they participated in the art workshop series. It is a benefit to the book that some of these artworks survived the sessions and can be shown, as art is intended to go with the creator or alternatively the institution. So, how did the artworks survive and why are there so few?

Plans for the art projects are presented at each site by the students and produced in a single session of the ten week series. Whatever the distinctive medium is for that session, participants can always simply draw freely instead. At the end of each session, participants are encouraged to take finished work with them back to their rooms or wherever they wish. Some do not want them, some present their work as a gift to a student, some are taken to hang on the walls by line staff attending the sessions, others are left on the tables (sometimes taken from the trash, which is always a little heartbreaking) where students gather them up to bring back to class. These are the ones we retain.

The following pages contain a selection of artworks from these sources, produced during the art and social interaction sessions. **Most project illustrations are available to view in color online at www.routledge.com/9781032972008.**

Art created by jail inmates
Art created by psychiatric patients
Art created by youth in the psychiatric hospital
Art created by troubled youth in facilities of the Dept. of Youth and Family Services

Reading the Picture

It is the nature of art to be able sometimes to speak in pictures more aptly than words when emotions are expressed. As in novels when a metaphor brings a statement to life, an image can strike directly at our hearts. If we as the viewer or reader of that art are sensitive and have empathy, the unspoken message of the picture will seep into the mind and we then

DOI: 10.4324/9781003592693-33

become aware of people, situations, the bitter *taste* of anger. It is no longer the sight or sound of something coming from afar. It is the taste.

Students are strictly advised not to analyze the drawings in any way, as they are not therapists, nor are they to engage in any therapeutic way with their subjects. Their position is to present their natural status as interested college students sharing their expertise in the joys and benefits of art activity.

There is no analysis given here of the drawings—again that is not within the purpose of the course, notwithstanding that it will interest viewers and possibly lead to a desire for further understanding which they might seek and find elsewhere—but there is a productive way to *look* at the drawings.

The reader is urged to *read* the art as you look at it. This is how to look at any work of art which interests you as you pass by it in a museum or gallery. *Say* what you are seeing (to yourself is fine). Often a cliché will come to mind (it's for good reason, cliché's became cliché's—they are usually universal emotions.

For example, in the first picture by a jail inmate serving time, what is seen is a clenched fist, about to strike something red and yellow which covers a quarter of the page: a brick wall. Hitting a brick wall, a cliché which expresses the frustration and helplessness this conjures.

Drawings by Incarcerated Men

These four pictures came from inmates at a county jail. Though some detainees, as they may be termed, are already serving time, others are incarcerated while still awaiting trial. The situation, accordingly, is tense.

Figure 25.1 depicts a clenched fist, about to strike something that covers a quarter of the page. It is assumed to be a brick wall. The hand is grey, the color of pallor but also steel, whereas the arm started off flesh color. Dark strokes run down to the wrist, possibly hair. There is nothing else in the picture. Reading what you see can lead you to the artist's intent and as you sense the rage of the person drawing, you may feel you know more about him than if you met him in person.

In Figure 25.2 the meticulously drawn head and torso of this woman, who could be a man, is frightening with her multi-horned headdress, fierce expression, dark, decorated brow and neck collar made of bones. A rabbit's tail for luck or hand grenade hangs down from a chain. Grasping a sword, the figure is armed to fight. The drawing is unquestionably beautiful in its rage.

In Figure 25.3, a humorous picture drawn by an inmate, we see the bare buttocks and flailing legs and feet of a burly man, who wears a belt like Santa, in a plunge down the chimney soon to land on flaming logs below. What a mistake he's made! But he can't easily change his course of action, he's in a hot spot. The chimney itself is carefully constructed—clear even stripes drawn to show this—with neat, well-organized things placed on the mantle. Even the logs are perfect. Everything is nice and tidy until he gets himself stuck there.

Figure 25.1 Inmate crayon drawing of a fist striking a brick wall

Figure 25.2 Inmate drawing of a woman with horns, and a neck collar of bones

Figure 25.3 Inmate drawing of man plunging down chimney toward the heat of burning logs

Figure 25.4 Inmate drawing of monster with hands like claws

In Figure 25.4 the head and arms of a bearded monster appears to glare at whoever dares to come near. His hands are poised to grip like sharp daggers. Out of his head grow two ram's horns, crosses and a sword. What should be his eyes are two menacing swirls shaped like frowning eyebrows.

Art by Patients in a Psychiatric Hospital

The next four pictures were produced by patients in the chronic ward (long term patients) of a psychiatric hospital.

Figure 25.5, titled "Burning Tree," shows what looks to be an eye clasped in the center of the tree as it goes up in flames.

Figure 25.6 depicts an open eye surrounded by what seems to be hair. It is, to this viewer, a study in puzzlement uttered with dots, dashes and slashes of bright paint.

In Figure 25.7 a horrified face looks down at a bright flower clasped in her small hand, which she is about to place in a vase. The vase already contains a multitude of leaves, a few falling out which lay beside it. The few faint strokes making up the body fade away before forming, so there is no actual body, only arms. The face is enclosed with a thick rim. The eyes and mouth are drawn with repeated circles around them and the pupils are heavily blackened.

Figure 25.8 is drawing by a psychiatric patient and shows a figure with head and arms but no body. The head has a dark eye and ear. The missing body has six dark buttons.

Figure 25.5 Psychiatric patient crayon drawing of an eye on a burning tree

Figure 25.6 Psychiatric patient painting of an eye surrounded by hair and dotted lines

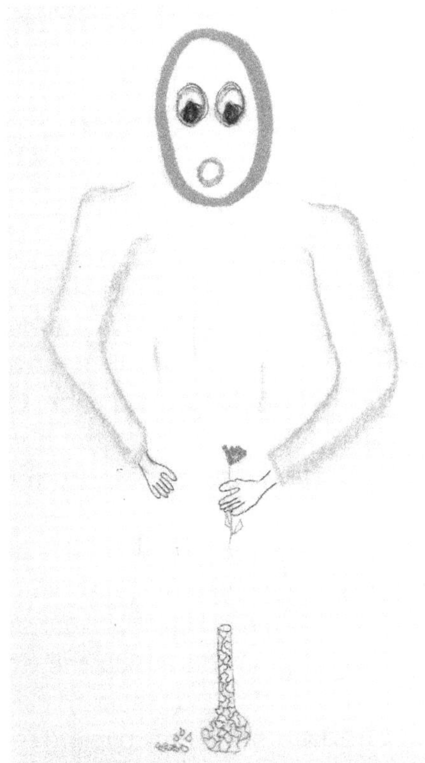

Figure 25.7 Psychiatric patient picture in mixed media of a woman staring, mouth open, at flower being placed in a broken vase

Figure 25.8 Psychiatric patient drawing of head and arms of figure with dark eyes, ear and buttons, absent a body

Drawings by Youth in a Children's Psychiatric Hospital

The next three pictures are by youth in a children's psychiatric center, a facility where dedicated professionals help children during long- or short-term stays heal from trauma.

Reading the picture in Figure 25.9 is painful by any standard. The abuse to every part of his body is made evident. Every feature of his face is broken, torn or bruised, he is hurt from head to toe where bare toes protrude from his ripped shoe. One arm has been severed and lies on the floor, the rips still showing. But his belt is tight, blazing black as are his boots, his mouth sneers with teeth bared and the words coming from the battered face is "I be back bud—y"

Figure 25.10 is a tissue collage picture of a house on fire made by an adolescent boy. He used the attribute of tissue bleeding color when it is dampened to express the violence. The upstairs rooms are ablaze with fire. The door, large, black and without a handle, is still intact but fire blazes in the back. The bright grass on which the dark emblazoned house stands seems untouched.

A different youth at the children's psychiatric hospital created the portrait in Figure 25.11. He too is bruised. The shape of his face is wobbly; he frowns and his teeth are bared. He is holding a knife in one hand and a chain in the other. He means to do business. He is obviously angry but he has drawn a figure intact, clothes fine, shoes neatly laced.

Figure 25.9 Youth drawing from Children's Psychiatric Hospital shows a horribly bruised boy threatening retaliation

Figure 25.10 Youth drawing from Children's Psychiatric Hospital, tissue collage picture of a burning house.

Figure 25.11 Youth drawing from Children's Psychiatric Hospital depicts a bruised child of 11 holding steel chain and knife

Drawings by Children Cared for by YCS, Youth Consultation Services

The last set of pictures was drawn by children living in a residence provided by the Department of Youth and Family Services having been removed from families for cause until the families could take safe care of them.

In Figure 25.12 the central figure stands in the water, mouth open screaming, arms stretched wide. In the foreground are large, menacing fish, all but one his own size or larger. They are pictured ferocious, teeth bared. One has in its jaws the bottom of the boy's leg which it has presumably torn off. A severed lower arm lies bleeding in the water. Both severed limbs of the boy are shown bleeding. Four birds and two butterflies are flying in the sky close to the boy as if watching—or are they there to somehow help—and a sun shines brightly in the corner.

Figure 25.12 Youth drawing from YCS of boy standing in water, screaming at monster fish who have torn off his arm and leg.

Figure 25.13 drawn by a boy in that same facility and similar circumstance includes the face only of a person. The eyes are huge, dark black, and from them two large tear drops fall from each eye. The mouth also is huge spreading wide with vertical and horizontal lines showing teeth bared. The artist has scribbled his name (not shown) and other markings over the large sheet of paper as if there was more he still needed to say.

The picture in Figure 25.14 might speak for them all. This is a collage in which shapes are cut out from magazines to make a picture. In this collage it appears a boy is being caught by the leg by a terrestrial monster. The boy has had a limb severed (as in other pictures seen in this collection by different teen and pre-teen boys); in the picture the torn leg is in the monster's mouth even as it attacks the other leg. The cry for help is as carefully cut and pasted as is everything else. The words occupy a large portion of one whole side of the picture. A terrestrial vehicle flies calmly above. The cut-outs (in color) on the monster and help sign (not on the boy) make a stark contrast to the black cardboard base.

Figure 25.13 Youth drawing from YCS of a face with bared teeth and streaming tears.

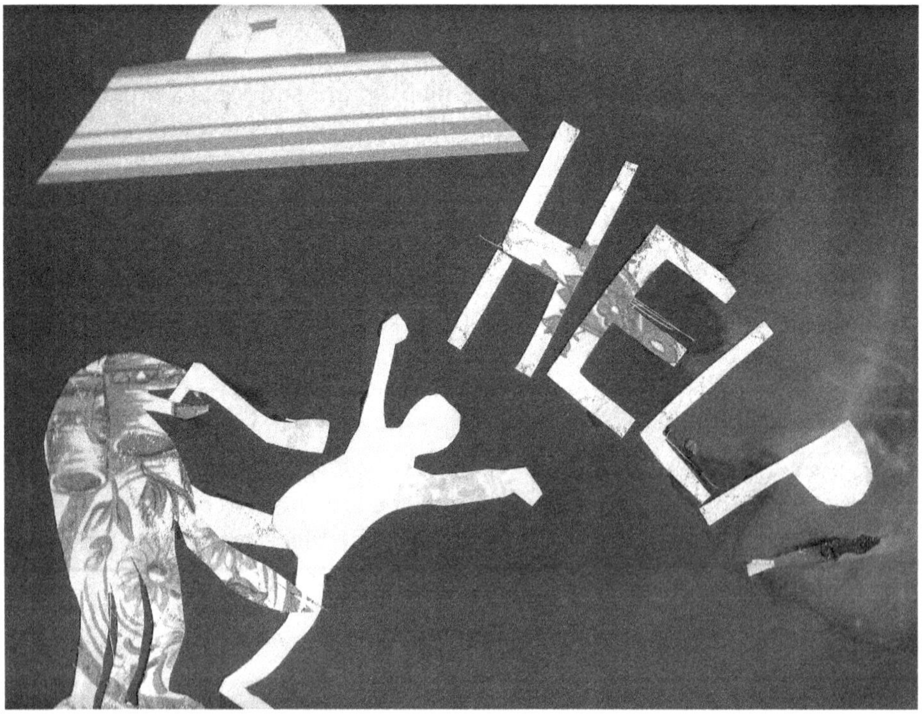

Figure 25.14 Collage by youth from YCS of a monster attacking a boy. HELP in large letters is cut and pasted on.

The Body Keeps the Score, Dr. Bessel van der Kolk has titled his seminal book. Certainly, the eruptions of the body onto the page that are seen here are almost *heard* as well, in the forceful evocations of abuse and trauma in the images.

But often, what is heard are whispers only, as the well-known resilience of children appears on their pages; the bloom of flowers more than the bleak of clouds; and rain, if it appears at all alongside children, might have umbrellas in the picture. Grown-ups do as much with humor. The pair of defenseless buttocks hurtling toward the steaming hot logs looks funny, but the mistake that Santa made to put himself in that position is anything but funny. And there is no going back.

No interpretation of participant drawings occurs during the art workshops. Students are not trained in such analysis, but other professionals available to the institution have such training and the art produced might provide a resource for understanding not otherwise available.

After Thoughts

What is evident in all the pictures is that an opportunity is afforded with the time, space and materials to make of this what you want and need. Not so in life but here the paper is your own, as is the hand, the eyes, the thoughts and the freedom to use it all. The freedom presents itself to allow you to control that aspect of your actions with whatever purpose is in your mind or heart, or with no purpose at all, only to feel okay and enjoy a passing feeling of joy. All that is enhanced in the act of making the picture—the freedom, purpose and joy—especially when you feel it safe to share with a caring person sitting beside you.

The opportunity exists for knowledge to pass between the artists, as presenter and participant create their pictures. That knowledge has wings to take each of you separately beyond the institution's walls to settle somewhere else. And who knows yet, where that will be?

Annotated Bibliography

Chermayeff, S. "The Shape of Humanism." In G. Battcock, ed. *New Ideas in Art Education: A Critical Anthology.* New York: E. P. Dutton, 1973, p 9.

A discussion of creative human concerns in the relatively unsympathetic environment of urgent contemporary issues.

Churchill, A. *Art for Preadolescents.* New York: McGraw-Hill, 1971.

An examination of artistic development in preadolescents, including projects for effective personal involvement.

Claxton, G. *Intelligence in the Flesh.* New Haven and London: Yale University Press, 2015.

Using neuroscience and psychology the author argues that functions of the body perform the intelligence for our moves—mind, body and emotions together embodying intelligence, not solely the brain which gets the credit. How as the natural doers and makers we are, intelligence is revealed in the craft of what we do, not solely cognitive function.

Edwards, B. *Drawing on the Artist Within.* New York: Simon & Schuster, 1986.

From the author of *Drawing on the Right Side of the Brain*, this book continues an emphasis on accessing natural creativity by releasing ingrained inhibitions.

Feldman, E. *Becoming Human Through Art.* Englewood Cliffs, New Jersey: Prentice-Hall, 1970.

Advocates the use of visual imagery in education along with its verbal associations.

Goffman, E. *Asylums.* Garden City, New York: Doubleday and Co., 1961.

A classic in the literature concerning the negative effects of institutionalization; a comprehensive description of the "total institution" and the people trapped within it.

Grandin, T. *Visual Thinking.* New York: Riverhead Books, 2022.

Visual thinkers are different, she argues, and contrary to belief may form a larger constituency than thinkers geared to the verbal. Education, parenting and hiring should be aware of this and make wider use of the productivity, innovation and problem-solving gifts natural to that way of thinking.

Gussak, David. *Drawing Time: Art Therapy in Prisons and Other Correctional Settings.* Chicago: Magnolia Street Publishers, 1997.

Provides a comprehensive history of art therapy in prisons and explains how uniquely beneficial art therapy can be.

Gussak, David. *Art and Art Therapy with the Imprisoned: Re-Creating Identity.* London: Routledge, Taylor & Francis Group 2019

Using interviews and discussions with inmates as well as art therapists and individual artists who have worked in prisons globally along with other avenues of investigation, the author explores the issue of personal identity among the incarcerated and how art can be effective.

Gussak, David *The Frenzied Dance of Art and Violence.* Oxford: Oxford University Press, 2022

An exploration of the potent dual nature of art-making as a way to mitigate violent inclinations and as a tool to regain control amidst turmoil.

Hammer, E. *Clinical Application of Projective Techniques*. Springfield, IL: Charles C. Thomas, 1958.
An examination of the use of projective techniques (patient drawing of the house, tree and person) in clinical evaluation.

Henley, D. R. *Exceptional Children, Exceptional Art*: Worcester, MA: Davis Publications, 1992.
Teaching art to special needs individuals.

Jenkins, T. S. (ed.). *Family, Community, and Higher Education*. London: Routledge, Taylor & Francis Group, 2012.
Explores the various ways in which the family unit influences and impacts college students.

Jonas, D. and Jonas, D. *Young Till We Die*. New York: Coward McCann and Goghegan, 1973.
A challenge to the elderly to maintain their place as society's elders to benefit society and themselves.

Johnson, R. N. *Aggression in Man and Animals*. Philadelphia, London and Toronto: W.B. Saunders, 1972.
Laboratory research and theory concerning aggressive behaviour with emphasis on the implications for contemporary man.

Kramer, E. *Art as Therapy with Children*. New York: Schocken Books, 1979.
A psychoanalytic approach to art therapy with disturbed, handicapped and normal children, using case histories to examine the interrelating ties between the therapist and patient.

Kransky, B. and Steffen, S. L. *Engaging Classrooms and Communities through Art: The Guide to Designing and Implementing Community-Based Art Education*. Lanham, MD: Altimira Press, 2008.
Describes the value of making art in the community and the cultural benefits of creativity and diversity in these endeavours.

Landgarten, H. *Clinical Art Therapy*. New York: Brunner/Mazel, 1981.
Offers a lucid and comprehensive insight into the breadth and depth of art therapy, including many case histories and numerous illustrations.

Lanier, V. "Art and the Disadvantaged." In G. Battcock, ed. *New Ideas in Art Education: A Critical Anthology*. New York: E. P. Dutton, 1973.
Argues for a kind of art education in ghetto areas unique to that culture and advocates confrontation with one's environment through art.

Lorenz, K. *On Aggression*. New York and London: Harcourt Brace Jovanovich, 1974.
An in-depth analysis of man's behavior patterns as compared with the action and controls and bonding affiliation demonstrated in aggressive animal drives.

Magsamen, S. and Ross, I. *Your Brain on Art*. New York: Random House, 2023.
Using research in neuroscience and body function, the authors reveal the enriching influence that engagement in the arts has on everyday life whether as arts maker or observer.

Malchiodi, C. A. (ed.). *Handbook of Art Therapy* (2nd ed.) New York: Guilford Press, 2012.
Informative chapters dealing with a multitude of situations where art therapy and imaginative problem solving were effective interventions.

Malchiodi, C. A. (ed.). *Art Therapy and Health Care*, New York: Guilford Press, 2013.
Demonstrates the benefits of creative expression for both youth and adults living with acute or chronic illness. Presents strategies to help patients cope with physical and cognitive symptoms, reduce stress and improve quality of life.

May, R. *The Courage to Create*. New York: W.W. Norton, 1975.
A defense of creativity as an inner power and a necessity for survival.

McNiff, S. *Art Heals: How Creativity Cures the Soul*. Kindle Edition, 2004.
A leader in the field of art therapy explains the ways in which art can heal.

Mehrabian, A. *Public Places and Private Spaces*. New York: Basic Books, 1976.
Observations on the psychological and sociological effects of the environment on self and community, as seen in public housing, public spaces and institutions.

Mella, D. L. *The Language of Color*. New York: Warner Books, 1988.
Describes emotional associations with various colors and how color association can be used in understanding personality and in healing.

Nietzel, M. *Crime and Its Modification*. New York: Pergamon Press, 1979.
A thorough discourse on crime and criminal behavior with its social, economic and psychological implications; includes studies concerning ways and means of modifying crime through penology and the law.

Peck, J. *Art Activities for Mind and Imagination*. Mahwah, NJ: Imagination Arts Publications, 2004.
Offers projects in drawing, collage, painting, sculpture and jewelry to encourage improvisation and originality; includes references to the association of brain dynamics to creativity.

Peck, J. *Artistic Crafts: Inventive Creations from Cast-offs*. Mahwah, NJ: Imagination Arts Publications, 2004.
Provides methods to create various projects in crafts with emphasis on using everyday materials and discarded materials in inventive ways.

Peck, J. *Sculpture as Experience: Working with Clay, Wire, Wax, Plaster, and Found Objects* (2nd ed.). Iola, WI: Krause Publications, 2007.
Using illustrations in color of completed work and the how-to of process provides instructions for working in a variety of three-dimensional media with methods requiring minimum technology, materials and space.

Proshansky, H. et al. *Environmental Psychology: People and their Physical Settings* (2nd ed.). New York: Holt Rinehart and Winston, 1976.
A lengthy text by several contributors dealing with the impact of the home, workplace, recreational and other environments on psychological well-being.

Rogers, C. and Weller, S. (eds.) *Understanding Caring Relations, Identities and Cultures*. London: Routledge, 2012.
Explores what care means in contemporary society, how it is practiced in different contexts and what resources we use to care about others and ourselves.

Ruben, G. *Life in Five Senses*. New York: Crown, Penguin Random House, 2023.
A personalized argument for the realization the author came to that her five senses accounted for much of her happiness. Citing the science involved in the five senses she offers practical ways to incorporate them into life's enjoyment and understanding.

Rubin, J. *The Art of Art Therapy*. New York: Brunner/Mazel, 1984.
A much read book by a leading practitioner in the field offering a general understanding of the need and use of art therapy with various age groups in diverse settings.

Sarma, S. with Yoquinto, L. *Grasp: The Science Transforming How We Learn*. New York: Doubleday, 2020
Far from an ordeal, humans are built as a species to learn, to take in the adventure imbedded in the world we live in that our curiosity arouses. Opening the reader to this notion and the ways to grasp it through neuroscience, cognitive psychology and more is the journey taken in this book.

Silver, R. (ed.). *Aggression and Depression Assessed through Art*: New York: Brunner Routledge, 2005.
Uses a draw-a-story technique and art to identify and help children and adolescents at risk.

Sommer, R. *Tight Spaces: Hard Architecture and How to Humanize It*. Englewood Cliffs: Prentice-Hall, 1974.
Examines the relationship of architectural space in institutions to the problems of its occupants and demonstrates how "hard" space reinforces negative behavior.

Sutherland, E. and Cressy, D. *Treatise on Crime* (7th ed.). Cited by Wilson, J. Q. in "Crime and the Criminologist," *Commentary Magazine*, 59 (l), July 1974: 48–50.
Argues that a primary cause of criminal behavior may be social factors including peer influence and the difficulties involved in counteracting these.

Sutherland, E. H., Cressey, D. and Luckenbill, D. F. *Treatise on Crime* (11th edition). Lanham, MD: Rowman & Littlefield, 1992.
This is the eleventh, expanded edition of *Treatise on Crime*, a much referred to book about the sources of criminal behavior.

Van der Kolk, Bessel, M.D. *The Body Keeps the Score*. New York: Viking, 2014.
An integration of brain science and knowledge of the body amassed through decades of clinical practice. The doctor delivers a trenchant understanding of trauma and stress and delves deeply into methods of healing. The book has become a vital resource for physicians and family in the grips of trauma and depression.

Wagner, B. (ed.). *Symbolic Transformation: The Mind in Movement through Culture and Society*. London: Routledge, Taylor & Francis Group, 2009.
Explores how culture and mind are related through symbols as we think, act, imagine, feel, dream and remember.

Wilson, J. Q. *Thinking About Crime*. New York: Vintage Books, 1975.
Analysis in straightforward language of types of crime, theories about crime and concepts of rehabilitation, reinforcement and deterrence.

Winner, E. *Invented Worlds: The Psychology of the Arts*. Cambridge: Harvard University Press, 1982.
Discusses the origin, import and impact of creative processes through examinations in the fields of painting, music and literature; includes consideration of child art and art of the mentally ill.

Yochelson, S. and Samenow, S. E. *The Criminal Personality: A Profile for Change*. (Vol 1). New York: Jason Aronson, 1976.
A heavily researched treatise offering knowledge and insights into criminal thinking and attitudes.

Appendix 1

Instruments for Class and Fieldwork

Appendix 1.A Course Syllabus

This sample syllabus from the program at Ramapo College will change in each section according to how a faculty leader designs the course. The structure, in its completeness, is offered for ease in adapting content to different constituents, focus and needs.

ART AND SOCIAL INTERACTION

Course Description

Students acquire the methods to work creatively with groups that for complex sociological reasons live peripherally to the mainstream of society. Students select one site for ten weeks of the semester and two additional sites as guest presenters to present weekly one-hour art workshops in small teams. Projects in drawing, painting, sculpture and selected crafts are learned in class sessions, as is the approach to informal join-in social interaction. Groups served include jail inmates, the frail elderly, psychiatric patients, hospitalized veterans, abused or disturbed youth in residences, youth of low-income housing developments, and women and children residing in domestic violence shelters.

Objectives for Students

The background, approach, projects and fieldwork are designed to:

A. Increase skills in perception, listening and observing.
B. Stimulate imagination and motivate productive creative activity.
C. Provide increased understanding of some of the complexities and problems of contemporary society: crime, drugs, old age, mental illness, poverty, domestic violence and veteran's issues by contact with individuals affected.
D. Encourage students to probe their own place in society, see themselves in a wider context, confront attitudes, determine values.
E. Permit a keener conceptual understanding of freedom—what it is, what it means and what endangers it—by meeting persons to whom freedom is limited.
F. Provide an exposure to the unique freedom embodied in art whereby memories and emotions can be liberated while the body remains in confinement.

G. Introduce approaches and projects that particularly emphasize evocative personal expression through visual art processes and product.

Objectives for Institutional and Agency Participants

The objectives in B, F and G are similar. The fundamental objective is to create an accessible program of artistic expression that is personal, informal and non-competitive, in which work on the projects and informal social interaction with college students may enhance self-esteem, encourage communication and form an effective bridge to mainstream life beyond the facility.

Course Content and Approximate Schedule

Class Schedule (Note: Classes Meet Twice Weekly)

WEEK 1: Introduction of students. Overview of course content and goals. Analysis of syllabus. Introduction of the project free form drawing. Short video: Art on the Outside

Home assignments: create an artistic personal Name Tag; complete the Fee Form Drawing adding color, obtain books.

WEEK 2: Background information about selected institutions and agencies. Methods for conducting appropriate critiques in institutions. Discussion of freedom and confinement and how this issue is seen within different institutions. Review of projects.

Introduction of projects, Collage and Oil Pastels

Student straw vote on site selection.

Home assignment: Photo Collage on a meaningful theme. Readings in *Art and Social Interaction*: Chapters 2 and 3. Readings on the effects of institutionalization, *Asylums*—Part I

WEEK 3: Analysis of site populations and related responsibilities. Review of projects and readings. Dinner Party project (in groups creating a picture of a meal as if seated with others at a dinner party).

Orientation on campus announcement: Room location and date Thursday regular class time. Representatives from participating institutions speak and respond to questions on the nature of their institutions and clientele. Students should bring their personal schedule of classes and work to be able to select days and times for their fieldwork. Master Chart is prepared; on-site Orientations are arranged.

Home assignment: Readings in *Art and Social Interaction* Chapters 4 and 12. Create Folder (a creative construction paper holder of your own artwork).

WEEK 4: Analysis of log writing with examples provided. Discussion of Master Chart: corrections and adjustments of student teams. Introduction of Strip Paper project; review of Folders.

Assignment: Theme drawing. Log submission related to on-site orientation. Readings in *Art and Social Interaction*. Chapters 5–6.

WEEK 5: Discussion of individual group responses to site orientations. Problem-solving. Further presentation of well-written logs if needed. Introduction of painting techniques in Watercolor. Introduction of journal-keeping for extra credit: for example, collecting news articles and/or book excerpts on crime, child abuse, domestic violence, old age, mental illness, drug abuse and related topics discussed in the course. Journal due at 13th class.

Assignment: Logs. Readings in *Art and Social Interaction* Chapters 10 and 13.

WEEK 6: Group discussion and problem-solving relevant to sessions at sites. Individual team meetings in faculty office about the progress and plans of the group at field sites. Review of Watercolor paintings. Introduction of Acrylic painting on paper and cardboard.

Home assignment: Readings (Chapter 24). Logs. Readings in *Art and Social Interaction* Chapter 14.

WEEK 7: Individual private critiques on writing: grammar and style; review of logs. Introduction of Tissue Collage project on paper and object.

Home assignment: Logs. Bring in theme-based Collage Cutouts collected in separate envelopes for use at sites; suggested topics: food, vehicles, furnishings, people, lifestyle, sports, emotions. Read *Thinking about Crime* on causes and effects of crime; be prepared to discuss this. Read Chapter 15 to study and begin to plan projects for workshops.

WEEK 8: Group problem-solving discussion and plans for sites. Small group planning for site presentations. Presentation of Sculpture Technique Clay and *Femo*.

Home assignment: Logs. Quiz on reading assignments.

WEEK 9: Quiz due. On-going site problem-solving techniques. Presentation of Sculpture Technique Foil and Plaster Wrap. Individual private writing critiques on writing grammar and style. Discussion of leave-taking at sites.

Home assignment: Logs. Complete Foil Sculpture. Read *Art and Social Interaction* Chapter 17.

WEEK 10: On-going site problem-solving techniques. Small group planning for site presentations Presentation of Sculpture Techniques Paper and Wood Shapes. Critiques of completed Clay and Foil Sculpture.

Home assignment: Logs. Complete Sculpture projects. Prepare journal—extra credit project.

WEEK 11: On-going site problem-solving techniques. Small group planning for site presentations. Presentation of Craft Technique Painting on Plaster. Individual critiques of logs.

Home assignment: Logs. Complete Painting on Plaster project. Plan additional two sites to visit.

WEEK 12: Small group planning for site presentations. Problem-solving. Introduction of Puppets. Planning final site sessions; optional certificate presentations to participants; final leave-taking discussion and effective procedures.

Home assignment: Found Object Jewelry. Logs; reflection paper.

WEEK 13: Journals due and discussed. Review of Jewelry project. Introduction of Copper Enamel Jewelry. Reflection paper due. Assembling art projects for final class.

Home assignment: Logs, make-up projects

WEEK 14: Evaluation of art projects done throughout the semester. Students leave all projects on tables with name visible, leave class and return to pick up work.

WEEK 15: Party for students, at College, professor's home or elsewhere to be announced.

Fieldwork

1 Twelve sessions in all (ten in each primary site plus two additional sites to gain wider exposure), each approximately 1.5 hours, including set-up, session and post-session discussion with representative. Students choose their sites from

participating institutions and agencies. Projects and materials for sessions are prepared during class time.

2 An on-site orientation to each of the primary sites selected is made prior to the start of the working series. These sessions count within the ten scheduled.

Course Requirements

1 Logs, written shortly after each fieldwork session and submitted weekly. Papers are due one week after the conducted session. Because timeliness is important for valid recollections, one grade point is deducted per week for lateness. The text *Art & Social Interaction* contains helpful components for writing comprehensive logs.
2 Completion of art projects.
3 A paper following the orientation to the facility, describing sensual and visual impressions, preconceived ideas, encounters, observations and reactions to the facility and its clientele.
4 (For suggested, extra credit): Informal journal kept throughout course including news clippings that relate current events to the experiences encountered in sites.
5 Preparation for take-home quiz and group discussions related to readings.

Required and Suggested Readings*

Butler, R. N. and Lewis, M. I. *Aging and Mental Health* (2nd edition). St. Louis, MO: C.V. Mosby Co., 1977. (Sug.)
Goffman, E. *Asylums*. Garden City, New York: Doubleday, 1961. (Req.)
Kramer, E. *Childhood and Art Therapy*. New York: Schocken Books, 1979. (Sug.)
Magsamen, S. and Ross, I. *Your Brain on Art*. New York: Penguin Random House, 2023 (Req.)
Peck, J. *Art and Social Interaction*. New York and London: Routledge, 2025. (Req.)*
Peck, J. *Art Activities for Mind and Imagination*, Mahwah, NJ: Imagination Arts Publications, 2004 (Req.) *
Peck, J. *Artistic Crafts: Inventive Creations with Cast-offs*, Mahwah, NJ: Imagination Arts Publications, 2004 (Req.) *
Wilson, J. Q. *Thinking About Crime*. New York: Vintage, 1975. (Sug.)

* All proceeds of Peck's publications included in the course taught at Ramapo are contributed to the Ramapo College of New Jersey Foundation.

Materials:

Tools, equipment and bulk materials are supplied. Students will have an expenditure of approximately $8.00 for a supply kit of emergency art materials.

GRADING (in order of importance)

1 Depth and thoroughness of logs and papers (double counted)
2 Management of selected field sites (double counted)
3 Class participation*
4 Extent and quality of art projects completed in and out of class.

*Class participation includes the following:

On time and consistent attendance
Responsiveness and participation in class discussion
Help and cooperation in assembling materials for field sites
Class participation in project preparation, critiques and cleanup
Quiz results

CEC EXPERIENTIAL COMPONENT
This requirement is not extra but built into the course, which includes substantial hours of experience outside of the classroom in the institutions served. Student teams should confer with an appropriate site representative after each workshop session for approximately 15 to 20 minutes to maximize this experience.

ELECTRONIC FORM OF COMMUNICATION
In accordance with college policy, students will be communicated about all course-related matters via Ramapo College email addresses (@ramapo.edu).

POLICY ON ACADEMIC INTEGRITY
Students are expected to read and understand Ramapo College's academic integrity policy found in the College Catalogue. Members of the Ramapo College Community are expected to be honest and forthright in their academic endeavors. Students who violate this policy will be referred to the Office of the Provost.

CELL PHONES AND TEXTING
Students will be given an opportunity in class for these communications but are not to use communication devices during class time. Consistent disregard of this proscription will result in a diminished participation grade.

STUDENTS WITH DISABILITIES
Students with documented disabilities registered with the Office of Specialized Services (OSS) should speak to the professor so that adequate arrangements can be made.

Appendix 1.B Log Cover Sheet

Log Cover Sheet

Your name ____________________
Name of site ____________________
Date of session ____________________
Date of writing log ____________________
Session number ____________________

Project for this session ____________________
Provider of materials for this session ____________________
Site representative present ____________________
Other students present ____________________
Number of participants at this session ____________________
If possible, indicate by name those who were present____________________
____
____
If possible, indicate by name those who were **not** present and why:____________________
____
____

Circle overall rating of the quality and effectiveness of this session:

1 Excellent
2 Above average
3 Average
4 Below average
5 Poor

Circle overall rating of the quality and effectiveness of the project:

1 Excellent
2 Above average
3 Average
4 Below average
5 Poor

Appendix 1.C Log Format

Log Format

Guidelines: Logs should be written the same day as the session or as soon after as possible. They are best written in narrative form using the outline below **only as a guide** to help you. **Each question need not be responded to but used to sharpen your observations.**

Part 1: The Log Cover Sheet (fill out completely).

Part 2: Observations about the content of the session.

1 Briefly describe the focus and intent of the art project.
2 Describe anything relevant about the preparation of material, the working area or logistical problems encountered in conducting the workshop.
3 What was your mood or general attitude that day?

4 What was your first impression as the session began? How were you received by the participants when you arrived? How were you received by the staff on duty?
5 What was the general mood or overall reaction of the participants to the session?
6 Was there anything unusual or different about this session?
7 Discuss any problems or difficulties with the session.
8 Summarize any significant conversations:
   i With participants
   ii With staff members
   iii With other students

9 Were there any distractions during this session?
10 Evaluate the success or failure of the art project by responding to the following:
   i Did the participants get involved?
   ii Were they motivated?
   iii Did they finish?
   iv Did they cooperate with you?
   v Did they cooperate with each other?
   vi Did they appear satisfied with their work? How did you determine this?
   vii What happened to the creative objects?
11 Compare this **art project** with previous art projects, giving it a number rating, using a scale of 1 (high) to 5 (low).
12 Compare this session with other sessions on a scale of 1 (high) to 5 (low).

Part 3: Observations of individuals. There may not be time during your session for this assessment; use these notes to lessen generalities and specify your observations.

1 Describe some of the individuals with whom you specifically worked.
   i Give their names, approximate ages and any relevant physical characteristics. Do not quiz them, ascertain through observation and conversation.
   ii If possible, pick up background from staff members.
2 Describe your personal impressions.
3 Describe the individual's attitude toward you and toward the project: initial reactions and later ones.
4 Determine the indication of any medication or health problems or extraneous family or social concerns that might have affected an individual's participation.
5 Can you get any feeling of daily lives and routines in the institution?
6 Describe any future- or goal-oriented comments made and any discussions pertaining to that topic.
7 Are there any indications that the sessions are affecting the regular activities of the participants outside of the sessions?
8 Describe the parting at the end of the session.

Appendix 2

Resources of the Pilot Program

Appendix 2.A Evaluators of the Pilot Program

Roger N. Johnson, Ph.D., former Professor of Psychology, Ramapo College of New Jersey, formerly teaching at Amherst College and Tufts University; author of numerous research publications, including the text, *Aggression in Man and Animals*.

Paul H. Humphreys, Ph.D., former Associate Professor of Psychology, Ramapo College of New Jersey, formerly teaching at University of Illinois; practicing psychotherapist.

Paul Elovitz, Ph.D., A Founding Faculty of Ramapo College of New Jersey teaching history, psychohistory and interdisciplinary studies; previously taught at Temple, Rutgers and Fairleigh Dickinson Universities. Among 390 publications on creativity, presidential psychobiography, psychohistory and teaching are eight books. He is a research psychoanalyst, founder of the Psychohistory Forum (1982–>), editor of Clio's Psyche (1994–>) and a past president of the International Psychohistorical Association.

Bernard L. Charles, Ed.D., former Dean of Academic Affairs and Professor of Education, Livingston College, Rutgers University. Program Officer for the Carnegie Corporation, Chairman of the Public Education Association, NYC; President of the Institute for Mediation and Conflict Resolution; Senior Advisor to the Governor's Advisory Committee on Black Affairs for New York State.

Spenser Jameson, Ed.D., Assistant Professor of Curriculum and Teaching, Teachers College, Columbia University; President of the Accelerated Program for Learning, NYC.

Eleanor Charles, M.A., former Assistant Professor of American Studies, Ramapo College of New Jersey. Head Arts Committee of the NAACP Legal Defense Fund, and fund raiser for Delta Sigma Theta Sorority, Inc., a public service sorority raising college scholarship funds for deserving students from the Harlem community.

Appendix 2.B References to the Art and Social Interaction Pilot Program

For all resources listed below, contact:
Dr. Judith Peck: judithpeck@optonline.net

1. Film: "Art on the Outside": a 17-minute, 16-mm color film presenting an overview of art and interaction. Scenes include classroom work and sessions with inmates in a maximum-security jail, residents in a nursing home and children in an urban housing project. (The film was a finalist in the American Film Festival, 1981, category of Education.) See below for video adaptation of the film.
2. Available 2014: A 9-minute YouTube video of the program: https://www.youtube.com/watch?v=zdjPyMonTd0.
3. The Places and the People of the Program, a chart listing facility, type of clientele served and location of site.
4. News media references to the program.
5. Taped student/participant interviews.
6. Representative evaluations of the program by members of the evaluation team.
7. Representative evaluations of the program by staff of institutions and agencies.

Appendix 3

Evaluation Instruments

Instruments designed to evaluate the effectiveness of the program in meeting its objectives for presenters, participants and institutions are offered on the following pages.

The letters, "P," "I," "E" and "C" refer, respectively, to "Presenters," "Institutions," "Evaluators" and "Clients" and indicate in most cases the intended source of the response. Note: the word "clients" is substituted for "participants" to avoid confusion in the letter designations.

All instruments should be considered **optional** and used only if evaluation is deemed necessary or desirable. Actual functioning of the program does not depend on evaluation, though funding and continuation in the institutions or the college may require some form of assessment of its goals and outcomes.

Appendix 3.A Evaluation Instruments for the Art and Social Interaction Program

"P" refers to Presenters
"E" refers to Evaluators
"C" refers to Clients (Participants)
"I" refers to Institutions

P.1. *Pre-program Background Information Sheet*, to be filled out by presenters before their exposure to the program to determine existing expectations and opinions.

P.2. *Post-program Information Sheet*, to be filled out by presenters after the series is over to determine any change in opinions and values.

P.3. *Log Cover Sheet and Log Format*, to be used as a guide by students or other presenters to evaluate each art and interaction session. The log format addresses all aspects of participation and progress (found as Appendix 1.B and 1.C on previous pages).

P.4. *Client Report Sheet*, a scaled assessment to be filled out by presenters and analyzed at the end of the series. The questions address (1) client attitude and involvement in the session, and (2) changes in client attitude and involvement observed from week to week.

P.5. *Observations for Measuring Program Effectiveness*, observations made by presenters concerning client attitude and responsiveness.

P.6. *Questionnaire for Previous Presenters*, a survey to be sent to former students several years after their participation to determine academic, career and personal values attributed to their experiences in the program.

I.1. *Advisement Letter to Institutions*, a document requesting evaluation input. The letter is not an instrument but prepares the groundwork for evaluation (Insert 10.2 in text).

I.2. *Guidelines for Final Institutional Evaluation*, for use by institutional representatives at the end of the series to assess client responses and indications of program effectiveness.

E.1. *Plan of Operation for Evaluators*, suggested procedures to use over the course of the series by outside evaluators.

E.2. *Format for Evaluation Team Report*, suggested categories of observation for outside evaluators' review of the program in its various sites.

C.1. Participant Questionnaire, a brief questionnaire designed to elicit direct response to the program, to be completed toward the end of the series or at the final session.

Appendix 3.B Evaluation Instruments for Presenters

P.1 Pre-program Background Information Sheet

1 Give some description about your background in art or art-related activities.
2 What prior experience or association have you had with institutional settings?
3 What are your expectations about this program and why did you choose to participate in it?
4 List any special skills, talents or directions which you hope to pursue in the course of this program.
5 Do you have any thoughts or feelings about the following? Use the reverse side:
   a Penal institutions and inmates
   b Psychiatric facilities and patients
   c Nursing homes and the aged
   d Delinquent youth
   e Abused children
   f Low-income housing projects and poverty
   g Domestic abuse shelters and spousal abuse

P.2 Post-program Information Sheet

1 Were your expectations of this program met or not met? Please explain.
2 With which of the following constituents were you most involved over the course of the program? Circle all those that apply.
a) Jail or prison inmates, b) Psychiatric hospital patients, c) Mental health clinic outpatients, d) Senior citizens, e) Frail elderly, f) Youth in need of supervision, g) Abused children, h) Children and mothers in domestic abuse shelters
3 Have your thoughts, perceptions or feelings changed in any way as a result of your participation in this program? Please explain.

P.3 Log Cover Sheet and Log Format

The Log Cover Sheet and Log Format are labeled Appendix 1.B and 1.C and are found on previous pages.

P.4 Participant Report Sheet

Date: ______________________
Participant's name ____
Facility ____
Circle the most appropriate marking:
Scale A: Your Observations about the Response to the Current Session
Mood: Excellent Good Fair Poor
Enthusiasm: Excellent Good Fair Poor
Sociability: Excellent Good Fair Poor
Involvement: Excellent Good Fair Poor
in Project:
Scale B: Changes you observed in progressive sessions
Mood and attitude toward session: Improvement No Change Decline
Socialization with presenters: Improvement No Change Decline
Socialization with other participants Improvement No Change Decline
Comments:

P.5 Suggested Observations for Measuring Program Effectiveness

Factors which add input to evaluation of the sessions are grouped into categories below: Some assessment can appropriately be made only by staff; others by presenters.

Arrival behavior:

Participant attendance as compared with other events.
Welcoming attitude: the nature of greetings; for example, remembering names, friendly smiles.
Demonstrations of anticipation: waiting for presenters before their arrival.
Arriving with work done during the week, such as art or poetry.

Admission to the program:

Are there waiting lists?
What are the reasons for wanting entrance: prior experience with art, seeing the opposite sex, diversion of everyday routine, word-of-mouth recommendations?

Sitting modalities:

Saving places for presenters.
Changes from sitting alone to sitting with others.
Sitting in the same familiar place with a sense of belonging in the group, or claiming established territory for the private art experience.
Hesitancy or enthusiasm about sitting down and getting to work.

Nature of discussions:

Changes in discussions about the future: goals, school, work, career; requests for information about opportunities.
Changes noticed in comfort with verbal socialization or confidence to engage in conversation.

Demonstrations of accomplishment:

Observed attempts at trying new things.
Disposition of finished work-discarded, left on tables, taken to rooms or homes, hung on walls, given as gifts (and to whom?).

Institutional interest:

Renewal of requests and new requests by institutions and agencies for the services of the program.
Increased participation or comments by staff during sessions.

P.6 Questionnaire for Previous Presenters

Looking back on the Art and Interaction program, how would you rate it?
(1) Extremely valuable; (2) above average; (3) average; (4) below average; (5) poor.
Has the program led to any changes in your life?
(1) Definite changes; (2) some changes; (3) minor changes; (4) no changes.

Please elaborate on any changes on the reverse side. Also check where appropriate below.
The program:

_______ helped me formulate career goals.
_______ caused me to change my previous career goals.
_______ helped me to get a job. (Name job).
_______ helped me determine a course of study.
_______ made what I learned in other studies more meaningful.

_______ had little effect on my career.
_______ had little effect on my education.

Please rate each of the following as:
1 = very important; 2 = moderately important; 3 = not very important

_______ learning the art projects.
_______ writing logs.
_______ seeing the various institutions and agencies.
_______ being able to know the client participants.
_______ developing friendships with other presenters.
_______ the satisfaction of helping others.
_______ improving my self-esteem and confidence.
_______ learning to work with others.
_______ becoming aware of social problems.
_______ learning responsibility and self-discipline.

Do you feel that you really helped at least some of the client participants?

(1) Yes, some in an important way; (2) Yes, some in a small way; (3) I don't think I had any effect on them; (4) I am not sure whether or not I had any effect. Please comment on reverse side.

Did any of the client participants have a lasting effect on you?

(1) Definitely, yes; (2) A slight effect; (3) No lasting effect.

On the reverse side, please name any client participants you can remember.

If you had it to do over again, would you participate in the program again?

(1) Yes, definitely; (2) probably, yes; (3) probably, no; (4) definitely, no.

Thank you for your help. Indicate your name if you wish (optional) and make any additional comments on the reverse side.

Year of participation in the program ____________________

Appendix 3.C Evaluation Instruments for Institutions

I.1 Advisement Letter to Institutions

See Insert 10.2 in text.

I. 2 Guidelines for Final Institutional Evaluation of the Art and Social Interaction Program

Please respond in narrative form on your own letterhead stationery, answering as many questions as pertain. You need not rewrite the questions. They are to be used only as a general guide. Please include your name and title on the evaluation and the names of staff most frequently in attendance during the sessions. Thank you for your cooperation.

1 What is your overall impression of the program and the quality of presentation?
2 Describe the atmosphere when the workshops are in progress.
3 How receptive are participants to the projects? Is work generally completed? Is completed work kept by participants or discarded? Do participants accept the encouragement of presenters in attempting new projects or resist it?
4 How receptive are participants toward presenters? What, if any, changes do you notice in behavior during the sessions, for example, in motivation or productivity; in social relationships with presenters, staff or fellow group members; in self-image; pride; talk of future-oriented goals; other?
5 Have you noticed any changes in behavior between sessions that you might ascribe to the program?
6 What is particularly good about the program and what could be improved?
7 What physical limitations interfered with the sessions, for example, TV; ping-pong; insufficient space, tables or seating; therapy and recreation scheduling; medication; shortage of staff; other?
8 Please list any comments that participants or staff have made about the program which you feel are significant.
9 Would you want this program to continue? Why?

Again, sincere thanks for your time and attention in completing this evaluation.

Appendix 3.D Evaluation Instruments for Outside Evaluators

E.1 Plan of Operation for Evaluators

1 Evaluators select the specific site or sites to follow through the presumably ten-week program.
2 Evaluators receive copies of presenters' Pre-program Background Information Sheets and their ongoing logs.
3 Evaluators meet the presenters at the college and review plans.
4 Evaluators make three site visits during the course of the series:
First visit, early on but not the first or second session.
Second visit, mid-series.
Third visit, toward the end, but not the final session.

All visits should be scheduled in advance notifying presenters and staff.

5 During site visits, evaluators make first-hand observations and conduct meetings with presenters and staff after each session to review participant progress and areas of success and failure.
6 Relevant clinical data on clients, where appropriate, are requested from staff; for privacy regulations, the data need not be made available to presenters.
7 Evaluators encourage staff to cooperate in filling out evaluative materials.
8 Evaluators keep the faculty leader informed about the content and progress of their observations via written reports, email or meetings.

E.2 Format for Evaluation Reports by Evaluation Team

Describe Site Activity

Project in progress
Number of presenters
Number of participants
Level of participation in projects
Level of social interaction
Appropriate and inappropriate behaviors
Discussions related to project and program
Significant conversations
Quality of completed projects

Describe Program Assistance

Adequacy of facilities: room, tables, chairs
Staff cooperation:
Preparing for the session: assembling participants.
During session: participating in project, handling distractions.
After session: dispersing group, holding dialogue with presenters

Distractions Impacting the Session

TV or radio on during session, music, singing, instrument playing. Ping-pong, pool or other game-playing activities of people not involved in the project.

Review of Logs and Other Observations and Evaluation Materials

Determine any observed improvements or setbacks during the series according to the following:

Participation in art projects
Socialization
Future-oriented goals
Learning; acquiring skills
Decision-making

Acts of responsibility
Verbalization of ideas
Satisfaction with finished art products
Acceptance of presenters
Relationships with staff

Note Successful Areas and Problem Areas of the Program

Logistics:

Travel
Collecting supplies
Disbursement of presenters around the room
Timing of session's beginning and end
Regularity of post-session discussion with site representative
Adequate makeup of group
Choice of projects
Topics of conversations

Describe Cross Observations between Sites

Effectiveness of art activity
Effectiveness of social interaction
Group and individual boundaries, closeness, distance
Increased/decreased attendance and involvement
Handling of logistics
Responsibility, reliability and capabilities of presentations
Staff involvement and support

Appendix 3.E Evaluation Instruments for Participants (Clients)

C.1 Participant Questionnaire

Name
Date
Location

1 Which art projects did you enjoy most? Why?
2 Do you look forward to the art workshops? Why?
3 How does this program compare with other activities you have and do?
4 Have you learned anything about yourself in these sessions?

5 Have your feelings changed about art or about anything else as a result of participating in the program?
6 Have you noticed any changes in how other participants in the program feel or think or act?
7 Do you have any new interests because of this program?
8 Would you join the program again if it were available and would you recommend it to others?
9 Do you have suggestions to improve the program?
10 If you have any other comments to make, please use the reverse side of this paper.

List of Figures

Color versions of many projects can be viewed online at www.routledge.com/9781032972008.

List of Inserts

About the Author

Judith Peck's sculpture is included in 80 public and private collections including the Yale Art Gallery and the Ghetto Fighters Museum in Israel. She holds a doctoral degree from New York University and two masters' degrees from Teachers College, Columbia University. Dr. Peck is a member of the Sculptors Guild, the Authors Guild and the American Art Therapy Association. She is professor emeritus of art at Ramapo College of New Jersey and author of nine books on education and visual arts techniques as well as two novels.

Peck designed Art and Social Interaction at Ramapo College of New Jersey believing that the freedom inherent in expressive art could be a rich resource for people experiencing confinement* and a means for undergraduate students to understand more about crime, mental illness, child and domestic abuse, economic disadvantage and a range of social issues by meeting people directly involved.

*Confinement covers diverse circumstances: physical restrictions as experienced by the frail elderly; restrictions in functions of the mind suffered by the mentally ill; steel barriers that enclose incarcerated men and women; the psychological constraints imposed by behavioral abuse in its many forms on youth and families; and the confinement of place and spirit wrought by poverty.

Acknowledgments

My pride is boundless in the students whose energy, talents and courage served so many through the years. They had not expected to leave so far behind their comfort zone enrolling in a college course. My gratitude for their commitment extends to the hundreds of participants with whom they shared the magic of the art and social interaction, sometimes life changing. I thank the faculty of Contemporary Arts for supporting the course, the vital ongoing support of Professors Jackie Skrzynski, Dean Kenneth Goldstein, and faculty from other areas of Ramapo College, Professors Kim Lorber, Dean Aaron Lorenz, Mitch Kahn, Sue Scher and others, who helped it gain academic credit in psychology, gerontology and social work and later as an interdisciplinary Gen Ed choice.

I thank the many institutional and agency personnel who welcomed the program and hosted it through the years. To those professionals who trusted the program at its start in the 70s I owe special praise, to open their doors to bright-eyed college students in wild hair and jeans, arms loaded with "things": Erroll Koesterich, psychologist at Rockland Psychiatric Center in Orangeburg, NY; Clint Dozier and Lt. Keith Ali at Essex County Jail; the forward thinking elected sheriffs of the Bergen County Jail Annex; Ellen O'Han of Rockland Children's Psychiatric Center; Archie Davidson of Catholic Family Services in the Paterson Housing Projects; Sandra Remos of Strengthen Our Sisters; and many more serving with skill and dedication those in their care.

I am grateful to the Department of Higher Education which provided a 3-year grant under Title 1 to support the program after its first two years of operation, giving it prestige as well as funding; thanks specifically to Robert Holmes who worked closely with us.

My thanks go to the able help of Tibor Csokasi for solving technical computer problems related to the book's photographic preparation and in short, being indispensable. I thank Julia Greco who squeezed in time from studies and internship to assist in typing.

I am delighted to recognize via photo captions those students appearing in the pictures in the early years, photos rarely taken, so wrapped up were we in running the program in our disparate venues. Immense gratitude to the students through the years who produced the inventive artworks that appear in Part Five. Most artworks are able to be credited in the captions, but my deep apology to those students whose art works, in the magnitude of productivity over the decades, were not identified despite countless weeks and months of searching records.

I am grateful to my Routledge editor Amanda Savage for the confidence she had in me, at times under difficult situations. My thanks to Sophie Dracott at Routledge for her patience, competence and kindness in our exchanged email messages never reprimanding for my delays, and to Alison Macfarlane for her superb expertise in the final shepherding of the book into print.

Lastly, I acknowledge with everlasting thanks the support of my four kids, Sarah, Jennifer, Joel and Sabrina, their beloved mates, and amazing offspring: That assemblage of accomplished young men and women and a few small children constitute an array of rousing noises always playing in my background.

Index

For Product Safety Concerns and Information please contact our EU representative GPSR@taylorandfrancis.com
Taylor & Francis Verlag GmbH, Kaufingerstraße 24, 80331 München, Germany

www.ingramcontent.com/pod-product-compliance
Lightning Source LLC
LaVergne TN
LVHW080807011026
849160LV00015B/1556
* 9 7 8 1 0 3 2 9 7 2 0 0 8 *